I0107736

LAST PLANE TO COCHABAMBA:

AN EXTRAORDINARY JOURNEY TO THE
FIVE CORNERS OF BOLIVIA

By

JOHN JOSEMARIA FULFORD

Last Plane to Cochabamba by John J. Fulford

Copyright © 2014 by John J. Fulford

Published by Astoria Press, Long Beach, CA

Author services provided by Pedernales Publishing, LLC
www.pedernalespublishing.com

Cover by Christine Di Natale
www.dinataledesign.com

Editing services by Barbara Ardinger
www.barbaraardinger.com

All rights reserved. No part of this book may be used or reproduced in any form by any electronic or mechanical means (including photocopying, recording, or information storage and retrieval) whatsoever without permission in writing from the author, except in the case of brief quotations embodied in critical articles and reviews.

Library of Congress Control Number: 2014946374

ISBN Number: 978-0-9831872-7-1 Paperback Edition
           978-0-9831872-8-8 Digital Edition

CONTENTS

TRAVELS WITH LILY

From Cuzco

Car

Puno

LAKE TITICACA
(12,500 ft.)

B O L I V I A

Bus

Copacabana

Strait of Tiquina

P E R U

Yunguyo
(The Farm)

La Paz

0   12.5   25   50

Miles

Bus

Guaqui

Tihuanacu

From Asunción

Bus
(Break Down)

Cochabamba

Plane

(20,000 ft.)

Plane

Oruro

Arica

Bus

L. Poopó

Sucre

To Antofagasta

Bus

0   25   50   100

Miles

Train

Condor Station
(15,700 ft.)

Potosí
(13,400 ft.)

N

LAST PLANE TO COCHABAMBA

Travels Through Bolivia

N

Porto Velho

Cachuela-Esperanza

Trucks to
Cachuela-Esperanza

Riberalta   **Guajara-Mirim**

B R A Z I L

P E R U

River Boat

Plane

Trinidad

Juliaca

L. Titicaca

B O L I V I A

Puno   Bus   **Coroico**

Bus

Boat

La Paz

Bus

Villa Tunari

Arequipa

Cochabamba

Arica

Oruro   Bus

Bus

**Santa Cruz
De La Sierra**

L. Poopó

Uncia   **Sucre**

Corumba

Potosí

**PACIFIC
OCEAN**

Bus

**C
H
I
L
E**

Uyuni

Tarija   Bus   **Villa Montes**

Calama   **Villazon**

Yacuiba

**San Pedro
De Atacama**

PARAGUAY

Antofagasta

Bus   Bus

Salta

A R G E N T I N A

| 0 | 120 | 240 | 480 |
Miles

Preface

When I first decided to write a history of Bolivia, it seemed only logical that I ought to travel to Bolivia and visit all the areas mentioned in the book. Unfortunately, at the time I was a penniless student in Vancouver without the faintest idea how to get to Bolivia, so for some years I could do little except study my books and stare at my maps and dream. But one sunny day my life changed. I had moved to California, where I married a fellow teacher, a blue-eyed blond named Lillian Christensen, who shared my interest in Latin America and had always longed to see the Panama Canal. She was an only child and her parents were very protective, and so when school was out in the summer of 1970, we told her parents that we were going just to Mexico City and would be back in a week or ten days.

After a couple of days seeing the sights in and around Mexico City, we took local buses and an occasional train south through Guatemala, Honduras, El Salvador, Nicaragua, Costa Rica, and eventually reached Panama, where we saw the great canal and took the train from Panama to Colon and back. It was quite an adventure. Lily, who had rarely been out of California, enjoyed every minute of it, so as we still had some money left and plenty of time, we continued on and eventually made our way by various forms of transport through Venezuela, Colombia, Ecuador, Peru, Bolivia, Chile, Argentina, Uruguay, Brazil, and Paraguay, where we ran out of time and money.

Traveling together Lily and I actually visited Bolivia twice. The first time, we arrived by land and explored La Paz, Tihuanacu, and Oruro, where we visited friends. The second time, after we had flown back from Paraguay, we managed to squeeze in the time to see Cochabamba, Sucre, and Potosí before Lily had to get home to go back to work. I had registered at the university as a graduate student and had until Christmas. This gave me the opportunity that I had always dreamed about. Lily and I had seen some of Bolivia together, but now I would have time to visit the rest of the huge country and to peer into those corners off the beaten track that tourists seldom visit.

Chapter 1: Lake Titicaca

Our first glimpse of Lake Titicaca was from the dock in Puno, Peru, where we had arrived in a taxi from Cuzco after an all night drive. There had been six of us squeezed into the unheated car, and while the others wrapped themselves against the cold and tried to sleep, I had sat wide awake, peering out the window as we made our way through the mountains and into a broad valley. All the little towns and villages we went through were silent and locked up tight as for hours we sped along, a lonely speck with its plume of dust, down the wide, empty, and almost treeless valley. I could see the snow-patched Andes gleaming in the starlight far off to the left. This was the valley down which the Inca Lloque Yupanqui had marched his army 800 years before, from the heights of Vilcanota to Lake Titicaca to begin his conquest of the Collasuyo, or what is now known as Bolivia.

We had been assured by every travel expert in Cuzco that the lake steamer to Bolivia would be waiting for us when we arrived, but there was no ship floating in the dark waters of the little harbor. The manager of the cafe where we sat in the sun, defrosting ourselves with hot chocolate, merely shrugged his shoulders and said, "What would they know in Cuzco? The boat leaves when the trains from Arequipa and Cuzco arrive. Probably tomorrow night."

Puno was a small, sprawling, unattractive town. Lily and I did not relish the thought of spending two days there, especially as we were counting the days and also counting our money. After discussing our situation with some French tourists who had just come from La Paz, we took a bus along the south shore of the lake. The driver guaranteed that we would reach the Bolivian border well before evening.

The bus was little bigger than a Volkswagen van. An official notice declared that it could take sixteen passengers, but that was a mere formality. There were at least twenty adults and numerous babies squashed into it, with folding seats blocking the aisle, which made it quite claustrophobic, although we had sideways seats, so at least we had knee room. All the passengers were Indians, with most of the women wearing the distinctive black bowler hats, long double braids, and heavy layered skirts, and everybody was very friendly. The children stared wide eyed and open mouthed at Lily's long blond hair and pale skin. It was obvious that some of the women had never been close to a blue-eyed foreigner before.

The road was dusty and pot-holed and, inevitably, the bus broke down. We had been able to catch only fleeting glimpses of the lake, but when the bus broke down, it was at the top of a small hill with a gorgeous view of Lake Titicaca. The water was a lovely shade of blue with only a tiny scattering of little waves that sparkled in the sun, and the shore was fringed with the bright green of giant rushes. It was too wide for us to see the other shore, but the snow capped Andes were reflected in the calm waters.

"It's so beautiful," Lily whispered. "I didn't realize it would be so big." We stood there for a while, hand in hand, admiring the view, and I thought of the Incas and the Conquistadors and many others, including Simón Bolívar, who had passed that way and could have stopped at that very spot to admire the extraordinary lake and its beautiful setting.

The rest of the trip around Lake Titicaca went relatively smoothly, though very slowly, and by the time we reached Yungayo, the border between Peru and Bolivia was closed. It was dark and the temperature had plummeted. There were no street lights and the town was deserted, and I was beginning to get worried when a well-dressed, middle-aged man from the bus, who had been fascinated by Lily's yellow hair and who knew a few words of English, cheerfully offered to find us somewhere to stay.

"Unfortunately, we have no hotel," he said in Spanish, "but we could look at the *pensiones*." The first *pension*, or rooming house, was a filthy hole full of drunks. We didn't even look inside. But the second was an extraordinary place, straight out of the 17th century. The front door led directly into a large open room, which was crowded with long wooden tables and simple benches packed with men, all of them eating or drinking and some rolling dice or playing cards. Half a dozen oil lamps hung from the high ceiling, and through the thick tobacco smoke I could see a gallery running all around the main room and what seemed to be dozens of small bedrooms. The only women in the inn were the solidly built servants in heavy skirts who squeezed between the packed benches with bottles of beer and plates of food. There was a gentle roar of voices, and the old oil lamps gave the scene a yellow tint exactly like a painting of a medieval inn that I had seen in a museum somewhere.

There was no room at that inn, and it was clearly no place for a foreign woman, so we turned away. Undaunted, our guide took us to a little restaurant where he was obviously well known. After a spaghetti supper in the warm kitchen and a long discussion with the owner, he looked at us and said, "You'll just have to stay at my place."

His place, on the outskirts of the little town, was quite a large adobe farmhouse with a thick thatched roof. In the starlight, the entire house seemed to consist of one enormous room containing not just his kitchen and bedroom but also his storeroom and his workshop and all his possessions. There were a large double bed and a smaller single bed, some bicycles hanging on the wall, a table and chairs in the middle, and sacks or boxes in all the corners. Clothing hung from wooden pegs, and one or two shelves held bits of china and glass. All the available space was well used, and by the candlelight I could see an extraordinary wide range of objects, including tools that I had last seen in a museum at an old Spanish mission in California. Our host used one of the candles to show us the toilet. That is, he simply opened a back door and pointed out into the yard, where I could see a solitary tree. That was the toilet.

That night, Lily and I slept in the large bed on a hard straw mattress under half a dozen heavy cotton blankets, the candlelight reflecting off hand-carved wooden agricultural implements and tools, clay jars, and hand woven clothing hanging from wooden pegs. Except for the shiny plastic battery radio, it could have been the 17th century. The blankets were heavy, but they gave no warmth, and it was a very cold night on a very hard bed for me. Lily was so tired that she fell asleep immediately. Next morning, she claimed that she found the bed cozy and warm.

She was entranced by the idea that she had slept in an Indian farmhouse on the shores of Lake Titicaca, and before we had even sat down for a breakfast of coffee and freshly baked bread, she whispered, "Do you think he would show us around his farm? Daddy would be fascinated. It's so different to the family farm back in South Dakota."

Our host was only too pleased to show off his farm and his business, especially after Lily complimented him in Spanish on the freshly baked bread. It turned out that he had a bakery attached to the house. He took us immediately to see his ovens and to meet his baker. The ovens were large brick and adobe affairs fueled by kerosene, and there were huge wooden troughs for mixing the dough.

The baker was a tiny Aymara Indian with a very dark skin and a serious expression that did not hide his obvious pride in his ovens and his skill. Each morning, he baked enough bread to supply half the town. He became quite excited when Lily told him that her father was a baker, too. For the next half hour, they were buddies, and Lily's Spanish improved immensely as they compared baking in Peru and in America and he showed off his mixture of ancient, hand-carved equipment and expensive gadgets imported from Argentina. It was obvious that the baker was having difficulty imagining that the father of this exotic, blonde American girl was only a humble baker, and he listened in awe as she proved that she knew what she was talking about. When she began to describe the stainless steel, automated, gas-fired ovens that her father operated, however, he shook his head and said something in Aymara that our host translated as, "If it is done with machines, where is the flavor?"

Suddenly, Lily gave squeal of delight. "Guinea pigs! Look at them warming themselves by the ovens. Aren't they darling?" Since she had a pet guinea pig at home, she immediately reached down to pick one up.

Our host caught another one and held it up. "Would you like it for breakfast?" he asked.

Lily understood before I could translate it, and with a horrified gasp she took the little animal from his hands and placed it tenderly near the ovens. It took me a while to explain that in America the creatures were kept as pets and never eaten. The baker found it hard to believe, but our host laughed loudly and we continued our tour of his farm.

It was a wonderful experience. I had read so much about farming on the *altiplano*, but to actually see it all firsthand was a rare and exhilarating experience. We went first into a walled yard where the little Andean potatoes where being turned into *chuno*. For about a week, the potatoes lie spread out to dry in the sun and freeze at night, and a small boy stirs them now and then with a wide wooden rake and keeps the livestock from eating them. We also saw sacks of the finished product, which looked like unappetizing little grey lumps, all bagged and ready for market. *Chuno* lasts for years and is the basic food for most of the people on the *altiplano*, but before it is cooked, it has to be soaked overnight. It is so bland that it is usually cooked with other ingredients and plenty of spices.

We also saw the oxen and the wooden plows and the great wooden wagon. "I don't need gasoline for this thing," our host said, "and she never gets stuck in the mud." Then he told us about his cattle and sheep and the potatoes and beans that he grew. It soon became clear that he was a careful farmer who stuck to the traditional way of farming but did not hesitate to use modern methods and equipment if they proved to be useful.

We were crossing the road to look at one of his fields when a string of llamas came by, each carrying a pair of flat, gray salt blocks. The llama train was tended by a group of Indians in traditional clothing. All of them, men and women alike, were spinning wool as they walked, with the long thread and twirling spindle dangling from their fingers. The women, as usual in their heavy skirts and bowler hats tipped at the right angle, all seemed to have babies buried in the shawls on their backs. The men were in calf-length, homespun trousers and wore llama-wool caps with long ear flaps. Although everybody was wrapped warmly for the overnight journey, they all had bare feet. No socks or stockings. Just a pair of open sandals with thick soles cut from automobile tires.

When Lily saw the llama train, she started to take photos until our host stopped her. "I must not take their pictures?" she asked.

"Not yet," he said, and he proceeded to line the people up in a neat row, even adjusting their hats to his satisfaction. Then he stepped back proudly and said, "Now you can make a nice photograph."

The sun was high in the clear blue sky before we eventually left the farm and resumed our journey. Our host went with us to the plaza and tracked down the Bolivian consul to get our passports stamped. He even found us the right bus for Copacabana. Needless to say, we were very grateful for his kindness, but he shrugged off our thanks with a wave of his hand and a wide smile for Lily.

COPACABANA

After a rough trip through the hills, we arrived in the famous city of Copacabana to find it a shambles. It was the day after a big national holiday, and the streets were littered with drunks sprawled in the remains of a grand celebration. Everything was closed. Nobody was interested in changing our Peruvian money or cashing a traveler's check or honoring a credit card. Between us, Lily and I had just enough to buy our bus tickets to La Paz.

Copacabana has been a spiritual center for the Indians around Lake Titicaca since long before the rise of the Inca empire. Here the Aymara had their gods and their places of worship, and when the Incas later superimposed their beliefs on those of the Aymara, they declared that this was the spot where the gods arose from the Island of the Sun and the Island of the Moon to create the world. Still later, Christian missionaries built a cathedral in Copacabana that became the center of worship and the most important center of pilgrimage on the *altiplano*. Legend has it that one pilgrim from far off Brazil took the name back to Rio de Janeiro and bestowed it on Copacabana Beach.

I was heartbroken to leave the city without even a quick visit to the cathedral, which we could see right in front of us across the plaza, but the bus was ready to leave and we had no money. At least we would be able to solve our money problem in La Paz, so we boarded the bus and promised each other that we would come back as soon as the opportunity presented itself. Unfortunately, the opportunity never did present itself.

Throughout the years, the Peruvian border has been a source of trouble for Bolivia. This is because Peru has always considered the entire lake to be part of Peru, whereas Bolivia has always insisted that the southern section, including the peninsula of Copacabana and the mouth of the Rio Desaguadero, is part of Bolivia. The two nations never came to blows over the issue, but the boundary has been altered a number of times, with Bolivia invariably losing more territory each time. Today, the border with Peru winds and twists erratically and cuts the Copacabana peninsula off from the rest of Bolivia so that the traveler has to cross at the Strait of Tiquina. The Bolivians have a joke about the border that they love to tell. "When they divided up the great lake," they say, "the Bolivians got the *Titi* and the Peruvians got the *caca*."

Crossing the strait was quite exciting. Before the bus was driven onto a small barge, all the passengers boarded motorboats, which sped across, leaving the top-heavy bus with all our luggage in it swaying dramatically on the barge through the choppy waters. One of the other passengers admitted that "once in a while" a bus is lost, but ours arrived safely, much to Lily's relief. Everywhere we looked, there were sailors enjoying the sparkling sunshine.

"Bolivia is a land-locked country, isn't it?" Lily said. "They seem to have more sailors than Switzerland."

So I explained, "The theft of their Pacific coast by Chile will never be forgotten in Bolivia. That's why Bolivia does indeed have a navy."

LA PAZ

Our arrival at La Paz was dramatic. We had been droning for two hours across a particularly flat stretch of the *altiplano* when the bus stopped in the middle of a small town of uninteresting buildings and dusty streets. This was El Alto, where many of the passengers got off. When we looked through the window, we saw that we were parked at the edge of an immense canyon at the bottom of which, at least a thousand feet below, lay the city of La Paz. The road down was steep and winding. Lily noticed that the driver crossed himself before we began the descent from the *altiplano* to the center of the famous city.

The great canyon in which the city lies is unique. Numerous mighty rivers flow down the east flanks of the Andes carrying their loads of sediment down to the Amazon, but only one, the Rio de La Paz (the Rio Chuquiapu), has eroded its way far enough to cut completely through the mountain chain and nibble at the edge of the *altiplano* to create this huge hollow. The city lies tucked into the feet of the high Andes, and the towering peaks with their great sheets of gleaming snow make a perfect backdrop. At sunset they shine bright pink and yellow over the city. The largest peak is Illimani, whose snow fields, when seen from La Paz, form the outline of an Indian woman carrying her baby on her back.

In many of the cities of the world, the rich tend to build their houses high on hillsides and pay extra for the view, whereas the poor have to be satisfied with the lower lying land. In La Paz, it is quite the opposite. Those who have the means try to live as far down the valley as possible, where it is noticeably warmer. The poor build their houses on the high slopes and live exposed to the freezing winds of the cold rim of the *altiplano*. Today, the valley of La Paz is almost completely filled and El Alto has become a major suburb.

La Paz is a crowded city of steep roads and busy markets, with buildings that range from the ancient to the modern, and heavy traffic that pollutes the air so that, at times, the entire city is hidden under a gray cloud. In 1548, on the site of the tiny gold mining village of Chuquiapu, Alonso de Mendoza founded the city of Nuestra Señora de la Paz to celebrate the end of the civil wars between the Spanish conquerors. Nearly 300 years later, the name was changed to La Paz de Ayacucho to celebrate Bolívar's famous victory. Since then, La Paz has seen scores of self-declared presidents and dictators, it has seen wars and Indian uprisings, it has seen riots, revolutions and bloody murders, and yet it still proudly calls itself the City of Peace.

TIHUANACU

The morning we decided to go to Tihuanacu blossomed into a beautiful day with a clear blue sky and a soft breeze. Just perfect for touring. The bus driver packed in the passengers to the point of suffocation, and there was even a woman with a baby on her back hanging from the door. After the bus had wheezed its way slowly up the hill, most of the crowd got off at El Alto. The road to Tihuanacu was not good. There were more hills than I expected, and so the two-hour trip was hot and very dusty.

When we arrived, we found that it was market day. There were bails of coca leaf, sacks of *chuno*, piles of bowler hats, and a wide variety of woven cloths in bright colors. The women were all dressed in their best and brightest outfits while the men were wearing dark suits with white shirts and shoes instead of sandals. Clearly, market day was a time to see and be seen, and it was remarkably quiet and businesslike. The church, which had been built with stones from Tihuanacu, has two massive stone idols from the local Indian ruins guarding its gates, and inside the heavily decorated statues also look very Indian.

About a mile away lie the famous ruins. They take up a large area, but centuries of looting have left very little to see except the foundations of what must have been a spectacular temple and palace system. Perhaps the Inca took a few stones for temple building, and then the Spaniards took a few for church building, and then thieves took carvings to sell to collectors, and museums took what they could get away with before the railroad builders arrived and took trainloads of beautifully cut stones to make viaducts and bridges and line tunnels and build stations. Fortunately, the magnificent Gate of the Sun still stands, along with a few other artifacts, and the grounds are well kept.

It was the silence and the emptiness of the ruins that most impressed us. A few tourists, mostly French, wandered quietly about, but there was no sound from the town, no dogs barking, no birds singing as the wind whispered across the silent and almost treeless land. Even the small boys selling clay copies of the statues were subdued.

We next took a bus to Guaqui, Bolivia's lake port, and found just a large village with many thatch-roofed houses, a brightly painted square church, and a dreary plaza with a few stores. The sun was hot, but a cool wind blew from the lake as we walked onto the dock, where we found some abandoned wooden rail wagons and an ancient steam crane that should have been in a museum. Floating silent and almost deserted, was the *SS Inca*, the second oldest steam ship on Lake Titicaca. She was built in 1905 and was still fit for service carrying passengers and a little cargo from Puno in Peru to Guaqui in Bolivia. A crewman appeared on deck, and we chatted as Lily took photos.

Suddenly Lily exclaimed, "Oh, look! Reed boats! I knew we would see some eventually."

In the distance were *balsas*, reed boats, among the high reeds, so we walked along the mole until we came to where some fishermen and their families were living in crude huts along with their sheep and some very hairy pigs. Despite all the tourist photos, we had not yet seen a single *balsa*, not even at the Strait of Tiquina. It seemed that the ancient reed boat has long since been replaced by the aluminum boat with an outboard engine. The women smiled shyly and the men offered to give us a ride on one of the boats, but although it was ten feet long and floated quite high on the water, it did not look very stable and we politely refused. Lily took photos of the graceful craft floating on the blue water with the snow-covered Andes gleaming in the distance.

Chapter 2: The *Altiplano*

The *altiplano*, or "high plain," surprised me, not only because of its huge size, but because the surface was nowhere near as flat as I had been led to believe. It was far from the barren wasteland that some writers have described. Because Lily and I had arrived in the middle of the Southern Hemisphere's winter, the dry brown land that we saw all around Lake Titicaca was actually fallow or unplowed fields waiting for the winter rains. As the buses and trains we took sped across the land, it slowly dawned on us that almost every acre of useable land was under cultivation and that even the steepest slopes were being used. In the Lake Titicaca and La Paz areas, many hillsides were covered with ancient terraces, and scattered over the land were the lonely farmhouses of mud brick and thatch, some with tin roofs, each with a low mud wall to shelter the livestock. Any land unfit for cultivation is covered in tufts of the hardy *ichu* grass that provides food for the llama. Much of the *altiplano* is covered by large shallow lakes like Lake Poopo, which shrink and expand according to the season. Huge areas are covered by salt pans, especially in the south.

ORURO

I had roomed for one year at the University of British Columbia in Vancouver with Ramiro Miranda, who was a Bolivian from Oruro.

He was studying mining engineering. His English was perfect and he was polite about my abysmal Spanish, and so we got on very well together. I had always had an interest in Bolivia, but it was Ramiro who made me really determined to visit and explore that extraordinary country one day. After graduation, he married a Canadian girl and went back home, but we exchanged letters and kept in touch.

Now that Lily and I were actually in Bolivia, we had had been trying for two days to phone Oruro, but the phone lines remained dead. Eventually Lily said, "Let's just take a gamble that they're home. If they're not home, a city that size should have a decent hotel. It would be fun to meet them." I agreed and bought bus tickets for the following morning.

Breakfast was hot black coffee and tea served by a curbside vendor who rinsed everything, including the cups, in the same bucket of water. But the hot coffee was much appreciated as we stood in the early morning sun, defrosting ourselves while waiting for the bus. It turned out to be a Spanish-made luxury bus, the most comfortable bus we had taken so far. There were not many passengers, and, at least for the first hour, the road was good.

It was one of those crystal-clear days when the Andes stand bright and sharp and seem so close one might touch them, and the *altiplano* stretches on forever. Lonely farmers tilled small, walled patches of ground with their oxen and wooden plows, and dust devils danced across the low hills. Now and then, an adobe church raised its square tower and tin roof above the farms, and many of the houses we saw had curious metal carvings fastened to the eaves to guard the property from evil spirits. Occasionally we saw the round houses of the Urus, the Indians who have survived here since before the Incas. In sharp contrast to all mementos of earlier days, alongside the road lay a shiny, new, steel pipeline bringing oil or natural gas from far down in the eastern lowlands.

Mining towns are never very attractive, and Oruro is a mining town as well as the main supply center for the mines all around it. The town sprawls up and around a small mountain that pushes up through the flat plains some distance from the Andes. When we arrived, we tried again to phone and were relieved to find that it worked and even more relieved to find that Ramiro and Barbara were home. They insisted that we bring our bags to their house without delay.

"This town has no hotel fit to stay in, yet," Ramiro said, and he gave us the address. His house was a traditional, single-story house with the front door opening directly onto the street, few windows, and numerous interior patios. It had been nearly ten years since I had last seen Ramiro, and he had not the faintest idea that we were in Bolivia, so we had a great reunion. His three children and three dogs added to the excitement.

Lily was fascinated by the problems that a modern, middle class Canadian woman had encountered when she moved from Vancouver to Oruro. First, there were the practical problems of unreliable electricity and water, dubious phone and mail service, shopping, and raising children. Then there were the strange medical problems, plus the cultural differences and social taboos. Lily and Barbara had much to discuss.

While they were talking about domestic details, Ramiro and I discussed high import duties, smuggling, and the problem of obtaining needed mechanical parts. We also exchanged news about old friends. We had supper, and after the children were put to bed, we talked until very late. It became very cold, and Ramiro produced a heater which we kept on all night.

Next morning, while Lily and Barbara discussed more domestic matters, Ramiro and I went to the garage where his truck was being repaired. In a land of vast distances and no services, plus bad roads and a scarcity of anything imported, a reliable truck is invaluable. His truck was partly disassembled, and each piece was being lovingly checked and cleaned. There were almost no spare parts. Ramiro explained that if something was broken, it was repaired, and what was beyond repair was manufactured right there in the garage. Not surprisingly, the mechanics were wizards at improvising. Ramiro showed me some vehicles that should have been in museum, but, he assured me, they all ran well. He drove a Land Rover, which he called "the Jeep." It had cost a fortune, and it had also taken months of complicated negotiations—and bribes— just to get the import permits.

We drove around the city for a while, then picked up Lily and Barbara and went to the market. Many of the market women had come in from other regions, so there was a collection of bright costumes. There were women from Cochabamba, with their tall white hats with wide ribbons and embroidered jackets and cuffs, there were women in brown bowler hats with little gold ornaments and long black skirts, and there were women in white berets, but they all wore sandals made from old car tires. When we saw skinned guinea pigs among the piles of vegetables and meats, Lily told Barbara about the one we had almost had for breakfast.

Barbara was astonished. She had always thought the animal was rabbit. Ramiro then looked embarrassed. He had never had the courage to tell her. I quickly changed the subject and bought Lily a piece of cloth that Barbara said was authentic Indian weaving using the traditional dyes.

Ramiro wanted us to visit Cochabamba and Potosí, but when we went to the bus station, we found that all the buses were fully booked and we would have to wait days for seats. At the railway station, we watched the two-car diesel train arrive and depart. It, too, was packed. The station master assured us that we would not be able to get seats for days. As nice as it was to be visiting friends in Oruro, we had been traveling for eight weeks and were beginning to run out of time. Lily had to be back to work in the States, so we decided to go at least as far as Santiago, Chile, before turning back. This would give us time to explore Bolivia at leisure. We went to the airline office and bought tickets from La Paz to Arica on the Pacific coast.

Ramiro tried to persuade me to stay and teach at the American school just across the street. He had gone there himself and had learned English there. They had done a good job at that school because I could never beat him at Scrabble.

Ramiro's children, two little girls and a baby boy, spoke to each other in Spanish but to their parents in English. Lily, who had a sharp eye and ear for such things, said, "Have you noticed that the girls carry their dolls on their back Indian style? And when I was reading a story to them, the little boy thought that the horses were llamas." As there was not a bookstore in town, our hosts were desperate for anything to read, which gave Lily a golden opportunity to unload all the books she had collected as we traveled. After supper that night, we watched Ramiro's slides and discussed international affairs. We learned that a plane from Lima to Cuzco had crashed, killing all the tourists on board. A careful check of our notes showed that it had been two flights after ours.

Considering all the places she had been, the food she had eaten, and the wide ranges of temperatures she had experienced, I thought it was marvelous how healthy Lily had remained. But that night she became cold and restless and complained of a sore throat and a stuffy nose. I was glad for her sake that we were going to go down to sea level and tropical warmth very soon.

Next morning, Lily slept late. She did not look well. The sun was brilliant, but it was very cold, and so we let her sleep while Ramiro and I went to buy bus tickets back to La Paz. First, we had to get police permits, as there was yet another political crisis happening in La Paz. An hour later, he and I left the city and drove out onto the vast plains that surround the city and into a strange silence broken only by the constant wind. The land was flat and dry, an immense ancient lake bed that would become a sea of treacherous mud in the rainy season. Here and there, we saw sand dunes and salt flats and large lake mirages. There were no trees, and we drove where we pleased. At one place, Ramiro stopped and pointed out a line of small brick pillars. "That's the old stage coach route," he said. "There wasn't any road in those days. It used to take up to a week to get to La Paz. It must have been a horrible ride."

Then we drove up the mountain, where we could see Lake Urus shining blue in the distance and watched a plane take off from the airport. Ramiro pointed up at the peak. "There's a light up there," he said. "It's some kind of monument, but we call it El Faro, the lighthouse. It's too easy to get lost out here, and that light is just about the only landmark around. Fantastic when you think about it. The only lighthouse in the world that's hundreds of miles from the sea."

On the slopes, I pointed out the horizontal lines of ancient beaches left behind by the retreating lake.

"Yes," he said. "Lake Minchin, the geographers call it. Some say that it drained off down the Rio de La Paz."

I looked at him. "You don't think so?"

Ramiro laughed and said, "Wait until you've seen the salt flats at Uyuni. Lake Minchin just dried up!"

Closer to Oruro, we passed some new buildings. Ramiro explained that they were a new university specializing in mining engineering, "And about time, too." he said. "This country depends on its mineral wealth, and I had to go to North America to get my training." After that, we drove past a small tin mine where huge icicles hung from the eaves of the buildings and a group of men worked silently in the sun.

Lily seemed to be better by lunchtime, so Ramiro and I drove out to see a new German-financed tin smelter that used natural gas brought in through the pipeline. After that, we visited a village where we watched a man sifting river sand for tin. The village church was quite picturesque, with its typical square towers of adobe brick and surrounding white-washed walls. There were even a few willow trees on the sunny side of the church, and Ramiro said that in the old days it had been a popular picnic spot. He explained that the priest used to come once or twice a year and perform all the marriages and baptisms in one day. In between these rare visits, the Indians had their own Sunday services and numerous saints' days services that were a strange mixture of Christianity and ancient traditions. In the cemetery, which was a short distance from the church, each little mound had a stone marker with a hole carved into it where relatives could leave offerings (usually coca) to pacify the spirits. Some had wrought iron markers which were not always shaped like the Christian cross.

On the way back, we stopped in the middle of a huge flat area that was covered in low mounds. These were the result of the Spanish excavation of an immense fortune in silver from the hill of Oruro. They had dumped the waste material out on the plains beyond the city. When the silver began to run out and tin suddenly became valuable, these dumped tailings were found to have a very high content of tin.

"My father started by working these tailings for Simon Patiño, the Tin King," Ramiro said. "Patiño became the richest man in the world. My father saved every penny he earned to buy a small lead mine in the mountains, and by plain hard work he made enough to send me to Vancouver to study modern mining." He paused, then added, "My brother has no interest in mining. He's in Madrid studying law. As if we don't have enough lawyers already."

THE LONG, COLD NIGHT

Lily seemed much better after lunch, so we sat around chatting until it was time to catch the bus, which was to leave at 6:30 that evening. We got the last two seats. It was not the luxury bus we had arrived on, but a well-worn older bus. About an hour out of Oruro, it broke down. The sun had set and the temperature dropped dramatically until we were both shivering. Lily put on both her sweaters and wrapped her Colombian *ruana* around herself, and I zipped up my parka. But they were not enough. It was a dreadful cold that penetrated through wool and kapok, deep into the bones.

With the engine not running, the bus got colder and colder. At first the passengers grumbled and shouted at the driver, then most of the men got out and urinated at the side of the road. The driver ignored everybody and with his boy assistant silently began to tinker with the engine, refusing any help and ignoring all advice. Gradually, everybody settled down for a long wait. The women produced blankets and wrapped themselves and their families in them and their shawls, but Lily and I had neither blankets nor woolen shawls. We sat shivering and hugging each other, with Lily trying to sleep and me worrying about her health. I was so cold that my shivering was quite violent and actually hurt. Now and then, I went outside to get some circulation back into my legs and wake up my frozen feet.

There was no moon, but I didn't need one. The sky was crystal clear and the light from the giant stars was enough. I had never seen so many stars, and never had they been so big…but I was in no mood to admire them. Breathing the frozen air hurt my lungs and in every direction the land lay flat and empty. Even the mountains were hidden over the horizon, and the road stretched away in both directions, narrow and deserted. There was not a sound except for the metallic click of tools as the driver still worked on the engine. At the side of the road, the pool of urine had frozen solid before it could drain into the soil.

We passengers sat and shivered miserably for three long hours until sufficient repair was made to enable the bus to creep slowly along the road. We stopped when we came to a roadside restaurant, where the driver went back to tinkering with the engine. The restaurant was locked up tight, so Lily remained on the bus with the other passengers while I paced up and down to keep from freezing and worried about her. She insisted that she was fine, but it was obvious that she wasn't. If I didn't get her into a warm bed very soon, I was sure she was going to be dangerously sick. At the side of the road, on the bare ground, in the middle of the bitterly cold night, I saw three Indian women sitting with their little trays of candy and cigarettes. They were hunched in their shawls, still and silent as statues, patiently waiting for the first rays of the morning sun.

After an hour, the bus was able to move again, but only at half speed. We crept slowly through the bitter night again until at last we could see the lights of El Alto. But it was half an hour longer before we reached the town. When we peered down at La Paz at 3:00 in the morning, it was a very beautiful sight indeed, and not just because of all the lights twinkling in the cold night air.

Both El Alto and La Paz were strangely silent, and there was absolutely no traffic on the streets. At the bus depot, the driver flatly refused to give us our bags and told us to come back in the morning when the office opened. That's when I lost my temper and threatened to climb up on the roof of the bus and get them myself.

But Lily stopped me. Despite the obvious curfew, there was a taxi waiting. I helped Lily into it, got in myself, and told the driver to find us a hotel, any hotel. He explained that there was martial law and a curfew and all the hotels were locked for the night, but he would try. We went from hotel to hotel, but they were all locked and dark. We were stopped at least five times by soldiers and had our papers checked. Eventually, however, the night clerk at one hotel took pity on us and phoned around. At the first place that he suggested, a woman leaned out of a window and shouted at us to go away, but we were lucky at the second place. A girl opened the door and listened to the driver as he explained our predicament. Without a word, she led us down a passage where there were men sleeping on the floor and into a large, cold room with two single beds. Then she showed us the washroom on the outside patio and silently left.

Lily, still shivering violently, was almost asleep on her feet, so I hustled her into bed half dressed, added all the blankets from the other bed and crawled in beside her. Together, we raised a little body heat, but it was still cold and my feet never did defrost that night.

FLYING TO ARICA

We were awakened to breakfast in bed brought by the silent girl, who seemed to be the only staff, but it was very hard to get out of bed. We were both feeling terrible by now. We could have stayed in bed all day, but we had a plane to catch. I made a quick visit to the American Embassy and picked up two letters, then I double-checked our ticket at the airline office. It was a brilliantly sunny day, and I was feeling much better by the time I went back to the bus station to collect our luggage, so I did not lose my temper with the manager and agreed with him that "rules were rules."

But I was impatient to get Lily down to the coast. I guessed, from past experience, that we would run into other problems before the day was out, so we set off for the airport early. The taxi driver squeezed five people into his ancient vehicle and set off up the steep road to El Alto. Half way up, the taxi had a flat tire. Naturally, the driver did not have a jack-stand that fit his car, so he spent some time rigging a wobbly make-shift stand out of bits of rock. When we reached the airport, of course, all the ticket counters and shops were closed, even the snack bar, and there was no central heating so we sat in the cold lobby and waited. An hour later, somebody arrived, but it was only to tell us that our flight was late.

When the plane finally arrived, it was packed, but I got us window seats with a magnificent view of Lake Titicaca. Warm at last, Lily relaxed in her seat. But there was still one more crisis ahead. The airport at La Paz is at 13,000 feet, and the plane has to climb another 6,000 or 7,000 feet to safely clear the coastal range of the Andes. From this point, the distance to Arica is only about eighty miles, and it's all downhill, making it the steepest drop made by a commercial airline anywhere in the Americas. We had completely forgotten that Lily had a bad cold.

The plane had hardly begun to descend before her ears began to hurt. In a few minutes, the pain had increased and she began to cry, so I called the stewardess. She was a pretty young thing and she smiled brightly, but she was absolutely helpless and not very concerned, either; all she could suggest was some cotton for Lily's ears. By this time, Lily had her hands pressed to her ears and was sobbing loudly and I was worried that her ear drums would be damaged. I shouted at the stewardess to find somebody who knew what to do. She came back with a steward, who carefully poured some oil into Lily's ears and plugged them with cotton. It seemed to work. Lily stopped crying and nodded her head when the steward asked her if she felt better. Later she said, "Oh, Lord! That was so horrible. I don't think I have ever experienced such pain in my life. It was worse than freezing on that damn bus last night." When we left the plane in Chile, she took out the cotton and found that she could hardly hear.

Chapter 3: The Tarapaca Coast

It was not much warmer in Arica, Chile, and there was a cool mist, too. We had been looking forward to tropical heat, but I had quite forgotten that the cold water of the Humboldt Current sweeps north along this coast as far as Ecuador, and, although it produces almost no rain, it also keeps the coast relatively cool. There were no palm trees and no tropical humidity. If we wanted heat, we would have to go inland about ten miles, into the desert.

The airport was far out of town and coldly efficient. Our passports were stamped, and I was told to get more pages put in, as it was too full. Then the women at Customs took over and went through absolutely everything, even the luggage of passengers in transit. And they took their time. The Chilean obsession about smuggling is well founded. Arica, Chile's northernmost city, was stolen from Peru during the War of the Pacific and populated by Chileans. It is heavily subsidized by the Chilean government and gets favorable treatment whenever possible. Otherwise, few people would want to live trapped in a desert, between the mountains and the sea, far from the heartland, and extremely close to the Peruvian and Bolivian borders. The high cost of transporting almost everything from the distant south results in high prices, and the nearby borders with Bolivia and Peru are temptingly easy to cross. Since both Bolivians and Peruvians believe that smuggling is an honorable profession and that smuggling in and out of Chile is practically a patriotic duty, the unguarded desert borders must be quite busy on moonless nights.

A taxi dropped us at the bus station and since there were a number of bus companies, we chose one with brand new Mercedes Benz buses and bought tickets for the 7:30 overnight trip to Antofagasta, then we left our luggage in the office and went touring.

There was not much to see. The only building of importance was the railway station, which was designed by Gustave Eiffel, the man who designed the Eiffel Tower and also the inside support structure for the Statue of Liberty. The station was not very impressive. Somebody said that Eiffel had also designed a church nearby, but nobody knew where it was.

The most popular car on the streets seemed to be a tiny French car which was assembled in Arica. All the taxis were those little things. We squeezed into one to go to the top of El Morro, a large rock overlooking the city where the Peruvians and the Bolivians made their last futile stand against the Chilean invaders. The view was excellent, but as the taxi driver proudly pointed out all the new factories rising from the desert sand, Lily pointed out the slums of little plywood shacks spreading over the dunes. He was proud of them, too.

Back in the city, we had a light meal of locally caught fish in a restaurant where the food was tasteless, the service miserable, and the price inflationary. Lily went into a store to buy some odds and ends later and came out laughing. "There's a shortage of small coins," she said. "I got an aspirin in place of a penny." Then she looked at it again and said, "Hey, it's probably more useful."

We left Arica at 7:30 that night on a luxurious bus with

roomy, tilt-back seats and good temperature controls. To add to our comfort, the driver's assistant brought around free candies, then little cookies, and she even produced cigarettes for those who wanted to smoke. "Now this is what I call comfort," Lily said as she relaxed back in her seat. "Wake me when we get to Antofagasta."

The well-paved road ran straight as an arrow through the rolling hills, where the encroaching sands were regularly bulldozed back from the road. In the moonlight, I could see nothing but extraordinarily barren desert so empty of any vegetation that it made the *altiplano* look like a meadow, or, as Lily commented, "Death Valley is a garden in comparison."

At 10:00, we stopped at a customs post out in the wilderness and every piece of luggage was inspected all over again. This took two hours. Lily, who still had a cold and whose ears were still hurting, was not feeling well. All she wanted was a glass of cold water, but there was no water available. I tried the water in the washroom, but it was tepid and salty, so I bought a bottle of Coke and sneaked it out of the store and onto the bus. During the night drive, the driver stopped now and then to take a quick nap sitting bolt upright in his elevated seat.

ANTOFAGASTA

We pulled into Antofagasta, a port city in northern Chile, early in the morning. A thin grey fog hid the sun, and the air was quite cold, and when Lily asked, "So where is the famous dry heat of the Atacama Desert?" I had no answer. Antofagasta seemed to be a fairly large town, but the center of the city was almost deserted because everything was closed for a national religious holiday. Even the taxi driver could not find us a restaurant that was open for business, so he dropped us in the main plaza. Eventually, we found a small coffee shop, where we had a makeshift breakfast. I left Lily in the coffee shop and tracked down the bus station. There I learned that every bus going south was packed and that if we waited until midnight we just might, perhaps, get seats.

Neither of us thought waiting till midnight in that closed-up city was a good idea, so we went immediately to the airline office and got tickets on the next flight to Santiago, Chile's capital city. That's when we found out that Chile was having monetary problems. When I tried to use a credit card, I was told that they would accept only cash. Only after a lot of persuasion, did they reluctantly agree to accept my traveler's checks. The flight was due to leave within the hour, so the office boy volunteered—for an exorbitant fee—to drive us to the airport, which was quite far out of Antofagasta and near the ocean. It was cold and windy there, and the blue Pacific was hidden under a fog bank.

When it arrived, the plane was a modern turbo-prop with Rolls Royce engines. Once we were in the air, we could see that while the fog bank extended only a few miles inland, it stretched down the coast like a great silver belt. The plane dived down into it and then up out of it as we stopped at a number of little coastal towns all the way down to Santiago. It would have been a boring trip except that the stewardess poured us a glass of Chilean wine after each take-off and each was from a different winery.

"Now this is what I call very clever advertising for the Chilean wine industry," Lily said.

We had intended to go just as far as Santiago, Chile, but the urge to go "just a little bit further" was too strong, and so we took a bus over the Andes and across the pampas to Buenos Aires in Argentina and Montevideo in Uruguay, then flew to Rio de Janeiro and took buses to São Paulo and the Falls of Iguassu, and then to Asuncion in Paraguay. Back in Bolivia, we had just enough time to visit Cochabamba, Sucre, and Potosí before we had to hurry to Lima to get Lily onto her plane for California.

Chapter 4: The Heart of Bolivia

The soul of Bolivia may be in Copacabana on Lake Titicaca, but the heart of Bolivia is deep in the high Andes at Potosí. Ramiro had insisted that, "Nobody has seen Bolivia if they have not been to Potosí," so when we returned from Paraguay, Lily and I visited Cochabamba, Sucre, and Potosí. We flew from Asuncion to La Paz and the very next morning got a flight to Cochabamba.

This was the first time that we had actually been in the mountains that loom over the *altiplano*, which made the one-hour flight exciting. There were no clouds, and we could see the peaks and the deep valleys, the tiny green lakes and the huge patches of snow, the glaciers and lonely mines high in the roadless land. Now and then, we spotted a tiny village at a ridiculously high altitude and remembered that somewhere in that maze of rock was the highest inhabited settlement in the world, where people lived (and breathed) at close to 18,000 feet. Air Force pilots are ordered to use their oxygen masks above 10,000 feet.

COCHABAMBA

From the small airport where we landed outside Cochabamba we took a taxi to the city center and found a nice little hotel with plenty of hot water. While Lily washed everything that could be washed, I went to check on buses to Sucre. There was nothing available for the next few days, and it was an eleven hour trip, too, so I decided that we would fly and bought tickets for the next day.

Cochabamba, which lies in a wide, fertile valley roughly halfway between the *altiplano* and the Amazon lowlands, was founded by the Incas, who marveled at the perfect climate and the rich soil in which almost anything would grow. They also saw the area as a good frontier post against the wild tribes of the eastern lowlands. In the 16th century, Geronimo de Osorio named it Villa de Oropeza to honor Viceroy Toledo, and it quickly became the breadbasket of the silver-mining towns. However, the fancy name was usually ignored and, to its citizens, it has always been Cochabamba, a relaxed pronunciation of the Kjocha-Pampa valley, from two Quechua words.

The city appeared to have some pleasant suburbs and the streets were clean, but beyond the main colonnaded plaza, which had a stone condor on a pillar in the center and lots of shade trees, there was little of interest. We saw crowds of school children, and as we strolled around, we found bookshops on almost every street. At one particularly well stocked bookstore, I was delighted to find books on the history and the geography of Bolivia in English. Lily found enough books in English to replenished her supply. We also came to a record shop with an excellent collection of Bolivian music, but we could not think how we would get the fragile records home safely, so we just listened.

What I particularly wanted to see in Cochabamba was the house that Simón Patiño built when he was the richest man in the world. Patiño (1862–1947) was born in Cochabamba and made his fortune by monopolizing the tin industry from mines to smelters. The Tin King, as he was called, built a fabulously expensive house in his home town, but never lived in it. Although he died in Argentina, he is buried in Cochabamba.

After lunch, we went to *Portales*, Patiño's house, only to find that it was now a school and we would have to come back in the evening. Next we checked on our airline tickets and learned that we would need a police permit to leave town, but nobody was quite sure where to get it. We eventually tracked down the official responsible, who turned out to be a pretty girl sitting at a rickety card table in the back patio of the police station. She smiled charmingly and assured us that there was no charge for the service.

Patiño's house was not huge, just large, but very impressive. We were the only visitors that day, and the young guide who showed us around spoke perfect English. It took five years to build the house, he said, and another two years to decorate it. Nobody knows just how many millions it cost, as everything except the bricks was imported and the expense of hauling the heavy and often fragile objects from Europe into the heart of Bolivia has never been calculated. The floors and fireplaces were of Carrera marble, the parquet floors were from France, the silk brocade wall paper and the tapestries were Gobelin. One room was copied from a room in the Alhambra, another was influenced by the Sistine Chapel, and the billiard room was Moorish. There were beautifully carved chests and wall paneling, there was stained glass, there was an indoor swimming pool and a hot house for Patiño's orchids, and there were even flags designed especially for him and woven by Gobelin.

It took us some time to see everything, and the guide waited to the end of our tour to finish the story of Patiño, who was the illegitimate son of a local girl and a Basque. It was because of his humble origins that the richest man in the world was snubbed by the local aristocrats and never moved into his lovely mansion. He left his native land, never to return, and neither he nor any of his family ever spent a night in the place. He died in Buenos Aires, but he is buried in Bolivia, the land of his birth.

That night, as it rained a soft warm rain, we dined in a Chinese restaurant that still had its Christmas decorations up. It also had a menu in English with only one error in it.

In the morning, we were at the airport by 8:00 only to be told that the plane would be at least an hour late. So we sat in the sun and waited. Lily had a bad throat and desperately needed a soft drink or some orange juice, but the best we could find was a rather dry orange that I bought from a small boy. Near the airport entrance there was a very 1930s German-looking statue dedicated to the pioneer commercial pilots who flew these perilous skies in the early days and *gab ihre Leben*, "Gave Their Lives." Germany did indeed provide many of the planes and most of the pilots, but Germany also used the arrangement to train hundreds of pilots for its own military air force during the 1930s.

SUCRE

When it finally arrived, our plane turned out to be an ancient DC-3. It was not full, and in fact there were more bundles of cargo than passengers. The takeoff was bumpy and so was the flight, which was fairly short. One of our fellow passengers was an Indian woman, complete with her bowler hat and baby in the shawl on her back. Rather than move the baby, she sat leaning forward the whole flight. After one spectacular bump, the flight deck door flew open. We could see the pilot reading a newspaper and his co-pilot sitting back, sipping a soft drink. This did not engender confidence on our part. Through the window ahead of them, we could see the jagged, snow-capped peaks rising and falling and occasionally twisting wildly as the automatic pilot battled the crosswinds and updrafts. There was no stewardess, and the door eventually slammed shut again.

Sucre, the legal capital of Bolivia, is the seat of both the Bolivian Supreme Court and the oldest university in Bolivia. It was in Sucre (Chuquisaca) in 1825 that Simón Bolívar declared Alto Peru an independent republic and named it Bolivia after himself. Sometimes called the City of Four Names, Sucre was originally known as Chuquisaca. In 1538, it was renamed Villa de La Plata (City of Silver), but throughout the colonial period it was more commonly referred to as Charcas. After independence, it was renamed Sucre to honor the South American great general, <u>Antonio José de Sucre</u>. Charcas became a rich and extremely powerful city during the Spanish colonial period, rivaling Lima and Mexico City, but during the wars for independence, it suffered terribly. Today it is a beautiful and pleasant city, but also a city that is off the beaten track and overshadowed by La Paz.

The airport at Sucre was on a small plateau away from the city. It was the crudest airport we had ever seen. The runway was just a strip of cleared ground with the edges defined by two rows of rocks that had once been painted white. After a bumpy, dusty landing, the plane taxied to the airport building to be refueled. The building was a corrugated iron shed with half a dozen oil drums stacked near it and a small locked storage shed nearby. We clambered down the iron steps, carrying our luggage, and watched some men refuel the plane while we waited for a taxi. Refueling was a simple procedure and horribly casual. Somebody climbed up onto the wing with a hose while a barrel was rolled into place. A hand pump was inserted into the barrel and everybody stood around it smoking cigarettes and discussing politics.

When he eventually turned up, the old taxi driver in his ancient Chevy explained that since the airport could not be used at night or during the rainy season, a new airport was being built. Or at least they had started to build it. "When will it be finished?" Lily asked. "Oh, soon, very soon," he said, and as proof he pointed out a little stretch of dirt and an abandoned bulldozer off in the distance.

Another passenger in the taxi suggested a hotel that turned out to be quite charming, with two colonial interior patios, lots of red geraniums in red pots, and even a fountain with very red goldfish. The owner had a passion for red and all the wrought iron grills and carved doors had been painted bright red.

It was a pleasantly warm spring day, and we went for a stroll along the strangely quiet streets, which were wide and clean and almost empty of cars and trucks. After the noise and air pollution of La Paz, it was quite restful, and we even came to some nice parks with shade trees. The main plaza with its ornate cathedral and equally ornate city hall was particularly attractive. There were a statue to General Sucre and also a couple of bronze lions that were well worn and shiny from children playing on them, and in one of the parks an army band was playing enthusiastically while the band master wiggled his baton casually against his leg, more or less in time to the music, as he made eyes at every pretty girl that passed.

After lunch, Lily took a nap while I went in search of the airline office. I learned there would not be a plane to Potosí for five days, so I went to the bus station and bought tickets to Potosí for the following day. It seemed that we were moving very fast from town to town and I was not pleased to be doing so, but we had almost run out of time. It was now only a matter of days before Lily had to be back to work. As she said, "It's better to get a quick glimpse than to not see anything."

That afternoon, Lily and I started out for the market but decided to stop at the American Express office on the way. Despite what it said in the guidebook, this office did not exist. A passing stranger helped us look for it, but the address in the book turned out to be a private house. "Guidebooks," said my wife, "are written by people who have never traveled more than a day's drive from home." I had to agree with her.

Near the market was a row of Indian porters sitting on a low wall and waiting for work. Like other Indians we'd seen, they were dressed in homespun clothes, with their ropes and blankets on their shoulders and heavy rubber-tire sandals on their bare feet. Like the market in Cochabamba, this market in Sucre sold almost only locally-grown fruit and vegetables, and there was very little by way of native crafts and no tourist souvenirs. What this market did have was a wonderful kaleidoscope of Indian costumes.

My friend Ramiro had warned us that many Indians are

superstitious about cameras and might refuse to be photographed. In this, we learned, he was correct. We were the only tourists there that day, and whenever either of us lifted our camera, the women would shyly hide their faces and the men would turn their backs. Some men even scowled angrily. Lily became quite frustrated and tried to sneak a few shots when nobody was looking, but it is very hard for a tall, blue-eyed blonde *gringa* to be inconspicuous in a crowd of short, very dark Andean Indians. When we put our cameras away and simply walked up to the Indians and admired their clothing, they smiled and were shyly proud, though only a few of them spoke Spanish.

Among the wide variety of Indian clothing, much was based on the clothing worn centuries before by the Spanish invaders. One tribe in that region, for example, has a colorful felt hat that is an exact copy of the helmet worn by 17th-century Spanish foot soldiers, and another has a chest panel of brightly decorated cloth that looks very much like a medieval tabard. Somebody in La Paz had told us that the famous bowler hat worn by the Indian women around Lake Titicaca was a copy of the bowler hats worn by English and other European visitors in the 19th century. Also, the tall white hats worn by the women of Cochabamba were copies of the hats worn by rich hidalgos of the colonial period. Unfortunately, as Lily pointed out, "the teenagers seem to prefer blue jeans."

On our way back to our hotel, we walked down silent streets lined with flat-fronted colonial-style houses, all painted in pastel colors and with their window shutters tightly closed. We guessed that they were vacation homes all locked up for the winter. The law courts and the university, one of the oldest and most prestigious in the Americas, were on vacation, and the dignified old buildings were silent and empty. It was here that the very first sparks of revolution against Spain had been fanned in 1809 and burst into a fire that lasted sixteen years.

As the sun went down over Sucre, the temperature plummeted. Back at the hotel, we discovered, to our delight, that there was plenty of hot water for showers, after which we dined on sausage and mash washed down with a huge bottle of Potosí beer. I liked that brand of beer because the advertisement was a little Indian boy dressed in a wool cap, poncho, and sandals, peeing into a mountain stream under the slogan "Don't Drink the Water."

By the next morning, Lily's sore throat had turned into a bad cold, the landlady was extremely unhappy about taking a traveler's check, and there were no taxis to be had. I started to carry our bags to the bus station, but at that altitude I was soon exhausted. Then a rather small boy suddenly appeared and shyly offered to carry our bags. In a minute, he had everything tied to his back and was trotting off down the road without even breathing hard. He asked two pesos for his labor, but when Lily gave him ten, we watched his face as he stared at the coin. "From the look on his face, that was probably more than he makes all week," she said. "But it was worth it."

The bus was a new Japanese mini-bus, and not only was there plenty of room, but it even left on time. The other passengers were a cheerful mix of Indians and businessmen who spent much of the time arguing about the age of a turtle that one of them was taking to Potosí to sell. The road was badly maintained, but the sun was bright and the seats were comfortable, and we were quite warm. Our route led up a narrow valley with spring blossoms on the trees, and now and then we passed old, crumbling haciendas, some of them faintly Moorish in style. Many of the fields were being plowed by patient oxen pulling wooden plows.

As we climbed higher, we left agriculture behind and entered a land of yellow dust and gray rocks and the occasional tiny village that we sped through in a cloud of dust. At mid-morning, when we stopped for a break, all the men headed for an alley to urinate while the women remained on the bus. There were no soft drinks anywhere, so I bought some rather worn oranges for Lily. Most of the villages had a tiny shack that called itself a hotel, but they were really just bars. Lily pointed out one that had a grass roof and was barely six feet square, but had a huge sign proclaiming itself the *Pension Potosí*. There were a few willow trees in the small fields, and many of them were being used to store hay or corn high off the ground. The bus windows were dusty, but we both tried to get a snapshot of these curious but practical treetop haystacks.

After a long climb, the bus crossed an ornately castellated bridge over a dry river, splashed across two or three fords, and came out onto a high, treeless plain with a few lonely farms and flocks of sheep scattered across the stony fields. We stopped for lunch at a little place where we had hot soup and sausages that were very spicy but very good and fresh baked bread.

Lily and I dozed off for the rest of the trip and woke up in the mountains where gangs of soldiers were repairing the road. Suddenly the bus turned a corner and the ancient city of Potosí lay right before us, gleaming in the sun and nestled at the foot of a great pyramid-shaped gray mountain, the fabled Cerro Rico de Potosí, the rich mountain of silver.

POTOSÍ

It was a little before three when the bus crawled up the cobblestone streets and deposited us in front of a hotel. This was a large, almost palatial, modern building with parquet floors and a wide sweeping stair case. Our room was big with a high ceiling, and there was plenty of hot water and even a portable electric heater.

Our first move was to go down to the railway station and buy tickets to Oruro on the Saturday train. That done, we walked back past a miner's monument and warehouses where the tin and silver and lead ores were stacked in big heaps of brown sacks. In the city center, we browsed around the market, looking for cheap film, and stared at all the old historic buildings. Most of the buildings now housed shops of various kinds, and on one street we came across an ancient colonial church that had been converted into a cinema. It was showing the latest horror movie.

The Casa de Moneda (the mint) was closed, and almost all the churches were tightly locked. As it was getting cold and the altitude was tiring, we headed back to the hotel to dine on the usual beefsteak and a very strange vegetable omelet. The temperature dropped rapidly, and the electric heater that had looked so good earlier proved to be almost useless in the huge bedroom with its high ceilings and polished stone floor, so we sat wrapped in blankets as Lily wrote letters and I stared out the window into the night.

It was hard to believe that we were in the Imperial City of Potosí, at an altitude of 13,000 feet in the middle of the Bolivian Andes. For years I had read everything I could find about Potosí, but I had never dared dream that one day I would actually go there. Lily felt that the Falls at Iguassu were the high point of our journey, and indeed they had been very beautiful, but I felt that this visit to Potosí was the high point. Now all we had to do was see as much as we could in one day, then get Lily home as quickly as possible.

Although she woke up coughing the next morning, and her eyes were red rimmed, she was cheerful. "Stop worrying," she said. "I'm fine enough to do some sightseeing." She set off at a good pace, despite the altitude, though she had to stop and rest quite frequently as we made our way back to the Casa de Moneda. There were other mints in Spanish America, but this was the most important and most valuable one in the empire of Spain and for many years after because it was here that most of the raw silver torn out of the Andes was minted into the flood of large silver pesos that financed the Spanish empire and were accepted as currency as far as China and Europe and the fledgling United States. It was the wealth that came from this building that indirectly financed the Industrial Revolution and changed the history of the Western world.

Over the main door in the inner courtyard is a huge painted carving of Bacchus, the Greek god of wine. "I can't count the number of times that I have seen that thing in books and magazines," Lily remarked, echoing my thoughts exactly. Legend has it that the artist carved it to look like the governor who had insulted him and took too long to pay him. We waited under the Bacchus' grinning face for the guide, along with an American backpacker in a coon-skin cap, a Bolivian family, and some French and German tourists. Although the old stone building was bitterly cold and the tour was quite extensive, it was so enthralling that nobody even noticed any discomfort.

The mint was a sprawling building, many of whose rooms had been turned into art galleries displaying great paintings ranging from early primitives to priceless classics of the colonial period. Some rooms also held a very good collection of Indian clothing from all around Bolivia. Each door was carefully unlocked to let us in, then locked again as we left, and no photos were allowed. The mint itself was astonishing. In the center was a great horizontal wheel with massive wooden beams that rose and fell to stamp the dies into the silver. Slaves or convicts pushed on long poles that looked rather like a ship's capstan to turn the massive device, which, like much of that building, was made of heavy timbers that had been hauled up from the eastern forests far below Potosí. The floor was unsafe in places, and we could clearly see the deep grooves worn in the floor boards by the bare feet of the wretches who slaved to work the machine. As we stood in awe, I could imagine the endless thump of those great beams pounding out the silver coins.

In other rooms, we saw the rollers that pressed the silver and the smoke-blackened, brick, smelting ovens where the silver ore was melted using charcoal brought up from the valleys below. We also saw all the other equipment used to ensure that the silver was 99.9 percent pure. There were racks of dies that had been used and worn out over the years and, in a separate room, a coin collector's dream: a beautiful collection of silver pesos dating back to the earliest and most primitive coins. They were all displayed behind thick glass and the room was securely locked when we left.

In a patio behind the mint, we saw a group of girls and women sitting in the sun and binding books by hand. It had been an excellent tour and it lasted until noon.

At lunch in the hotel, there were a number of Japanese and German businessmen talking with some Bolivian dignitaries. They were discussing mining and minerals in meticulously enunciated English and switched to perfectly pronounced Spanish whenever it was necessary. It was a pleasure to eavesdrop on them as we ate.

That afternoon, we took a bus that was supposed to go to the top of the mountain. The Cero Rico de Potosí, which has produced silver since its discovery nearly 500 years ago, is honeycombed with so many mines that they could never be mapped. Today, only vague estimates can be made of the enormous fortune the hill has given up. It still produces a little silver as well as tin and lead. The bus only went as far as one of the mine entrances, where there was a statue of a miner holding a gun. The hillside was torn up, muddy water gushed from pumps, and machinery was scattered everywhere. Like colorful ants, Indian women were scavenging the tailings for any little bit of ore while the coca chewing men with their green mouths pushed loaded wheel barrows. The place looked like a war zone while, far below, the tiled roofs and towers of Potosí shone in the sun.

When we were back in the city, I asked a group of taxi drivers if anybody would take us to the very top of the mountain. I explained that Simón Bolívar had made a speech from the top and somewhere I had read that there is a statue at the summit that I wanted to see.

Almost all the drivers claimed that the road was too dangerous and, anyway, it did not go all the way to the top. "He must have gone up on horseback," said one. "I'll give it a try for fifty dollars American." said another. "Don't even think about trying to walk up," said the first man. "You were not born here. You couldn't handle the altitude." No such thought had ever crossed my mind.

Still in town, we found a famous Jesuit church with its fantastically carved doorway created by Indian students, but it was locked and nobody knew who had the keys. "I think it's always locked," Lily said. "I have never seen a picture of the inside, just the doorway."

Most of the people who crowded the streets of Potosí were Indians, probably mine workers. Women in warm shawls sat at little stalls along the streets selling pins, coins, and jewelry they claimed was solid silver, but, judging by its weight, was probably made from tin cans and thinly coated in silver. Mixed in with everything else were bright plastic children's toys and bales of coca. Some of the street corners had a traffic policeman in a little booth, but all the drivers ignored the one-way traffic signs and failed to hear the policeman's whistle. Strangely, this did not seem to bother him.

At sunset, all the electricity in the hotel went off. We dined by lamplight, and candles were placed on each step of the winding stairs so that it was quite romantic for a while. But then it began to get cold. The waiter told us that it happened quite often and added cheerfully that we were lucky because a few weeks earlier it had snowed quite heavily. Lily thanked him politely for that bit of useful information. There was a candle in our room, too. The electric heater was, of course, entirely useless, so we squeezed into a single bed with extra blankets and kept each other warm. The lights came back on just as we were falling asleep.

We got up early to pack, then sat in the sunshine to thaw. "I think you should change our tickets," Lily said. "I really don't think I should come anywhere near Barbara and the children with this cold."

So I went to the train station only to find that the section from Oruro to La Paz was fully booked. We would have to stop in Oruro. While I was there, a very old train chugged by, a big, black wood-burner pulling a freight car and three wooden passenger cars, one of which seemed to be a restaurant car. Nobody could tell me where it was going, so as the engineer waved proudly, I took a photo.

While waiting for our train, we bought some oranges for Lily from a peddler. Soon we heard a band warming up in the parking lot. It was a wedding and no expense had been spared. There were eight giant decorative arches, each completely covered in ribbons and silver objects of every kind, from tiny coins to massive serving dishes, forks and spoons, and necklaces and rings. Every scrap of silver had been collected from the groom's relatives to show the bride's family that the girl was going to a good home. It was a dazzling sight. I was peering at a string of priceless old silver pesos, each with an ugly hole punched into it, when our train arrived.

It was a modern Japanese diesel with two streamlined cars, and it was crowded and very warm. The conductor, a pompous little man with a red face, found us a pair of seats that gave us a last long view of the towering peak of the Cerro de Potosí and the shiny silver wedding arches as the train pulled out of the station.

When it was built, the line from Potosí to Oruro was the

highest rail line in the world, climbing to 15,700 feet above sea level, a thousand feet higher than the Mollendo to Lake Titicaca line. Within an hour, we had climbed out of the mountains and reached Arctic tundra, where we crawled across a wide, wind-swept land of eroded rocks. It was bleak but strangely beautiful, with patches of ice gleaming in the sun. Here and there we could see bright green hummocks of *yaretta*, a plant that looks like moss but can be used as fuel, and I thought of the long trains of llamas that had used this route for centuries to bring out the silver from Potosí. To Lily's delight, the llamas were still there. Scattered across the land there were small herds of them living semi-wild and somehow finding enough food in the wilderness.

The passengers in our carriage were a cheerful Saturday crowd. The only other foreigner was an Englishman with an expensive camera. A little man with a worn broom repeatedly swept the floor, and the loudspeaker blared Bolivian music while waiters wriggled through the coaches with sandwich lunches and soft drinks on trays. The women were naturally curious about Lily and her blond hair, and when they saw that she had a bad cold, a number of them offered suggestions. One woman brought some Vaseline for her red and sticky eyes. One tiny child came up close and stood staring at me for a long time until I went cross-eyed at her and she ran off giggling at the strange foreigners. Neither of us felt like eating, but the air was extraordinarily dry and so we drank a lot of Coke, and I tried to persuade Lily to sleep.

As we crawled back down to the *altiplano*, we began to see small villages and mining activity, and when we reached the flat land the engineer made up for lost time. At one point, the track had been laid right through Lake Poopo. All around us, the shallow water of the lake was covered in flocks of birds. There were thousands of pink flamingoes with black wings and tall white herons, as well as flocks of gulls and many tiny water birds, all so busy feeding that they didn't notice the train. The flamingoes especially fascinated Lily, who found it difficult to imagine these tropical birds so high on the *altiplano*.

FROM ORURO TO LIMA

When we pulled into Oruro just before sunset, I phoned Barbara Miranda to explain that Lily was suffering from a cold. Barbara insisted that we come to the house right away and not worry about the children. Ramiro was up at the mine, she added, but due back that night. His father, who was at the house, suggested shots for Lily, but I did not know what she was allergic to and did not recognize the medicine, so I politely turned down his offer. Instead, Barbara made hot soup and found a portable heater, and we sat and talked about our adventures until almost midnight, at which point we hustled Lily into bed, where she had a good night's sleep.

Because Ramiro had arrived after driving mountain roads all night, we let him sleep until noon. Then we went to his garage to check the Land Rover. He had had a flat tire, and now the spare was flat, too, so he got out the truck and picked up Lily and the luggage. We thought we were late for the bus, so our farewells were brief, but when we got to the bus station, there was a problem. They had already lashed down the luggage on the roof, and we didn't have tickets, but Ramiro argued with the driver and sat Lily down in the door of the bus while I dashed off to get the tickets. Then we dragged our luggage inside the bus. It was very crowded and the driver was furious, but we were safely on the bus.

As the sun set on Oruro, the bus bounced across the open countryside on the old gravel road to the brand-new road that has just been finished. An old man explained to us that this was the only completely surfaced road in Bolivia and nobody was supposed to use it before the official opening ceremonies which were scheduled for next week. "But," he said, "why waste a perfectly good road?" The driver put his foot down on the accelerator and made no stops until the lights of El Alto appeared on the horizon. Then he drove back onto the old road.

La Paz looked very pretty in the night, with all its lights twinkling in the great basin. We chose a hotel that seemed to be warm, but the radiator in our room was stone cold, so I demanded that they find a good electric heater or we would move immediately to another hotel. They produced one, and while I was testing it, the maid took a look at Lily and asked if perhaps she needed oxygen. She offered to bring a cylinder, but Lily politely refused and insisted that she was better than she looked.

Lily did seem better in the morning. I made a quick dash to the U.S. Embassy for any letters. The marine on duty reminded me that it was Labor Day back in the States. My heart nearly stopped. School started the day after Labor Day. There was no hope that Lily could get back in time. I just prayed that the letter I had mailed some days earlier, in which I claimed that there had been an airline foul-up, had arrived and that Lily's school had a substitute standing by.

The plane to Lima was due to leave at 1:30, but we left extra early just in case anything went wrong. And of course it did. Halfway up the road to El Alto, the street was blocked by a line of police in riot gear and a crowd of students shouting and waving placards. I gathered that this was partly a political demonstration and partly a demand for more money for schools. It took the police half an hour to clear the road to allow the long line of stalled traffic to get through. I gave a hand to help shove rocks off the road. True to form, the plane was nearly an hour late and exit taxes took almost all of our Bolivian currency.

Before we boarded the plane, I realized that I was coming down with a cold, too. Lily produced some cotton for our ears, and we just hoped for the best. She also produced a large thermometer which she shoved into my mouth. "How accurate is this thing?" I mumbled, thinking about the altitude. "It's very accurate," she replied. "I use it on my cats quite regularly." She caught the look on my face and laughed, "Just a joke." If Lily could make jokes, she was not sick.

Our flight had originated in Buenos Aires, and sitting in the plane was a large, overdressed woman who started to complain about a shortage of air. When she got quite excited, the stewardess brought her a small cylinder of oxygen with a plastic tube in it. The lady sat back sucking happily on her bottle for a few minutes. Then Lily began to giggle. "That cylinder has a gauge on it," she whispered in my ear. I looked and nodded. "It reads empty," she whispered. "Anyway, I don't think you take oxygen by sucking on a straw." When we were airborne, the stewardess took back the cylinder with a straight face.

The flight to Lima was smooth and we got a fine view of Lake Titicaca. The next day, I saw Lily safely onto her plane for Los Angeles. Back at the hotel, I planned my trip to Arequipa and back to Bolivia and worked out exactly where I hoped to go in the short time available to me.

Chapter 5: The Peruvian Coast

After I had seen Lily (clutching an armful of souvenirs) safely onto the plane to Los Angeles, I returned to the hotel to plan my route. I was already feeling lonely without Lily. Traveling without her would not be the same. We had been together through good days and bad days for nearly three months, traveling thousands of miles through seventeen countries on every form of transport from ancient buses to luxury airlines. We had seen Machu Picchu and the falls at Iguassu, the Panama Canal, Rio de Janeiro, and Lake Titicaca. We had sweltered in tropical heat and frozen in the mountains and slept in everything from a luxury hotel on the Caribbean to a mud brick Indian farm house on the *altiplano*. I would miss having her beside me.

As I had the beginnings of a cold, Lily had made me promise that I would not go back up onto the *altiplano* until I was quite healthy. So I slept late, then headed for the bus station to see about transport to Arequipa, which is in southern Peru. I had planned on taking a communal taxi, which would cut the long trip from nineteen to only fourteen hours, but they were all full, and so I had to take the bus, which was half the price. After a long wait, the bus eventually arrived late in the afternoon.

The bus was not too crowded. The passengers were a mixed bunch that included a black couple across the aisle, and, in front of me an Indian woman with her hat perched on her head, who sat bolt upright all night long , never once leaning back. The bus was reasonably comfortable and had plenty of leg room. I had come prepared for a cold night, but it was actually not too bad, barely tolerable. Everybody else had brought warm blankets, but my sweater and a jacket were enough for me.

The coast of Peru is pure desert broken only by an occasional oasis wherever a river reaches the Pacific. Little towns and villages suddenly appear near the rivers and banana and orange trees bloom for a mile or two, then it is back to rock and sand. It never rains here, so the houses of the poor have woven straw roofs and are usually just mud-plastered sticks. Some are made entirely of woven straw mats. Only the affluent have real roofs. As we drove south, a series of villages came and went in the dark, and whenever we stopped at one, the bus was instantly surrounded by children selling bananas or huge juicy oranges they carried in plastic bags.

For supper, we stopped at an inn by the beach. Almost everybody else filled up on the usual chicken and rice, but I was not hungry, so I bought a bottle of Inca Cola and strolled down to the water. In the starlight, huge rollers, gleaming and flashing, crashed with a constant roar onto a beach that seemed to stretch for ever.

The road was well engineered and mostly flat, but wherever the mountains reached down to the sea, the road either twisted and turned in hair-raising curves or tunneled right through. At one particularly dangerous bend, the bus stopped. We peered out the windows and down about 500 feet at the remains of a vehicle that had not quite made the curve. It appeared to have been a bus, but there wasn't much left of it.

Here and there, nitrate ore showed where it had been exposed by bulldozers. It has little value now, but once, not so long ago, men struggled in this wilderness to dig it up for fertilizer and high explosives.

During the night, an army officer took the seat next to me. He wore his hat all the time and mumbled about the bus being late. I would have preferred Lily next to me. She does not sleep with a hat on. Woolen socks, sometimes, but never a hat.

Breakfast was at a straw-roofed Chinese restaurant that served no Chinese food. I had coffee and rolls and talked with the driver, who explained that, since he had no passengers for Mollendo, he would go straight to Arequipa. "Anyway," he said, "why would you want to go to Mollendo? There's nothing there."

I didn't bother to explain that it was from Mollendo that the Spaniards shipped much of the enormous fortune in silver that came down from the silver mines of Potosí, and it was also just off Mollendo that the English and Dutch pirates lurked, waiting for that same silver. I learned that during the night we had sped through Nazca and the gigantic, mysterious markings in the desert.

The coastal fog burned away as the road climbed up from the coast to the foothills and the little oasis villages became fewer. It also got much hotter. The soldier took off his jacket, but not his hat, and the Indian woman pulled her blanket more tightly around her. It was a long slow climb. I could see the dormant volcano, El Misti, three hours before we arrived.

There was a sudden sharp line between arid desert and green cultivated fields, and five minutes later we reached the plateau and entered Arequipa, the second largest city in Peru. Arequipa sits comfortably at the foot of El Misti, a 19,000 foot active volcano.

AREQUIPA

We had been on the bus for twenty hours, and the floor was inches deep in orange peels. Everybody was quite glad to get off and stretch their legs at the inevitable police road block. Out in the desert, the heat was fierce, but at 7,000 feet, the city is nicely cool. Arequipa looked like an attractive town of gleaming white buildings with clean and tidy streets. A helpful taxi driver showed me the hotel recommended in the guidebook. It was so grubby, however, that we didn't even stop. He took me to a tall, brand new hotel where the prices were quite reasonable. I was given a luxurious room on the ninth floor with a spectacular view and plenty of hot water, plus a bottle of mineral water, compliments of the Jesus Mineral Water Company.

There has probably been a settlement at Arequipa since long before the time of the Incas, who valued the region for its tropical agricultural products and sea foods. The Spanish also appreciated its pleasant climate and well irrigated soil and its ideal position on a steady trade route far enough inland from the coast to be safe from pirates. The white volcanic stone was easy to quarry, and the city grew quickly as merchants and rich Hidalgos scrambled to build fine houses. Lima may have been the capital and the seat of power, but Arequipa was by far the more comfortable city in Peru.

I spent a long weekend wandering about the city and sunning myself in the plaza, drinking lots of orange juice and gulping aspirins until I was quite sure my cold had gone.

Arequipa's Plaza de Armas was quite lovely, with two-level arches on three sides and the cathedral on the fourth. There were trees and flowers, and I was not the only one enjoying the perfect weather. I did notice that there were not many tourists and that most of the foreigners were German or American businessmen.

The old part of the city has been well preserved, and I spent hours strolling past numerous Spanish houses built in a similar, slightly Arabic style. They were usually single-level homes built directly on the street with the minimum number of windows, which were protected by heavy wrought-iron grills. Their façades were dominated by huge wooden doors, wide enough for a man on horseback, some even big enough to allow a carriage through, and they were almost all built of the white volcanic rock which gives Arequipa its nickname, the White City. All the churches and many of the old houses had intricate stone carving around the doors and the windows, and many of the doors were also beautifully carved. I peered into every door that I could and saw that they usually opened onto a charming patio. Some of these patios were small jungles of carefully tended trees and flowers in giant containers, while others had beautifully carved arches. They were not tall houses, and quite a few of them had, over the years, settled in the soft soil and their foundations were now below street level. Some of the houses had domed roofs. Considering that the city lies in an active earthquake zone a short distance from a very large volcano, it is not surprising that the Spanish kept their buildings low. Most of the houses in the suburbs of Arequipa were made from the white volcanic stone. All of them had TV antennas on the roof. The cathedral, like the famous Jesuit church in Potosí, had a doorway carved by Indian masons in the unique, highly intricate pattern of intertwined leaves and flowers that they developed. It was a fine building with two very short towers. The loveliest old 17th-century building was the British consulate.

On Saturday night there was a religious celebration in the street opposite my hotel. There were three large bamboo towers covered with fireworks, and the rockets flew wildly in all directions while the occasional Catherine wheel spun off crazily down the street. Through the smoke and drifting sparks, El Misti gleamed in the moonlight.

On Sunday I was listening to the band in the plaza when a man from Uruguay struck up a conversation with me. Lily and I had visited Montevideo and had not been impressed, so when he boasted of an eighty percent literacy rate in his country, I suggested that perhaps a decent garbage collection system and efficient sewers might be of better use to the citizens. He was quite puzzled at my strange North American values and soon walked away.

THE TRAIN TO PUNO

Even if there had been a bus, I would have taken the train to Puno and Lake Titicaca. Not just because I like trains, but because this line, which runs from Mollendo at sea level to the great lake at 12,500 feet, was one of the great railway building feats of the 19th century. The first section, from Mollendo to Arequipa, was one of the first railroads built in South America. Before it even reaches Arequipa, the train has to climb 7,500 feet in barely 100 miles. A gradient of seventy five feet per mile is impossible, so the track twists and turns in a series of loops, hairpin bends, and switchbacks, sometimes turning on itself like a snake in order to gain just a few more feet of altitude. At Arequipa, the train still has 200 miles to go and 5,000 more feet to climb.

It was a cool morning when I arrived at the station, and the first thing I noticed was that many of the train's windows were stuck open. The train was built by the British and was relatively new, with a buffet car and lots of green leather. It was also quite clean. There were eight coaches, and the second class was packed, while the first class coaches were nearly empty, with only a handful of tourists. Most of the second-class passengers carried their goods in bleached flour-sack bundles and stood on the platform, making their farewells long after the station master had clanged his large bell. The train had just started when the conductor grabbed a boy selling hair clippers and led him by the ear back to the second class carriages, but almost immediately the boy was replaced by a man selling altitude sickness pills. At times there seemed to be more people selling things on the train than in the central market.

As we left the city, we saw brilliantly green fields of onions and women cutting wheat with sickles, but very quickly we were out in the desert where the only vegetation was the cactus. The train was quite fast and climbed steeply in wide curves around a snow covered range, and now and then we passed a tiny oasis, brilliant green in all the brown. But the desert was far from dull. There were steep canyons and the occasional tunnel and tiny streams that had cut deep gullies through the rock. There were pretty yellow flowers growing on ugly scrub, blossoms on some varieties of cactus, and wild flowers hiding between the boulders. At a whistle stop called Green Hills, there was a handsome horse with an expensive silver saddle and large wooden stirrups tethered to a tree. In the background, snow covered mountains loomed everywhere.

The train was cold and drafty, so I wrapped up in my sweater and parka again and snacked on a cheese sandwich and coffee. About mid-morning, we stopped on a wide, desolate plateau where tough yellow grass grew between the rocks. This was the Pampa de los Arrieros, or Plain of the Mule Drivers. It was here that the long trains of llamas transferred their precious loads of silver to the mules that would take the silver down to sea level. Both mules and llamas were given time to rest and nibble at the tough grass, then the llamas, loaded with imported goods, would make the long journey back to Potosí. The *arrieros*, or mule drivers, walked every inch of the way alongside their animals, often as many as fifty mules in each string.

A trickle of silver made its way south to Chile and Argentina and some went directly to Lima, but the bulk of it went down to the Pacific. There were half a dozen places along the coast where the silver could be loaded onto ships that would carry it north to Panama, but most of these "ports" were merely slight indentations in the desert coast line. The Mejillones/Antofagasta area was the best port, but that route lay across the salt flats of Uyuni, through the volcanic coastal range of the Andes, then down across the widest part of the Atacama Desert. Even the llama must eat and drink, but vegetation and water were scarce (and in some seasons non-existent) over most of the route. The most popular route was along the shore of Lake Titicaca, then down to Arequipa and Mollendo. This was at least twice as long, but there was plenty of grass and water on the *altiplano*, and the mules could be used for the last extremely rough section. Mollendo was also nearly a week's sailing time closer to Lima and Panama and thus a little safer from the pirates.

There was no harbor at Mollendo. The men walked out into the surf and loaded the cargo into small boats, which then took it out to the ships anchored as close to the shore as they safely could. It was hard and difficult work, but almost every ounce of silver that was exported and almost every necessity or luxury that was imported was carried through the surf and loaded immediately onto the sturdy backs of mules that had probably been raised far away on the Argentine pampas around Salta.

All the second-class passengers got off the train for lunch at portable stoves set up near the track by Indian women. Out in the distance there were two or three small buildings, a mixed herd of sheep, goats, and llamas, and dust devils dancing across the plateau. The passengers ate quickly, then hurried back onto the train, which set off across the plateau and began to climb again.

It got much colder, and then is started to snow. I tried to close all the windows, but some were jammed, and all I could do was pull down the blinds. Three or four times, we stopped at unmarked spots in the wilderness where a lonely figure would climb down from the train, saddle bags or flour sack luggage slung over his shoulders, and, vanish into the Arctic tundra. In some places, tiny groups of women and children huddled in blankets against a stone wall stared at the train, and now and then a small herd of llamas ignored us as we passed. It was so cold in the drafty, unheated train that my feet began to hurt again, and I paced up and down the carriage thinking of the wonderfully warm city I had left just that morning.

But the train continued to climb and I continued to be astonished that people lived in that desolate land.

The train stopped for a few minutes at Cruzero Alto. At 14,660 feet, it is the highest point on the line, and at that time it was constructed, it was the highest point on any passenger rail line in the world. There was nothing there except a couple of low buildings slowly being covered with snow. Now the train started its descent. Actually, it was only a drop of 2,000 feet to the *altiplano*, but it seemed like much more as the snow quickly turned to light rain and it seemed to be less cold.

The land on the east side of the coastal range was less arid than on the west. We passed two or three large lakes, one with black ducks on it, and there were signs of agriculture on the slopes. Here and there, we passed a village where farmers were attacking the damp ground with wooden plows and awkward looking hoes. At one tiny village, I saw a tin roofed shack claiming to be the "Gran Hotel Santa Lucia," but some body had painted over the "Gran." We saw a few trees alongside a small river, then we were out onto the *altiplano*, where herds of sheep and cattle and small villages showed through the late afternoon mist and every patch of ground seemed to be under cultivation.

It was dark by the time we reached Juliaca, where a swarm of vendors climbed onto the train carrying every variety of alpaca poncho or blanket, and small boys scoured the train for plastic bottles and old newspapers. With a lot of whistle blowing and shunting, our train was attached to the train from Cuzco to make a sixteen-car train. Then we crept along the remaining few miles to Puno and Lake Titicaca.

A few years after I'd made this trip, I read that the passenger train from Mollendo to Puno had been discontinued. The train could not compete with improved roads and a regular bus service that made the trip in half the time and was much more comfortable. Today the famous rail line carries an occasional freight train up the ancient trail where, many years ago, the mule drivers guided their long strings of patient animals bearing the silver that built and sustained the Spanish Empire.

THE LAKE STEAMER

When the train pulled into Juliaca, I took the precaution of hiring a sharp looking 14-year-old boy who had clambered onto the train while we were still miles from Puno. He wanted to learn the English words for "Carry your bag, Mister?" I thought that was very enterprising of him. After I hired him and when the train first stopped in Puno, he dragged me off the train and into the very first carriage. Then, when the train moved onto the docks, we were first off the train, and he dragged me through the dark into the customs shed, where I was the first customer. My bags went onto the boat, and I had to line up again at least three times, but my guide hurried me along, and each time he either wriggled me to the head of the line or took my passport and slipped it neatly onto the top of the stack to be stamped. After making sure that he was fluent in "Carry your bag, Mister?" I was quite happy to pay his fee and go aboard the SS *Inca*.

There were a lot of passengers that trip, most of them foreign tourists who had come from Cuzco. There were Germans and French, Americans and English, three Spaniards, a Mexican, and a Brazilian, and they ranged from businessmen with polished shoes to hikers in heavy walking boots. The Latinos all wore suits, while the foreigners nearly all wore parkas and warm sweaters. We were ushered straight into the boat's large dining room, which had two long tables. Supper was served immediately. It was a good, hearty meal of soup, rice, and meat that went down well with a bottle of beer. I dined with a Spaniard from Valencia, a French couple, and a Peruvian woman with four well-behaved children. Everybody was very cheerful, communicating easily in a mixture of English, French, and Spanish. The Germans formed their own beer drinking group at the end of the table. There was a second sitting for supper, so we retired to the lounge, where I found myself talking to a Catalan from Barcelona, where I was born.

The *SS Inca* is not a large ship. She was built in England in 1905, sailed around the Horn, then brought up from the coast in pieces and assembled in Puno. The brass portholes had red velvet curtains with gold tassels, the woodwork was painted white, and there were green velvet cushions and charming brass "pie mold" light switches. There was also an English sideboard with a large mirror and a clock. The heating was supplied by just two skinny radiators, but the ship was comfortably warm.

The old ship was so well maintained that nobody noticed when we pulled away from the dock and quietly slipped out onto Lake Titicaca. I only realized that we were sailing when I happened to look out a porthole and saw that Puno was just a cluster of lights in the distance.

That night, I slept on a very narrow bunk in a cabin off the dining room, which I shared with two American youths who came in late and very drunk. But it didn't affect the wonder I felt. There I was, sailing across Lake Titicaca on the famous steamer, living the dream I had had for so many years. I slept very well.

By 6:30 I was up and out on deck with my camera. The water was gray and choppy, but otherwise it was a fine day, and the view of the lake and the mountains in the background was spectacular. We passed through the Strait of Tiquina, where all the small boats made way for us and a sailor dipped our flag as we passed the Bolivian navy base. I had a quick continental breakfast and hurried out on deck again, where I stood under the billowing black smoke from our tall funnel and spent two hours watching islands go by and soaking up the fantastic view.

At Guaqui, the *SS Inca* slipped smoothly into her berth, where we were greeted by a lone policeman in a battered German helmet painted white. There were no customs or immigration; instead, there was a mad scramble for seats on the two-car diesel train. My bag was grabbed by a boy who said he would take Peruvian money and would save me a seat while I haggled with a money changer and, as usual, lost the argument.

When the train stopped at Tihuanacu so the passengers could take a quick look at the ruins, a boy peddling fake artifacts told me that the train only stops at the ruins twice a week and doesn't bother stopping if it is late. My little guide had found me a wooden seat which seemed quite comfortable, but after half an hour I offered it to a lady with more padding than I possess and, feeling virtuous, I stood for the rest of the way. At El Alto they attached two engines to hold the train back as we made the steep descent into the city. It was a slow, careful descent that took 45 minutes.

It was fortunate that I took that boat trip across the lake because a few years later the historic boat trip was no more. Today the tourists travel around the lake by bus and the oldest boat of the fleet, the *Yavari*, is now a floating restaurant in Puno. The *SS Inca* was broken up.

Chapter 6: The *Atacama* Desert

Ramiro and Barbara Miranda had very kindly offered to make their house in Oruro my base for exploring Bolivia. Together, we agreed that I should certainly visit the real *atacama*, not just the northern tip, so I bought a ticket on the night train to Antofagasta. It was a modern, two-car diesel train on which I had an empty seat next to me. It was almost midnight when we left Oruro. The conductor handed out huge tartan wool blankets. At first, the heating seemed to be adequate, and I used the blanket as a pillow, but at Uyuni the heating system quit functioning. The conductor simply shrugged his shoulders and the train became very cold. The blankets were put to good use.

UYUNI

The southern part of the *altiplano* has a number of large salt flats, but I particularly wanted to see the salt flat of Uyuni, which is the largest salt flat in the world, covering over 3,000 square miles. In a land of mountain peaks, Uyuni is probably the flattest place on earth. It is also the end of the line for the water that drains out of Lake Titicaca through the Rio Desaguadero, and in the rainy season it becomes an immense lake that is only a few inches deep. For centuries, it was considered a useless wasteland with scorching hot days and freezing cold nights, but recently geologists have discovered that the great salt flat contains lithium, which is used in electrical batteries. Today, the world's most valuable deposits of lithium, a very "modern" metal, lie here in this ancient land.

Our train moved smoothly and quickly through the night, skirting the edge of the salt flats, and although there was no moon, the stars were bright enough to see quite clearly the Andes looming to the east and the salt gleaming white to the west. I thought how the railway builders must have enjoyed putting down miles of arrow-straight line across a perfectly level plain after having struggled to lay the line thousands of feet up and onto the *altiplano*. The engineers soon found that it was cheaper to ship in thousands of wooden railway ties from Europe and North America than to bring them up from the Amazonian forest.

Many of the passengers got off at Uyuni, and I wondered why. It was not a very large town, and it wasn't very attractive, either. It seemed to me, situated as it is on the edge of the huge salt flat that is treeless, waterless, and subject to temperatures that could range seventy or eighty degrees in twenty four hours, that it must be one of the worst places to live in Bolivia. It is an important railway junction. There is no agriculture, and the only thing that might interest a tourist is the railway junkyard outside the town, which bears the interesting name the Railway Cemetery.

When the train stopped, the porters were wearing gloves and scarves and their breath steamed in the night air. Some German tourists and I found the extra blankets and snuggled down to sleep as the train headed for the Chilean border, and three large, overdressed women from La Paz fussed about the carriage, looking for places to hide their contraband and talking loudly all the time.

Soon we were so far out on the wide, white flatland that even the highest peaks of the Andes were below the horizon.

OLLAGŰE

I woke to find that we were in the coastal range of the Andes, where all the hills and mountains were clearly volcanic. Their yellow, dry cones were everywhere, and there was not a speck of vegetation anywhere. It was still cold and cloudy and as lonely as the surface of the moon, yet, astonishingly, there were a few llamas and I even glimpsed a tiny farm house.

Ollagŭe proved to be nothing more than a large mining village with a railway siding. Our train parked near the Chilean train, and then somebody collected our passports and told us to switch over to the other train. The three ladies were horrified. They immediately gathered up their contraband and scurried back and forth across the track, still talking excitedly all the time, while the German tourists smiled and pretended not to notice.

Unlike our earlier train, the Chilean train was delightful. It was still clearly labeled Antofagasta-Bolivia Railroad Company and had been built in 1910, but the old wooden coaches were pulled by a modern diesel engine. There were four sleeping cars and three first class cars, and the restaurant car in between had a little chimney on the roof. The two-way seats were cast iron but had comfortable, green, English leather cushions, and there were also brass hat racks and wooden windows with shutters that kept falling down. There were cut-glass panels on the doors and the WC was white tiled, although there was no water in the English pull-chain toilet. The train was beautifully made and still rode smoothly, with only the slightest screech of wheels on the tight bends. I spent much of the rest of the journey wandering up and down the train and leaning out the windows for a better look at the scenery.

When we stopped at a tiny station in Chile, a man wearing blue jeans and carrying a six-shooter on his hip gave us back our passports, then the customs men came down the train. Ignoring the Germans and me, they headed straight for the three women from La Paz, who began protesting loudly. Five minutes later, the customs man left with an armful of small packages. The women were wonderfully silent.

It was a slow, careful ride down to the coast, most of it spent winding down a valley with volcanoes on all sides. None of them were active, but I did spot steam escaping from fumaroles, and there was ample evidence of volcanic activity in the very recent past. It was a wildly savage and very beautiful land with small salt flats, dried up lakes, and rocks carved into strange shapes by wind and sand. The high Andes were bright with snow, but this stretch of the coastal range was mainly dry, with only an occasional patch of snow very high up.

At lunchtime I dined with a Bolivian business man in the charming restaurant car, whose brass fittings included flower holders with plastic flowers in them. The car was clean, the service was good, and the meal was also good, but there were only a few diners.

Everywhere I looked, I saw signs of mining activity. The desert was criss-crossed with tire tracks, some of the hillsides were pock-marked with exploration holes, and here and there blocks of salt or sacks of some mineral were piled alongside the train tracks. Once we passed a siding with a dozen freight cars loaded with chunks of brilliant yellow sulphur. It was startlingly bright against the brown hillsides. I saw not a drop of water anywhere. Although it warmed up by the time we came out of the mountains, there were still no trees nor even any grass.

CALAMA

Calama, Chile, is a big, dusty, ugly mining town lying under a cloud of pollution. It is an oasis town lying on the Rio Loa, but I could see no water in the river. Most of the passengers left the train at Calama, and so I finished the journey almost alone.

The line went straight across the desert, but the scenery was not very interesting, and a slight wind blew fine sand into the train so that I was soon covered in dust. Even my glasses were coated. In the distance, there was a ridge of low hills along the coast. I could see the top of the coastal fog bank drifting over the crest of the hills only to vanish in the dry desert air. It was very like the fog that rolls into San Francisco at certain times of the year.

ANTOFAGASTA

We entered Antofagasta high on the hillside with the sea port spread out before us. The city looked very dusty, the temperature dropped as we descended, and the sun had set before we arrived at the station, where I took a crowded taxi to what I was assured was the second best hotel in town. This was an old building that had plenty of hot water, enough to wash the dust off my skin and out of my hair. Then I dined in solitary splendor in the huge hotel dining room.

Antofagasta had not impressed Lily and me when we were there the first time, and now, after a day spent wandering around the city, I still did not like it. It is an old city with a few modern buildings in the center, but the rest was mainly lower income housing, with slums creeping up the hillside. Many trees had been planted, and there were flowers on some of the streets, but they did not make the city more attractive. It was a cold and windy day, and the city was sadly lacking in decent restaurants or even modern cafes. In one square, I found a monument to English friendship, nearby I found a bandstand dedicated to Yugoslav friendship, and I noticed that the mailboxes were the English red pillar boxes. Otherwise, it was all very dull. The few people I spoke to were rather surly and spoke a terrible Spanish with a strong Chilean accent and too much local slang. (In fact, of all the Latin American countries that Lily and I had visited, the Chileans spoke the worst form of Spanish.)

The one bright place in Antofagasta was the market. The prices were very high, but the quality of the fruit and vegetables was excellent, with huge yellow bananas and luscious grapes all very obviously imported from far to the south or from overseas. The fishermen's wharf was picturesque, with women buying the gleaming fish straight from the boats, but when I asked about a good fish restaurant, nobody could think of one. There was a public beach, but it was dirty and huge waves were crashing onto the sand.

I dined in the hotel again that evening. There were three dozen tables, but only two customers. The plants in their oil barrel pots were dusty, and the train timetable on the wall was twenty years out of date. At that point, I decided that I had seen enough of the coast and decided to backtrack to Calama and go further into the desert to San Pedro de Atacama.

Next morning, I took a very crowded bus to Calama. It was nice to be away from the foggy coast, even though it was not hot and there was even a slight breeze. Calama proved to be a bustling mining town, dirty, expensive and dangerous with narrow streets and corrugated iron buildings everywhere. Groups of rough looking men stood lounging around, and even the women looked hard and grim. The bus driver told me that there was no bus to San Pedro that day, "Maybe tomorrow," he said, so I checked in at what seemed to be the only decent hotel in town. It proved to be very modern but very expensive, and I shuddered when I saw the prices in the restaurant.

Since there was nothing to see in Calama, I walked out to the river. The Rio Loa is unique because it is the only river to cross the *atacama* and usually has some water in it when all the other streams have dried up long before they reach the Pacific. Before this land was stolen from Bolivia, Calama was a popular oasis village on the trade route from the *altiplano* to the Pacific at Mejillones or Antofagasta. Today, the little river cannot supply enough water for a mining town, and water has to be brought great distances through aqueducts that reach far up and into the coastal range of the Andes, where the water is collected from the melting snow.

The river I saw was barely ten feet wide and blocked behind a concrete dam. There were some scraggly trees and some painted concrete picnic tables, but it was not very inviting. I took the ramshackle bus back to town.

When I arrived, I saw a notice in the hotel lobby that invited visitors to tour the great copper mine at Chuquicamata, which is close by. I decided that I would see the mine before going to San Pedro de Atacama, but to be on the safe side, I bought the bus ticket first. On the way back to the hotel, I noticed a restaurant in a converted private house and decided to gamble on lunch. I was lucky. The food was excellent, the service was excellent, and the price was not too high. That night, it was pleasantly cool, and I slept in a modern bedroom with a bathroom that positively gleamed with modern plumbing.

I was up early the next morning and squeezed into the crowded bus for "Chuqui." We raced along a dead-straight road across the desert and suddenly found ourselves facing an enormous slag heap that was a hundred feet high and at least a mile long. Just behind it, two tall chimneys were belching smoke. Beyond a gateway guarded by armed police was a small town with a theater, a stadium, some stores, and a large hospital, all coated with dust. Along the main street a few skinny trees struggled to survive. This was Chuquicamata.

There was a suspicious lack of truck traffic, and when our little party of foreign tourists reached the public relations office, we found it locked. We waited in the hot sun for about an hour until an official who spoke perfect English arrived and told us that the miners were on strike and that there would be no guided tours for the next few days. Waiting at the bus stop for the ride back to Calama, I chatted with an Italian who claimed that Calama was the most expensive place in the whole of Chile. I had to agree with him.

SAN PEDRO DE ATACAMA

The bus for San Pedro had not left, so I hurried to the bus station. But I need not have worried. It was the usual half an hour late. This bus was the strangest vehicle that I had ridden in so far. Its front half was a bus with seats and windows, but the rear half was an open truck bed with straps to hold down the mixed cargo. I found a seat between a stolid Indian woman and a very fat businessman who did not talk. For a few miles where the road was surfaced, our driver (an army officer in a tight uniform) drove quite sedately. But when the good road ended abruptly and degenerated into little more than a track of broken rock and sand, he handed over the driving to a boy who looked hardly more than sixteen and drove with his foot flat down all the way.

The desert was mostly quite flat, and we could see the smoke from the smelter at Chuqui for miles. There were vast stretches of sand broken by piles of colored rocks, long sand dunes smoking in the wind, and ranges of hills carved into strange shapes by the wind and blowing sand. Huge chunks of black pumice poked through the yellow sand. There was not a blade of grass, or a tiny cactus, or even a dry twig to be seen anywhere. It was a fantastic and extraordinary scene, as eerie and strange as the surface of the moon.

After about two hours, we bounced over a low hill and there

below us was a large area of vegetation with the top of a church poking through the green trees. This was San Pedro de Atacama, the oldest town in Chile. There has been a human settlement in this tiny oasis for many thousands of years. The Tihuanacu empire probably did not know of its existence, but the Inca did and used it as a welcome rest stop on the route to their lonely southwestern frontier. When Almagro and his unhappy army of conquistadors arrived in the 16th century, they were returning to Lima, having found absolutely nothing of value in Chile. It is quite possible that it was in this peaceful little village that the "men from Chile" plotted their bloody revenge on the Pizarro brothers and started the civil wars that plagued the Spanish empire in the New World for over a decade.

When I was there, San Pedro de Atacama was a very quiet little town. The bus was the only vehicle on the street, and I walked two blocks to the hostel without seeing a soul. I came to a clean and modern hostel with five separate chalets and only a few other guests. Its low walls were made of white volcanic rock and decorated with pumice carvings and cactus wood, and the glass walled dining room offered a superb view across the desert to Mt. Licancabur, the local volcano.

After I had dropped my bag in my room, I went for a walk to the edge of the town, which is in an oasis. Out in the desert, some men where loading blocks of brilliantly yellow sulphur onto a truck, and when I asked where it came from, they pointed vaguely into the range of volcanoes in the far distance and said, "Across the border, in Bolivia." As I wandered around, waiting for the sun to set in order to get the best photo of Licancabur, I met a teacher from the local school. He was young and enthusiastic, and we walked to his school, where we climbed to the top of the new football bleachers to get the best view of the mountains. While we waited for sunset, he told me that the latest explorations showed that the Incas had made human sacrifices on the cold, high summit of the volcano.

Licancabur was the most perfect volcanic cone that I had ever seen. It towered 19,000 feet over the bare desert, with just a few patches of snow on its steeply sloping sides and as the sun set it glowed pink, then bright red, then purple. Then the huge desert stars appeared in the crystalline air, and the volcano became a giant, ghostly shadow.

That night I dined very well and slept like a log in the absolute silence. It was such a quiet night, in fact, that I overslept in the morning. After a quick continental breakfast, I hurried out to do some sight seeing. The first thing that impressed me was that most of the buildings in San Pedro de Atacama were quite low. The private houses were packed close together and built of sun dried adobe bricks, but the fashion was to build just high enough for comfort and no further. There were very few windows, the roofs were flat, and the doors were barely high enough for a tall man to get through without cracking his skull. Many of the houses were painted white or blue, and much of the woodwork was obviously light cactus wood, which has so many holes and hollows that it is barely useable. Most of the little stores had no windows and their walls were covered with old advertising that the sun had long ago reduced to tatters. These stores seemed to carry nothing but the bare necessities.

Down the middle of many of the streets there were tiny

irrigation ditches carrying a steady flow of surprisingly clean-looking water. Now and then I passed a garden hidden away behind a mud wall with large thorns set into the top, and I also glimpsed fig and pear trees and some corn. It was Saturday, but the town seemed fast asleep as I made my way towards the main plaza. Even the few lonely horses with their light saddles and large wooden stirrups outside the stores seemed to be sleeping in the hot sun.

The plaza was tiny, but wonderfully cool under its huge pepper trees. There were flowers carefully fenced against the goats and a little bandstand, but, thankfully, no huge bronze statues, just a little bust to some long-forgotten general. Near the plaza was a very old tumbledown building. An elderly gentleman who spoke some English explained that it was a hospital built by the conquistador Valdivia in the 16th century. "Since it was the first permanent building erected by the Spaniards," he added, "we can claim that we were the first European city in Chile." He was so proud of his charming little town that I did not point out that the land had originally been part of Bolivia.

He and I strolled over to the small, white-washed church with its short tower, and my guide pointed out that the walls were six feet thick at the base. "Look at the roof," he said. I looked up at the brown ceiling supported by thin beams. "It's just adobe," he said. "Just clay spread on twigs." He laughed at the surprised look on my face and said in Spanish, "Well, it never rains here. At least, it has never rained in my lifetime and my father's lifetime, although they say it snowed for a few hours in 1908. That could be the original roof that the Spaniards put on when they built it in 1550." Then he added in English, "Which makes this the oldest church in Chile."

One of the pleasures of wandering though this little town was the absence of flies or other insects. It must be too dry during the day and too cold at night for the pests, but I wondered how the crops got pollinated because there were quite a few well tended fields, all of them surrounded by low mud walls. I also wondered about the water supply because the wide bed of the Rio Atacama was bone dry and had not seen water for many a long year.

Behind the police station I saw two trucks marked *Geografico Militar* and half a dozen horses and mules, which made me wonder what geography the military were studying. As I stood staring across the desert, one of my questions was answered when I caught a flash of water and spotted the irrigation canal that came down alongside the dry river. It seemed to come a very long distance from very high up in the mountains. I wondered just how old it was and whether or not the Incas had built it.

Standing there, I could also make out the road, actually hardly more than a track, that zigzags up past Licancabur and crosses 300 miles of mountain wilderness to make its way eventually to Salta in Argentina. It's probably one of the worst drives in all the Americas. It was just such a mountain crossing by the conquistador Almagro, 400 years ago, that had left a trail of frozen corpses. It was such a terrible experience that Almagro never again crossed the mountains, preferring to reach Lima by the route through the *atacama.*

At noon, I went back to the hostel and washed everything I could. Thanks to the arid climate, every garment was bone dry within the hour. After lunch, at the suggestion of the hostel manager, I went to the museum, which was an old adobe building with a mud roof run by Padre La Paige, a Belgian Catholic priest. When he heard that I was a Canadian, he was excited because he had not been able to converse in French for years. But I disappointed him. Not much French is spoken in Vancouver, and although I had lived in Montreal, I could hardly speak a word. "*Tant pis*," he said, "a pity." He had worked in the Congo for some years and, since I had been there quite briefly, he cheered up and showed me around.

The padre was short and pleasant and wore a tattered khaki shirt and a large silver cross. His Spanish was excellent, as was his English, and he talked nonstop as he showed me his extraordinary collection of artifacts. There were pots and arrows, cloth and woodwork, and unusual artifacts from all over the *atacama*. There were also drawings and sketches that the padre himself had made, plus some very detailed maps. Although the museum was packed from floor to ceiling with things he had collected over the years, most intriguing was his collection of mummies. There were dozens of them sitting around in cardboard boxes, and thanks to the climate they were nearly all beautifully preserved. Traditionally, the dead were buried sitting down and hunched up. I wandered from shelf to shelf and box to box, staring at well preserved cloth and hair and skin while my guide pointed out details.

It was clear that the padre loved his job and loved the desert, too. Sitting on a bench in the shade, he spoke to everybody who walked by and it was obvious that all the small boys admired him. He also told me a story. When he began his archeological and anthropological work, years before, he found that while skeletons out in the desert were very well preserved, the bodies of Christians buried in the hallowed ground around the church were decomposed.

The Atacama Indians saw this as an ominous sign and it took some time for the padre to explain to them what was happening. The reason was obvious. Over the years, well meaning people planted flowers or shrubs in the cemetery and sometimes watered them. The Indians would never dream of wasting precious water on the graves of their ancestors.

By late afternoon there were more people on the streets and quite a little crowd in the plaza, where I watched some men playing a game that looked easy but wasn't. The players threw steel pucks at a target that was just a large box of damp clay. It was rather like pitching horseshoes and just as difficult. There were vendors selling fruit and homemade candies, but at sunset everybody went home. That night, I slept under a couple of blankets.

Next morning, I was up at six and tip-toed out of the hostel to the football bleachers, where I hoped to get some good sunrise pictures. It was cold and I shivered on my perch for an hour only to find that in that crystalline air, the spectacular sunrise was much too brilliant for my little camera. The bell in the church soon began to ring, but I was too cold to visit, so I hurried back to the hostel for a hot breakfast.

Everybody was quite vague about the bus schedule, though it was generally agreed that it would arrive "soon." I sat in the plaza, watching the citizens walk up and down with the children all in their Sunday best. Finally, in the middle of the afternoon, the bus arrived and the driver went off for an hour to have a drink. It was a regular bus, covered in dust inside and out, but there was plenty of room and we eventually headed off across the desert back to Calama. The plume of gray smoke from the smelter at Chuquicamata was clearly visible across the desert an hour before we got there. After a mediocre but expensive spaghetti supper at the hotel, I watched a Salvation Army band playing on the street corner. They were a rag-tag bunch dressed in bits of uniform, and they were not very good, but there was a large crowd, almost entirely men, stolidly listening to the fire and brimstone preacher. I gathered that the Salvation Army was the only entertainment in town that Sunday night.

I am glad that I visited San Pedro de Atacama when it was a half-forgotten little village. Today, it is an extremely popular holiday destination for Chileans, with bars and discos and all-night parties with amplified music. Modern new buildings have sprung up, and the village has completely lost its charm and character.

THE COPPER MINE AT CHUQUICAMATA

Next morning, I took the bus again to the mine at Chuquicamata, hoping the strike was over. I was eager to see the famous copper mine and smelter built on the site where, centuries before, Spanish explorers had stopped to make crude horseshoes from the chunks of raw copper they found among the rocks. The tourist office was open this time, and a smartly dressed young man showed us a slide show, gave us all hard hats, and then took us in a minibus to the edge of the pit. It was enormous! We stood on an observation platform and stared down into what must have been the biggest manmade hole on earth. I had seen the great hole at Kimberly in South Africa and a few others, but this hole was not only deep, it was wide, too, so wide that it took the little bus nearly two hours to drive all around it. Below us, scores of giant trucks climbed slowly up the winding road that cut through the hundreds of steep terraces. We could barely see the huge machines at the bottom that were ripping out the copper ore. The guide claimed that there were 100 miles of railway track in the pit alone. Over everything there hung a haze of dust, and whenever the wind changed, great clouds of foul-smelling smoke rising from the smelter chimneys blocked our view. The land all around was horribly torn up and the giant slag heaps and other heaps of rubble slowly crept out into the ancient desert. The guide would not take us into the smelter and banned any photographs of the smelting process that we could glimpse, but we did see the great sheets of pure copper stacked up and gleaming like red gold, a brilliant contrast to the dust-coated gray buildings and the smoke-filled sky.

Some of the visitors who had a car offered me a lift back to town. They told me that the miners earned five times what the average Chilean earned, but since Calama was the most expensive place in Chile, their high wages did them very little good and strikes were quite common. When we passed the large hospital, the woman in the group said, "Yes, they need this hospital. Most of the patients are children, and eighty percent of them are on oxygen because of the pollution."

Back in Calama, I bought a bus ticket to Arica, then waited in the hotel lobby. The bus to Arica was modern and comfortable, the road was well paved, and we went directly to Arica with no stops except for the usual passport check in the middle of the night.

ARICA

After our bus arrived in Arica early in the morning, I found a small hotel where I slept until noon. Back at the station, I learned that the next train to Bolivia was next morning, so I had the remainder of the day to see Arica. Lily and I had been there before, but we had not been impressed and had left very quickly. My first task now was to change some money, which proved quite difficult. I tried three banks before I found one that would change a traveler's check, and then they only gave me half the posted exchange rate and were rude when I complained. It seemed that the country was experiencing financial problems and the exchange rate fluctuated daily. Prices were so erratic that nothing in the shop windows had a price tag, and even the restaurants had their prices in chalk so that they could be quickly changed.

Down at the fishermen's wharf, the sun had broken through the mist and black cormorants sat on the lighters, carefully watching the line of yellow-painted fishing boats tied up to the dock. There was a beautiful display of gleaming silver-blue fish of all sizes with plastic bags of fish roe among the little crabs and octopus, and crowds of people were buying directly from the fishermen.

The town looked very busy. There were new shops and apartment buildings, and I found a fruit bar selling blender-mixed pure fruit juices that seemed to be very popular. I also came to a little shrine at the roadside that was covered with bunches of flowers with a small pyramid of melted candles in the center. An old Indian man was carefully adding another candle. One of the cards on the flowers said *Gracias*, but when I asked the man what it was for, he ignored me.

At the dock I had asked about a good fish restaurant, and that evening I tracked it down and ordered a full meal. I was in for a surprise. The soup came with the head and the tail of the fish in the tureen. It was delicious. Next came the rest of the fish, baked to perfection and wonderfully flavored with a few vegetables. It had been a large fish, easily enough for two or three people, but it was so fresh and so tasty that I sat and ate the whole thing, leaving nothing but polished bones. I could tell from the wide smile on her face that the manager was impressed by my performance. I still think that was one of the best meals that I have ever eaten.

Before I went to bed that night, I looked out the window and noticed that many of the houses near the hotel had roofs made only of split bamboo canes or canes covered in a thin skin of adobe. It seems that there is at least one advantage to living in a region where it never rains. Another advantage is the complete absence of mosquitoes.

THE TRAIN TO LA PAZ

There was a small crowd of passengers waiting patiently with their luggage at the train station the next morning, but the customs agent never turned up. As we boarded the single passenger carriage, I saw we were a very mixed bunch of Bolivians, Chileans, English, French, Americans, and a young Swiss couple who seemed to be on their honeymoon. I sat next to a Bolivian student who said he had exchanged American dollars for fifty Chilean pesos in Santiago, but only twenty pesos for travelers checks. I told him that I had not even received that much. Across the aisle was a little old Bolivian nun with a huge bottle of wine peeking out of her black bag. The American woman had a teenage daughter in dental braces. Neither of them spoke a word. The most interesting people in the carriage were two retired English teachers who were worried about altitude sickness. They were very capable looking ladies. I told them that Lily and I had never had any trouble, and the Bolivian student agreed that altitude sickness was greatly exaggerated. A few days later when I met them again in La Paz, they were tackling the steep streets like mountain goats and enjoying every minute.

The train was just our one passenger carriage with what I took to be a baggage car behind it and a large diesel engine pulling us. The line is famous for being a cog rail line, and when it climbs the mountains or went around very sharp bends, it was possible to see the third rail, but we did not seem to be using it. The first few miles went along the coast through mist and fog, then we turned up a long, wide valley and headed into the desert sun. There was some irrigated agriculture in the valley, but no villages and so we made no stops. The train climbed quickly and smoothly until, quite suddenly, we were in the mountains and I caught a glimpse of a snow-capped volcano far to the north in Peru.

I made my way through the carriage to the diesel engine, then past the giant, noisy engines to the engineer's cab. The engineer did not want me there, but before he chased me away he explained that the cog rail was not necessary for such a light train pulled by such a heavy engine. Only heavy freight trains used the cog system. There was a pipeline running alongside the track, but he did not know whether it carried oil or natural gas or whether it was being imported or exported. His only interest was his train and his schedule.

Soon there were volcanic peaks all around us. The steward appeared with an excellent lunch, which told me that part of the baggage coach was obviously a kitchen. Another surprise was in store at the border: we did not stop and there were no formalities. In fact, if it had not been for the sudden change in scenery, we would never have known that we had crossed the border into Bolivia.

Suddenly we were on the *altiplano* with its familiar adobe farm houses and women in derby hats staring silently at the passing train. There was a herd of llamas in the distance and flamingoes stood in the little river the train was following. The sky was huge and bright with thunder clouds hiding the peaks of the coastal range. Far in the distance, the afternoon sun sparkled on the snow clad peaks of the Andes.

The rest of the trip was quite fast. After a brief stop at the railway junction in Viacha, we soon arrived in El Alto, where our train wound down the mountain side to La Paz without another engine assisting. In the crowded station, the porter cried out the numbers on our luggage like a Bingo caller. After a short hunt, I found a suitable hotel where, although there was no heat, the beds had plenty of blankets. It was hard to get to sleep with the noise of the busy city and the high altitude, but it felt good to be back in Bolivia.

Chapter 7: A Visit to a Small Lead Mine

When I returned to Oruro after my trip to the *Atacama*, Ramiro said to me, "I'm going up to the mine in a couple of days. Care to come along?" I jumped at the chance. I had been down a copper mine in Africa, a coal mine in England, and a salt mine in Colombia, and I had peered down into a diamond mine in Africa. I had also toured a gold mine in South Dakota, a copper mine in Chile, and an aluminum smelter in Canada. Now I could go down into a lead mine in Bolivia and perhaps (with a bit of luck), a tin mine, too.

Because of the distance and the difficult road, Ramiro had not yet taken his family up to the mine, which was up in the highest part of the Andes overlooking Oruro, nor did he go himself more than once a month (and in the rainy season even less), so we spent a day checking his Land Rover and picking up things for the mine and its workers, which included everything from spare parts to a couple of large bales of coca. At the market, he handed me a few coca leaves and said, "Here. Try some."

I took a few of the greenish brown leaves and stuffed them into my mouth and chewed them. Nothing happened. "Rather like trying to eat hay or dead leaves," I said, and spat out the mess.

Ramiro laughed and said, "I bet every tourist who comes here says those exact words. You have to chew a whole wad of the stuff for hours before you get any juice out of it. I never use it myself and nor does anybody in my family, but it's part of the miner's pay. They won't work without it."

Barbara woke us at 4:30 the next morning and fed us a heavy breakfast. It was still dark and cold as we drove through the silent streets to the mine manager's house. Nava, the manager, was born and raised in the Andes, and his ancestors had been there since before the Incas. His family has been miners for countless generations and he has worked for Ramiro and his father before him. Short, copper dark, and barrel-chested, Nava sat in the back seat of the Land Rover and kept up a cheerful chatter throughout the long drive to the mine, sharing his inexhaustible fund of anecdotes and legends regarding the mountains, the minerals, and the men who seek them.

There was ice in the puddles as we drove toward the mountains, and the starlight showed us fresh snow on the peaks. Suddenly, just as we reached the foothills, the stars went out and the great golden sun rose dramatically. Within minutes we had shed our heavy jackets and Ramiro put on his sunglasses.

The road had been well engineered, but time and weather had ruined the surface, and it was some time before I could adjust to the teeth-rattling jars and bumps, but the magnificence of the scenery made up for mere physical discomfort. The bare, rolling hills were golden brown and utterly treeless, and there was no sign of human habitation, not even birds, just the empty road winding away into the distance. We gradually climbed high into the very heart of the Andes.

Even in the most inhospitable land, some people will find ways to survive. About mid-morning, as we drove through a small village of adobe and thatch homes scattered haphazardly in a bleak mountain hollow, Nava pointed out the clay pots stacked at the roadside. They seemed to be well made. He explained that the village survived by making pots and trading them for the necessities of life. "They only trade," he said. "They don't like to use money. It's not much use to them up here."

Just before noon we crossed a high ridge and zigzagged down to Sacaca, a provincial capital with a population that is almost entirely Indian. Sacaca lies in a fertile valley where every inch of land, no matter how small or steep, seemed to be cultivated. Walls of rock protected the fields while stone lined irrigation ditches less than a foot wide carried the precious water from field to field and ran down the middle of the town's stone-paved main street. Herds of sheep, goats, and llamas were everywhere.

I saw quite a few people on the streets of the town, and we stopped in the main plaza to stretch our legs. The plaza was big, with plenty of shade trees and rose bushes, each with its own little irrigation ditch. Near the plaza was a huge church, but its doors were locked. Nava said, "Inside the church I have seen some very old paintings. They are very big, but they are in poor condition and some have been damaged by children. It is only open for special fiestas."

After a quick soft drink, we got back in the Land Rover and headed out of the town in its fertile valley. Soon we were back in the mountains where on a very narrow stretch of road high up a steep mountain side, we came on a long string of pack llamas. Since llamas will use any excuse to panic and scatter, we inched past them slowly and quietly. Each of the animals carried two small bundles, and their ears were tipped with colored wool. They were carrying salt from the *altiplano*, Nava said, in two twenty-pound blocks each. "They will probably take a week to travel the same distance that we are going to cover today," he added. We spent the next hour discussing the importance of salt in every culture and the immense distances over which it has always been traded.

As we climbed higher, the rock became more colorful, with areas of red and yellow or patches of white with blue-green streaks. Although there was very little grass growing between the rocks, there were flocks of sheep and long-haired black goats tended by very small children. Invariably the shepherdess was squatting in the lee of a pile of rocks, muffled in her shawl and long black skirt, immobile and almost invisible in the wild scene. Now there were also numerous traces of mining activity.

Where the road ran along a mountain crest, we stopped to admire the breathtaking view. In the crystalline air, range upon range of mountains fell away into the distance, some of them looking almost close enough to touch. Great patches of snow hid from the sun behind the rocks and, except for the sigh of the wind, there was absolute silence. We were at the top of the world. Nava pointed into the distance and said, "If we had some binoculars, we could see the tailings dump from the tin mine at Llalagua. It's about fifty miles over there." Then he turned around and pointed in another direction and said, "We could probably see the Cerro of Potosí, too."

In the midst of all this lonely splendor, we met a bus. Naturally, this happened on a particularly steep and narrow stretch, but Ramiro, with plenty of advice from the bus passengers, carefully inched the Land Rover to the edge of the cliff and the bus driver, with long experience and a dark, expressionless face, squeezed between the cliff and the car. Neither vehicle lost any paint.

About noon, although we were still well above the tree line, we began to descend a little, and suddenly Ramiro veered off the road. It took me some minutes to realize that we were on a track, not just bumping across the open hillside. It was a ten-mile-long access road that had taken Ramiro over a year to build. It was rough, but good enough for a truck or a jeep. We soon saw more signs of past mining activity, like small exploratory holes in the colored rock, yellow tailings, jeep tracks winding into the peaks. It was a world fit only for geologists and miners, yet here and there I spotted another little shepherdess huddled behind her stone shelter and some gray sheep blending into the ancient landscape.

In almost every culture, the gods live on mountain tops. The Andean Indians have always liked to keep the gods happy, so whenever an Indian reaches the top of a pass or the crest of a hill, the grateful traveler sets a small stone onto a cairn as a symbolic offering. These cairns ranged from little heaps of pebbles to enormous piles that must have taken generations to accumulate, plus one or two small altars painstakingly built of large flat rocks. When I asked Nava about the tradition, however, he declined to discuss it.

The few Indians we passed were dressed in the traditional, calf-length, homespun trousers with heavy woolen ponchos, and their heads protected from the wind and sun by high, sand-colored, felt hats over their familiar, knitted woolen caps with ear flaps. As usual, their feet were almost bare in crude rubber-tire sandals, and on their backs they carried pouches or tied bundles of wool. Almost everybody, men and women alike, twirled spindles as they walked, making thread for weaving, and some of the men had rawhide slings looped around their waists. The women wore heavy skirts, and instead of the men's rugged sandals, they wore tiny slippers that looked absolutely useless on the rocky roads.

We spotted Ramiro's mine from about five miles away. High up the side of a hill, two or three yellow tailing slopes pointed arrow-like to the dark entrance to the tunnels. When we reached the entrance to one of these tunnels, I saw some rails leading out of the small hole and a solitary Indian shoveling dirt through an upright sieve. He and Ramiro exchanged a few words in Quechua, and then we drove on down the hill to the valley bottom. Ramiro was very proud of this section of road, which was a fine piece of engineering. We stopped to admire it as he described the hours he had spent mapping out the route.

"But who actually built it?" I asked.

"The miners," he replied, "With picks and shovels. They needed a bit of dynamite in places, but not much, considering."

I pointed to the neat, stone retaining walls. "And those?"

He kicked the stones to show how firmly they were in place. "The stonework they did entirely by hand," he said, "with a lot of patience and the biggest pile of stones in South America." He gestured toward the surrounding peaks. "Seriously, though, these people were working stone before the Inca arrived. All I did was give them the tools and then leave them alone. Notice how they allowed for runoff in the rainy season. This road will last a century."

At the bottom of the tiny valley, in a sheltered spot at the side of a little river, there was a working area of about 200 square yards. It was a pretty site, with two or three trees by the river, a couple of tiny corn and potato patches, and, below the site, the remains of an old Spanish grist mill with a couple of huge granite millstones lying in the sun. A nine-inch sluice brought water from further upstream, and above the work area a windowless adobe house served as combination store, office, and manager's house.

As Ramiro and Nava vanished into the office, I walked over to the workings. Half a dozen Indians shoveling gravel or directing water into little runways stared shyly at the bearded stranger, then politely ignored me, There were various sieves and washers and three concentrating pits, or "puddles," which Ramiro had described but which I had never seen before. The puddle is an ancient but wonderfully simple ore concentrator.

Only one puddle was being operated that day, and I watched a man carefully shovel finely ground ore into a narrow, stone-lined water channel. A tin spout allowed the muddy water to fall exactly in the center of a stone-lined pit about five feet wide and three feet deep. As the mixture fell, the water washed the lighter sand to the outer edge of the pit while the heavier ore settled in the center. The water then drained off through the stonework. I knelt beside the puddle in fascination. There, right before my eyes, a cone-shaped hill of gray ore with a yellow fringe around it was forming in the bottom of the pit.

I must have knelt there for half an hour, watching this marvelous process. The pit was about half full when Nava appeared and the water was cut off. He studied the ore for a long minute, then called over another man, who knelt and carefully scooped out the bright yellow sand with small tin scoop and dropped it into a bucket. Then he scooped out the center of the ore and dropped the purest lead into another bucket. The rest of the ore went into a third bucket.

"We will put the ore through the process again two or three times," Nava said, "until we have extracted as much lead as possible." He explained that by constantly washing the ore they hoped to get it at least 70 percent pure and, hopefully, 75 percent. I was astonished that such a primitive system could turn out an ore purified to such a high level.

Almost everything in the mine, except for the narrow rail lines and the wagon, was either made from stone or carved of wood and could have been exactly as it had been in the time of the Spaniards or even the Inca. While I was looking around, Nava called me over to the crusher.

I had seen rock crushers in other mines, and usually they were enormous machines costing thousands of dollars that gave off clouds of dust and made an ear-splitting noise. This crusher, by contrast, was half of an old millwheel. It stood about three feet high on a smooth slab of rock, and there was a long pole attached to the flat top so that the contraption could be rocked. A sturdy-looking Indian grasped one end of the pole and began to rock the stone as, squatting on the ground alongside, another man slipped pieces of rock under the rising and falling stone. He held a wooden scraper and poked at the crushed rock until he was satisfied, then quickly scooped the dust into a bucket and slipped some fresh stones under the mill wheel. He had to work fast because the man operating the rocking pole could not see his hands and continued rocking the millstone.

When Ramiro called me, I climbed through a potato patch to the house. It was only fifty feet up the hill, but I was panting heavily when I arrived. We snacked on canned tongue and canned corn washed down with sweet black tea brewed on the camp stove, then Ramiro talked Nava into playing a few tunes on the *charango*, a small eight-stringed instrument like a mandolin and traditionally made from the shell of an armadillo. It is played very rapidly, Nava gave us a few traditional songs, and although he complained that arthritis had begun to slow him down, he was very good.

The sun was still high in the sky, so I walked along the stream and saw a small girl herding her sheep on the other side, accompanied by her even smaller brother. She was using a sling identical to the sling used by the Biblical David and placed pebble after pebble only inches from the nose of any animal that dared to wander from the flock. When she noticed me watching her, however, she gave a shriek, threw her shawl over her head, and hurried her flock on down the river, her bare feet seeming not to notice the sharp rocks. It is quite possible that I was the first bearded white man she had ever seen.

Ramiro and I took the Land Rover back up the hill to where the lone worker was still screening gravel, and there was a long discussion in Quechua. When it ended, Ramiro explained that most of his workers had not yet returned from a two-day fiesta. It had been a particularly wild celebration, he said, and three or four women and boys had turned up to take the place of their hung-over wage earners. Ramiro was philosophical about the situation. We drove to another mine entrance, where he sent a boy to find the foreman. Pointing over the steep edge of the mountain, he said,

"Down there is a mine at exactly the same level as my mine, yet, would you believe it? he is working a nice vein of tin. Right now tin is nearly ten times the price of lead." He shrugged. "That's mining for you."

While we were waiting for the foreman, we stood and looked at the spectacular view. He named the peaks and the two small lakes we could see in the valley and pointed out where the village lay, then he rattled off figures and prices and explained how the rise or fall of just a few cents for lead or tin on the world market could mean a profit or bankruptcy. It was obvious that he loved the land and the mine that he and his fathers before him had dug out of the hard rock.

Near where we stood was a neatly shaped, square pillar about waist high. The top was dusted in gray ash, and there was a jumble of crosses of all sizes carved into the stone. When I asked Ramiro what it was, he quickly changed the subject. Later, I asked Nava, but he, too, evaded my question.

When the foreman finally appeared, he explained that the boy had taken one look at my beard and had reported that, "Señor Miranda has brought his father, or perhaps it is his grandfather." I was puzzled for a moment, and then it dawned on me that since American Indians don't normally have beards unless they are very old, the boy must have thought I was ancient. Then the foreman found some carbide lamps in a small shed and led us to the mine entrance. Since nobody had a miner's helmet, the lamps were handheld. First, we carefully tapped out the old carbide on a rock that was white with ash, then we put in some fresh fuel and a drop of water and waited until the gas hissed. Finally, we spun the lighter wheels to create the flame. It took a while to get the old brass lamps to function correctly.

Then we stepped into the mine. The tunnel was so low I had to walk stooped over, and the lamplight was barely bright enough for me to see where I was going, but my eyes adjusted quickly. It seemed a long hundred yards, and my back was aching, by the time we came to a small opening at the side of the tunnel. By the lamplight, I saw Ramiro and his mine boss sit down on a pile of rocks in front of two small statues. These were Tio and his wife, La Vieja, and they were made from the first ore taken from the mine. They were about ten inches high, quite crudely made, and decorated with tissue-paper clothes. Miners the world over are a superstitious fraternity, and the Andean miner, although nominally a Catholic Christian, is probably the most superstitious. His is a hard and dangerous life with the constant risk of sudden death or serious injury and always the fear of seeing that tell-tale speck of blood when he coughs. Over the years, he has learned to carefully placate the old gods as well as the golden haired Madonna in the village church.

As I squatted down beside them, the foreman placed a few coca leaves on an already quite large pile at the foot of the statues, while Ramiro and I lit cigarettes and placed an extra one in Tio's mouth. If the cigarette went out, that meant that Tio did not want us in his mine. While we watched and waited, Ramiro explained that each year, on the Friday before Carnival, the miners come to the mouth of the tunnel and dance to show Tio that he will not be forgotten during the celebrations. The great spectacle in Oruro, the famous *Diablado* with its devils' heads and fantastic costumes is actually a continuation of the ancient miners' dances that drive away evil spirits from the mine. To this day, the groups of whirling, leaping dancers start at an old mine entrance that has long been covered over by a church. This is the miner's church, Nuestra Señora de la Socavon (Our Lady of the Mine).

Tio was not displeased by the presence of a stranger (me), and he smoked his cigarette down to the filter. Unfortunately, Ramiro had important things to do around the mine, so I contented myself with taking a few flash photos of Tio and then made my way back into the brilliant sunshine. It would have been too dangerous for me to explore the mine by myself.

Paying respect to the ancient idol is not mere superstition. On the contrary, it is quite sensible and very important. Ages ago, even before the Inca arrived, the Andean miners learned that poor ventilation and a lack of oxygen could kill them. They also learned that fire will not burn without oxygen.

At a sharp bend in the road down to the concentrator, the ground was torn up and a pile of ore lay scattered among the rocks. Some weeks previously, a truck driver who had had a few drinks took the curve too fast and was killed when his truck went over the edge. Life is short and hard in these mountains, and what the coca cannot deaden, alcohol can. Two days before we arrived, there had been a fight in the village during the Fiesta of Todos Santos, and one of the miners, a belligerent, one-handed individual, had gotten the better of another villager. Later that evening, the second villager had pushed one-hand over a low wall, and his sister had hurled a rock at one-hand. The man died of a smashed skull.

At sunset, I went back down the hill. The sluice had been turned off, and the yard was deserted except for a boy who earned his room and board by making himself useful around the camp. He was the brother and sole relative of the truck driver who had been killed and had nowhere else to go.

That night, we left our imported canned goods on the shelf and dined on *chuno* and *charqui*, which Nava prepared. *Chuno* is the popular freeze-dried potato of the *altiplano*, but even the best cook can not give dried potato much flavor, so it is usually spiced with *aji*, a sauce made of some of the most violent peppers ever to burn the mouth of an unsuspecting stranger. *Charqui* is the original Spanish name for jerky, or dried meat, and ours was mutton barbecued to perfection. The rarified air had given me quite an appetite, and I tore off strips of the stringy dry meat and washed them down with steaming mugs of sweet black coffee. After supper, Ramiro fiddled with a battery-operated short-wave radio and Nava immersed himself in a pile of well-thumbed Chilean and Argentine comic books.

About 10:00, the foreman dropped in for a chat, and we were soon discussing whether or not there were condors in the area. The foreman claimed that he had seen an albino condor when he was a boy. He also claimed that there was a type of vampire bat further down the valley in the direction of Cochabamba, but Nava scoffed at the idea. What everybody agreed on was that there was a cougar in the area and that it probably lived on the rodents that live among the rocks.

The foreman also mentioned that there was a strange village nearby where the people lived in caves which they reached by ladders or rough steps. The villagers, he said, were very shy and existed by caring for the male llamas, which are always pastured high up on the mountain away from the females. This mysterious village, he continued, was so primitive and isolated that no anthropologist had ever visited it. I found it all very interesting, but at the mention of llamas, the conversation switched abruptly and the men began comparing their bad experiences with that curious and quite unpredictable creature.

About half of the small house at the mine was used as an office and a storeroom where the orphan boy slept. The other section was mostly taken up by a huge bed covered in llama wool blankets and a couple of black sheepskins. Nava took half of this bed and soon disappeared under his blankets, but Ramiro unrolled an expensive Canadian sleeping bag on his side of the bed. I made do on a smaller bed, and slid, almost fully clothed, under a pile of rough woolen blankets.

The temperature dropped swiftly as the oil lamps were extinguished, and I was soon glad I'd kept my socks on. The blankets had weight, but not much warmth, and whenever I moved, an icy draft would sneak between the covers and bite viciously at any exposed part of my body. It was a very cold night. Next morning, Ramiro and Nava were up bright and early, but I lay in my cocoon of blankets and waited for the sun to show its face over the mountains. When the sunshine reached the door, I washed in the icy waters of the sluice and breakfasted on a bread roll and a huge mug of hot *api*, a sweet purple drink made of maize and flavored with cloves. On a very cold morning, a mug of *api* can be much more welcome than coffee or tea.

As Ramiro was busy handing out the pay, I went down to the workings and took some photos. The Indian miners were shy at first, but soon relaxed and were even eager to pose for me. At least the men and the boys were. The women and girls either broke into giggles and hid their faces or stood stiff and stern-faced, paralyzed with embarrassment.

The Land Rover caught up with me as I walked slowly up the hill to the next section of the mine, where Ramiro tried to speed up the work on a small adobe hut. "The heavy rains are due very soon," he explained, "and I want the roof on before then. All the men are still not back to work, and I've got mostly boys and women." He pointed to three women who sat just outside the mine entrance, where the short rail lines ended and the single ore car dumped its load. Two of the women had babies tied snugly on their backs. "They're sorting the ore," he said. "Actually, they do it quite as well as the men."

The women each had a hammer and a wooden scraper and were picking lumps of rock from the pile and reducing them to the size of large marbles. As they worked, they picked out bits that were, to them, obviously just useless rock and tossed them to one side. The rest they scraped into a pile that was shoveled into a bucket by a boy who carried it off to the crusher. The women worked quickly and silently, never taking their eyes off the valuable ore. I picked up a few bits and examined them. To me they were just gray rock. Ramiro watched me with a grin on his face. "It's easy to become an expert," he said. "Just have four years of university like me or have 400 years of experience like them."

When the foreman appeared, he looked at the sorted ore but said nothing. Then we went around the mountain and down the side to where a new shaft was being dug. It was only an exploratory tunnel, and as we approached, a young boy came out pushing a wheel barrow. Although he was short, he was bent almost double and his rough clothes were muddy from contact with the walls. I borrowed the boy's carbide lamp and Ramiro and Nava shared a lamp and we entered the shaft. It was too far to crawl, so I did the best I could bent over in an awkward crouch, stopping every few yards to rest my back and force some air into my lungs. When I caught up with the others, they were lying down and talking to the miner who was half hidden in rubble. Unlike the other men who had been politely friendly and eager to stop and chat, this man continued his slow deliberate hammering on the end of a long steel bar. He was drilling a dynamite hole in the face of the shaft.

They spoke in Spanish, and I gathered that Ramiro was trying to speed up the drilling by offering a bonus, but in such a way that it would not reflect on the miner's skill. He praised the man's work but pointed out that the rains were only weeks away and the foulness of the air, heavy with rock dust and dynamite fumes, indicated that a ventilation shaft would soon have to be dug. With carefully chosen words, Ramiro suggested that if the work were finished by Christmas, a hard working miner should be able to celebrate in style. Nobody promised anything, but the dark figure with the wool cap pulled down over his ears, stopped hammering, shifted the large quid of coca in his cheek, and said something quietly in Quechua. They all seemed satisfied, so we turned to leave. Since I was the last in, I had an unobstructed view down the long tunnel. In the far distance, the opening was just a speck of yellow light centered perfectly in the middle of the tunnel. This shaft was arrow straight and, according to Ramiro's instruments, was accurate to within a few centimeters. The only guide the miner had was a narrow pillar of white stones that he had erected about ten feet in front of the tunnel mouth. I could see why Ramiro valued him.

I was standing outside the tunnel for a moment, stretching my cramped muscles, when Ramiro asked, "Would you like to see inside the mine?" It was an unnecessary question. "Well, you asked for it," he said, and he led the way down to what I considered to be the main entrance among the four or five entrances scattered across the hillside at various levels. Half-way there, we came across the truck stopped in the middle of the road. There seemed to be an ignition problem. Ramiro immediately reached into the innards of the vehicle. That truck was the most valuable and most important single item in his whole operation. Everything depended on it. It had to be kept running at any cost.

While everybody else gathered around the truck to watch Ramiro, I strolled down the road to where there was a low stone wall that enclosed a small cemetery whose graves were marked by rounded stone or clay markers and wooden crosses, now tilted or warped into strange postures. Each grave had a niche at its foot, smoke blackened from countless candles, and some still retained the remains of flowers in tin cans or small jars. A number of the newer crosses were still draped with black and purple wreaths of paper flowers that rustled slightly in the breeze, a forgotten reminder of the Fiesta of Todos Santos. At the side of the road was a large brown rock that had been roughly carved into a block. Its top was covered in a series of small depressions from which led drainage grooves. I could make out the ash of burned carbide in some of the holes and guessed that it had some religious significance, but when I asked some of the men standing around the truck, they were very vague and some pretended not to see the rock. It was obviously something that should not be discussed with strangers.

It was quite hot in the sun by now, so I walked over to the mine, where the foreman found me. We picked up a couple of lamps. Tio had been visited earlier in the day, and now we went directly into the heart of the mountain. My eyes gradually adjusted to the gloom. We were in a fairly narrow tunnel through red and gray rock. There were a few side tunnels, but it was strangely silent. The foreman assured me that there were a dozen men working in the mine, but I could not hear a sound. It was cool, and the floor was quite level but damp and slippery and, since the rail lines and the ore car were in another tunnel, it was not difficult to walk stooped over under the low roof.

The foreman stopped at a black hole in the floor. By the lamplight, I could just make out the top of a ladder. With smooth skill, he vanished down the hole, which was about eight feet deep. I was holding my lamp in one hand and had my camera and a flash unit dangling around my neck, so it was not quite so easy for me to go down the ladder, especially as it was homemade and rickety. At the bottom, I found myself in a maze of workings, with tunnels of various sizes leading off in all directions. Some were narrow and rough walled, others were quite wide and smooth walled, but all of them were silent and sinister in the yellow light. I followed my guide, or rather, stumbled after his boots, which I could just make out with my head bent low. Here and there, he stopped and pointed out how waste rock had been used to fill worked out areas or to shore up a weak point in the roof. There were no timber supports

and no wooden roof supports, just the bare rock. I shivered when
he aimed his lamp at a section of roof and pointed out that it clearly
needed some support. The empty tunnels were surprisingly clean.
They lacked the muddy tangle of pipes and wires and track that I
had seen in other mines, and the deep silence was not broken by the
clatter of pneumatic drills or the rumble of machines.

We stopped at another hole in the floor that was only a few feet
across and had no ladder. When the foreman sat on the edge and
slipped off into the darkness, I saw that it was only about six feet
deep. I did not feel like jumping down a six-foot hole, so I lay on
my belly, clutched my camera and flash unit and carbide lamp, and
slid down. We had reached a working level. There was broken rock
underfoot and what looked like little piles of lead ore.

As we slid and wriggled our way along, I thanked my lucky
stars that I was not claustrophobic because in some places there
was just barely room to get through. I had to be very careful not to
crack my head on the rough ceiling. Suddenly the foreman stopped
and pointed out a black streak about four inches wide. It contrasted
sharply with the red and gray rock. Even I could see that it was
a seam of something. The little tunnel twisted and turned as it
followed the seam and—at last—we came to a miner.

At this point, the seam had widened to almost three feet,
though it was not as pure as the narrower part had been. The miner,
wearing muddy clothes and his woolen cap pulled low over his ears,
was kneeling and patiently chipping at the seam with a steel chisel
and a heavy hammer. Every few minutes, he would sort through the
rock he had removed and place the bits with lead in them to one
side. He tossed the useless rock to the other side. He worked quickly

and rarely took a second look. Considering that he was working only by the feeble light of his carbide lamp, his performance was astonishing.

"How does he see the ore in this light?" I asked.

"Many years of experience," the foreman said, "and also he feels the weight. The lead is heavier than the rock." He then explained that the discarded rock would be shoveled into abandoned tunnels and only the ore would be taken out of the mountain.

We left the miner patiently chipping away and as we made our way further along, we passed a side tunnel where I could just faintly hear another miner working alone in the dark. Then we came to the hoist. Instead of the great steel cages and giant winches or huge wheels that I had seen in other mines, here there was only a four foot hole in the floor and a thin rope disappearing into the dark below. Somewhere above us stood a hand winch operated by two men, who had to lift the heavy buckets of ore forty feet through six levels. As the gray bucket rose slowly and vanished overhead, the foreman explained that the new shaft would eliminate any need for the hoist. The ore would simply be dumped into the hole and removed from its bottom. I could see why Ramiro was eager to get the new tunnel finished as soon as possible.

Without my guide, I would never have been able to find my way out of the mine before my carbide ran out, but soon we were back at the main entrance, though I did have a desperate moment or two at the pit with no ladder. It would have been tricky with both hands free, but the foreman, who was much smaller than me, proved to have muscles of steel and hauled me up with one hand.

Back in the blinding sun, I brushed some of the mud off my

clothes and found the other men sitting in the shade of the now-repaired truck, eating imported Chilean sardines on bread rolls and talking about mining. I asked if the mill near the mine was really of Spanish origin and everybody assured me that not only did it date back to the 16th or 17th century, but there were countless other old sites in the region. Nava listed six or seven nearby mines that had been originally discovered by the Spaniards, and Ramiro added, "If you go prospecting anywhere in the *cordillera* north or south of Potosí, you will find that some Spanish prospector was there first, a couple of hundred years before you."

Everybody agreed, and somebody said, "They were extraordinary men. But there is still plenty of mineral wealth here, enough to make us all rich. No?"

We would have gone on talking for the rest of the day about the fortunes hidden in the high Andes, but Ramiro looked up at the sun and said. "Well, we've done all we can for this trip. Let's get back to Oruro."

On our way back, we detoured across the bare hillside to the edge of a steep valley where, far below, we could see a little cluster of buildings and a truck, a 1936 Leyland. "That's my father's truck," Ramiro said. "He bought it new. We're waiting for some spare parts from England, then she'll be running fine. Should get a few more years of use out of her."

An hour later, a bank of clouds that had raced ahead of us now stood squarely across the road. I wondered aloud what a deluge would do to the already very bad road, but Ramiro just smiled. "It's too early for rain," he said. "Probably just hail." And just then, the cloud dumped its entire load on us. It was frightening and slightly dangerous, but at the same time it was very beautiful. The whole countryside was soon covered in two inches of tiny hailstones, all gleaming white in the rays of brilliant sunshine while long streamers of hail still drifted from the clouds and dragged slowly over the hills. To add to the scene, a herd of llamas, ears up and noses high, stood silhouetted on a hillside, pretending to ignore this insult from the sky. In a few minutes, we were out of the storm and a turn in the road brought us back to a world of dry, red, and brown mountainside.

As we approached Sacaca again, we saw small groups working the fields, hurrying to get the land ready for the rains. Sometimes it was just one farmer steering his wooden plow behind a pair of black bulls while his wife and children followed behind, breaking the larger lumps with wooden mallets, but more often it was a group working in cooperation with three or even four plows. We stopped near one very colorful group to get some photos, but they all stopped working to stare at us and a swarm of little children poured down the hillside to beg, so we hurried on.

We stopped to stretch our legs in the Plaza in Sacaca, and both Ramiro and Nava spent a few minutes greeting various people before we went into a cafe. The back dining room was cool and dark, with no windows, and the walls were decorated with the usual collection of old calendars. A little girl with bare feet served us Bolivian made soft drinks with a strong strawberry flavor and lunch was served by a woman in a derby hat and full skirts. I asked Ramiro if the women ever took off their hats. He thought about this for a minute, then said, "I guess it's rather like Muslim women who keep their heads covered in public. But it's certainly not a religious thing." The soup was vegetable soup with a strong flavor that I did not recognize. Ramiro stirred a large spoonful of *aji* into his. "Here, try this stuff," he said with a suspiciously straight face. I took a little *aji* on a spoon and sniffed it. There was no strong flavor, so I popped the rest into my mouth. Immediately my mouth was on fire. I began to hiccup violently as beads of sweat formed on my forehead. Ramiro waited while I emptied the bottle of soft drink, then said, "Scientists say that peppers originated on the east side of the Andes, here in Bolivia. They have found some that make those Mexican things taste like nothing in comparison." Then he calmly took another spoonful and mixed it into his soup. When the woman brought chicken with rice and potatoes, I politely refused the bowl of *aji* that the little girl brought from the kitchen.

Outside, a large crowd had gathered to welcome the bus from Oruro. There was a pile of luggage and brightly wrapped bundles and families were greeting returning relatives. A small crowd just stood and watched. Ramiro and Nava had many friends and business contacts to greet, so I wandered back toward the church. It was large, built of cut stones and bricks, with an arched gateway and a massive tower standing well away from the church. In Bolivia it is not unusual to build the tower away from the church, but this one was at least a hundred yards away. The huge wooden doors were locked and the whole building had a run-down look, although it sported a brand new corrugated iron roof that clashed horribly with the ancient stonework. These churches are all over Bolivia, many of them small and made of adobe, but all of them are beautiful in a simple, rugged fashion.

Back in the Land Rover, Ramiro said that he had been consoling the mother of the one-handed man who had been killed with a rock. She had not heard about the fight, and it was Ramiro's job to break the news to her. We were silent as we climbed back into the mountains toward Oruro. Now and then we caught a glimpse of the road winding snake-like ahead of us, miles of thin brown ribbon, and once we saw the dust from another vehicle, miles ahead, but we never caught up with it. Nava was coming back with us and would hitch a lift back to the mine in a day or two. He knew everybody in Oruro who regularly traveled that road, and when I asked him if the government would ever improve the road, he surprised me.

"Yes," he said, "that would be nice. But then there would be more traffic. I like it the way it is." It was clear that he did not like the idea of more traffic taking away the wild, lonely beauty of the land.

High on a windy plateau, we pulled up at a small stone hut where a little boy came out and Ramiro asked him if there was any gasoline for sale. Away from the cities and the major highways, there are no service stations, but there is usually somebody who has a small supply of gasoline and motor oil for sale, and nobody begrudges them the small profit that they make. I took the opportunity to slip on my jacket and sweater. As we drove on, the sun set in an extravagant display of orange and yellow, and then we made the remainder of the journey in pitch dark with the headlights alternately illuminating the gray cliff face or shining out into space. I thought Ramiro drove a bit fast, but he knew the road well.

Nava also knew the road well. I livened the trip by asking him what lay around the next bend. He told us exactly and even how many miles it was to the object he described. He knew every mile of the road as a city dweller knows every store or house on his street.

The rocks and ravines were like phone poles, mailboxes, and street signs to him. Suddenly we topped a rise. In the far distance below we could see a huge cluster of lights in the blackness. The air was so clear we could make out the red signal light at the railway junction over twenty miles away. We were soon speeding across the plains with the car heater on at full strength.

After the solitude of the mountains, the city of Oruro was another world. Saturday night crowds thronged the streets and bright electric light shone through the open doors of the shops and onto the crowded pavement. The traffic was thick and noisy, and children ran and played wildly in the streets. Despite the coldness of the night, the plaza was full of people. Servant girls with an evening off were dressed in all their colorful finery, brilliant skirts and shawls and tiny ballet slippers, with their brown or black derby hats tilted rakishly forward, smiling coyly at the soldiers in their smart green uniforms and shining boots who pretended no interest. Children played on the statues of the fountain while their parents gossiped on the green benches. But we did not stop. After dropping Nava off at his house, we headed directly for home where we were welcomed by Barbara and the children and the wildly barking dogs. A good supper and a hot bath rounded off my visit to a small lead mine.

THE HOT BATHS

The next day, Barbara and Ramiro decided that we would all go to the thermal hot springs about fifteen miles out of town. Just after lunch, when the sun was high and it was quite warm, we squeezed the children into the Land Rover and drove about twenty miles into the foothills near Paria. This was a lonely spot with just a few buildings huddled at the foot of a cliff. When we got out of the car, we realized that, despite the bright, clear sky, a bitterly cold wind was blowing down from the mountains. Instead of their swimsuits, the children were handed their warm jackets, although Ramiro and I both grabbed towels and our swimming gear. There was a large, open pool surrounded and protected from the wind by small private baths and dressing rooms, and the old stone buildings were in good condition. Everything was spotlessly clean and tidy. In the dressing room, there was a sunken bath with four stone steps down and a wisp of steam that showed that the water was hot. I changed and cautiously tip-toed in. It was delightful, and I could have spent the rest of the day there, but Ramiro called to me and I stepped out into the icy wind. It did not take me long to reach the edge of the pool and jump in.

The water was very warm, almost hot, and the algae clinging to some of the walls gave the water a greenish tinge. But there was no taste of sulphur and no chlorine taste. A couple of very brown Indian boys had been swimming when we arrived, and they kept staring in wonder at the two white men with bodies like ivory but sunburned faces and hands. Barbara and the children stood all wrapped up, sheltering from the wind. It took some courage for me to climb out of the pool to get onto the diving board, but my courage was soon rewarded by the warm green water and, for nearly an hour, the two of us played around in the pool with little more than our noses above the water. The children got restless, however, and before we were ready, it was time to climb quickly out of the water and dash for the changing rooms. Before getting dressed, we spent another twenty minutes soaking in our individual hot tubs. We realized just why the Incas loved their hot springs and why the Romans, too, spent so much time in their hot baths.

The hot water came in through a stone channel. As I sat there, luxuriating, a dark hand appeared in the gap and placed a neatly carved stone in the channel to cut off the flow of water. This was a polite way of telling us that visiting time was over.

After the exercise and the hot water, I felt quite invigorated. We all walked behind the buildings to see the hot water bubbling up in its little pools and the neat stone ditches that led the water to the baths. "The Incas used them, then the Spaniards used them," Ramiro told me, "and then towards the end of the 19th century, somebody built these bath houses and they were very popular for a while. They aren't used much these days, but I think that they'll soon become popular again as more people get cars."

He then drove us to the foot of the hills and pointed out some towers perched on the hill tops. "Guess what they were for," he said. "The Spanish built them. Some are still used occasionally." I couldn't even guess, so Ramiro explained. "They're wind-powered smelters. There is always a strong wind down this valley, and the towers face into the wind. They burned mostly llama dung, and they had to squeeze every bit of heat out of it. Quite a bit of silver was smelted that way."

ORURO AND THE ORE EVALUATION

Ramiro took me out to a tailings operation the next morning. We drove across the *altiplano* for about half an hour to a place where a muddy river came down from the hills and lost itself on the flat lands. There were two or three small farms there, but must of the land was badly torn up, with holes and piles of rock everywhere and scores of little water channels snaking in and out. "These people are farmers," Ramiro said, "but they can make more money working the tailings." I looked where he was pointing. "The mines upstream have been dumping their tailings in the river bed for ages. Every rainy season, the floods wash much of it down to this spot, where it settles. There's probably $12,000,000 worth of alluvial tin under here."

I looked again at the sea of yellow mud, "And no big mining company has tried to get it?" I asked.

Ramiro laughed. "You bet they have. Lots of people have, but there is such a tangle of ownership claims with everybody from the original mines down to the little farmers all claiming it. Who owns the mud left behind by a flood?" He laughed again. "The lawyers just love it."

We drove to one of the farms. While Ramiro talked business with some men, I wandered around, looking at the handmade tools, the wooden plow, the stone mortar and pestle, and the adobe storage shed where the ancient rafters were tied down with rawhide thongs. One of the rafters was an old ox yoke, and there were small bottles of alcohol and tufts of llama wool hanging under the eaves to keep the evil spirits away and keep the good spirits happy. I was peering down the well in the yard when Ramiro came over and said,

"That's nearly two stories deep. There's water under the *altiplano*, but it's a long way down." I stepped back from the well.

Eventually, an agreement was made and four sacks of very heavy tin ore were loaded into the Land Rover. We set off back to Oruro. "It might look very primitive to us," Ramiro explained, "but they're getting at least fifty percent of the tin out of those diggings and it's between fourteen and eighteen percent pure tin. Which is pretty good. They're actually making quite a good living."

We drove back to the miners' cooperative in Oruro, where Ramiro's lead ore was going to be tested. In a large, high-walled yard, a huge sheet of steel lay in the middle of dozens of neatly piled sacks of ore. Four serious looking men were standing at the edge of the metal slab, all dressed in tight black suits with ties and dark hats. They greeted Ramiro solemnly and walked over to his stack. One of them chose a sack at random, and a laborer dumped the sack in the middle of the slab. Two men quickly spread it out with shovels, then divided it into four equal portions. One of the dark suited men then chose a portion at random and the rest was quickly shoveled back into the sack. The ore was again spread out and neatly divided and yet another dark suited judge chose a section. This went on for five or six divisions until all that was left was a very small portion and the judges had to peer closely to make their decisions. Finally, they were satisfied and the little sample was carefully swept into a glass container and carried off into what I took to be the laboratory.

During this whole procedure, Ramiro had been standing silent and grim faced, but when the sample disappeared into the lab, everybody relaxed and smiled. I gathered that the judges had been impressed by what they had seen.

"They did it this way when my father was a boy," Ramiro said. "We do it this way today, and I suspect they will be doing it this way for another hundred years." He added that it would take a day or two to get the results, so after a short discussion about prices we drove back to the house, but not without a stop to buy small presents for Barbara and the children.

Chapter 8: A Visit to a Large Tin Mine

Very early the next morning, I set off to visit the largest tin mine in the world. This is Llallagua, the mine that made Simon Patiño's fortune. It was the profits from Llallagua that enabled him to take complete control of the global tin market at a time when tin had become vitally necessary to the armies of the world.

Along with twenty other people, I squeezed into a micro bus that had little head room and even less knee room. As the overcrowded vehicle sped across the *altiplano* and started to climb into the foothills, it very quickly became hot and stuffy. It was a long, zigzag ride with no stops up through wild, treeless country onto a wide plateau and then down a winding valley with a dry river bed and no farms. It was not the most exciting scenery I'd ever seen. I soon dozed off.

LLALLAGUA

When I woke again, the bus was crawling up a hill past huge gray mountains and yellow tailings and rows of ugly little houses. When we stopped in a small plaza, I got out of the bus and looked around. Llallagua was a very depressing town with rows of dilapidated buildings on untidy streets, everything covered by a thick layer of dust and grime. There was an air of neglect and abandonment over the town, and the streets were crowded with poorly dressed people, mostly women and children, who didn't smile much. Over the whole town hung the strong smell of human excrement, as if no water had flowed through the sewers for a long time.

It was hot, and the altitude tired me quickly, so I made my way immediately to the town hall where a young clerk explained that although the mine was in Llallagua, the concentrator was in the nearby town of Catavi. It was the mine that I wanted to see, so I walked toward the mine office past rows of small, unpainted, miners' houses and a cinema where a crowd of children were struggling to get in to see old Hollywood films at a children's special price.

The miners' houses had a communal latrine, and, as I needed to relieve myself, I went into the men's. During my travels, I have experienced an extraordinary variety of lavatories, but this one was certainly the most primitive. It was a large shed with a concrete trench down the middle. The men simply straddled the trench and did their business. There was no privacy and, of course, no toilet paper. The stench was overpowering. It was clear that no water had flowed through the trench to keep it clean for many weeks. I did not use it.

At the mine office, a clerk said that I needed a permit from headquarters, *la gerencia*, to enter the mine, and the *gerencia* was in Catavi. Outside the office, I came upon a crowd of men who were using only their muscles to get a large ore car back onto the rail tracks. I followed the tracks past the crusher to the enormous mountain of tailings that loomed over the mine.

I had come upon a moonscape of holes and caves and molehills and trails across the completely barren sides of a manmade mountain. On the higher slopes, women were bent low, poking among the tiny bits of rock and now and then tucking a stone or two into their shoulder bags. They were lonely dabs of color on the huge bare landscape. The gully below was small stream of gray, mineralized water with tiny sluices leading to small pits dug in the river bed where men labored with shovels and wheel barrows, working their unofficial claims the way men have mined riverbeds for thousands of years.

It was an extraordinary sight. The brilliant colors of the rock, reds and greens and yellows shining in the sun, made a startling contrast to the grayness of the town and the mine buildings. I slid down a slope toward one of the miners who looked friendly and who was soon joined by his neighbor. Between them, they explained that they had worked in the big mine but had not liked it. "We are out in the open air now," said one. "We are free." He waved his hand at the brilliant blue sky. "And we make about as much as we did in the mine," added his friend, who had a wad of coca in his cheek. When I asked if there was much tin in the tailings, they both said that there was plenty. "Yes, sir, still a lot of tin here." I scrambled back up to the road as high overhead a double line of dump buckets continued to carry more tailings far up the rapidly filling valley.

Back in Llallagua, I found a small, clean-looking hotel, where I had a late lunch of fried eggs. The manager said there was transport to Catavi at the corner. The transport consisted of a pickup truck with a couple of planks in the bed for seats, but as the fare was only a few cents, I didn't complain. The pickup stopped at several houses to collect workers, then bounced for ten minutes along the road to Catavi, where it stopped in a small plaza.

CATAVI

Catavi was much better than Llallagua. Simon Patiño had built it as a company town with rows of houses for the miners and all the facilities that he thought his workers should have. Although it had a neglected, run-down air and was covered by a layer of dust, it was cleaner and did not stink. The little plaza was surrounded by offices and industrial buildings which included a company store where, from what I could see, the prices were lower than in Oruro and the women who crowded the store were all paying with coupons. Just down the road was the Simon Patiño Theater. This was a classical Greek-style building with steps and columns and Patiño's name in large letters over the portico. It must have been very impressive when it was built, but now it just looked old and worn under its layer of dust.

At the *gerencia* I wondered how I was going to talk my way into a guided tour of the mine. In Northern Rhodesia, where I went down a giant copper mine, I had simply walked into the first office I came to and said, "Please, can I go down your mine?" It had worked there, but I doubted if that approach would work in Bolivia. So I started by asking for the public relations department and was sent upstairs to an official who listened to my story that I was writing a history of mining in Bolivia. He passed me along to another official who also listened to my story before passing me along to yet another man. By this time, I had changed my "history" to a Ph.D. dissertation. The third man sent me down stairs to see the Big Boss, as he called him, and I waited for an hour in a room with a wide assortment of other people, each with a very good reason to see the Big Boss.

Eventually, I found myself in a nicely paneled office talking very good English with a gentleman who had once worked in Timmins, Ontario, to get experience in Canadian mining. Since I was a Canadian and had lived in both Montreal and Toronto, he was very pleased to see me and we chatted for a few minutes about mining in Canada while his secretary collected various sheets of figures on tin production in Bolivia. After this, he gave me permission to tour the mine and passed me on to the legal department. The lawyer, however, had different ideas and he spent nearly half an hour trying to dissuade me from going into the mine, citing safety and health and insurance and everything else that he could think of. Eventually, I gave up and he went off, with a smug smile, to the Big Boss. A few minutes later, he returned with a very red face and angrily slapped a release form on the desk for me to sign. This form gave me written permission to tour the mine. The lawyer told me to be at the entrance at 6:30 in the morning.

Back at the hotel, I was given a room that was clean and contained a fairly new bed but lacked soap or towels. Although the toilet was outside, there was a stand with a bowl and a jug of water in the room. I also found a chamber pot under the bed. It was not exactly the Ritz, but it was better than some places I have slept in. I had a chicken supper and took a look at the town. It was very dirty, with wicked roads that all seemed to be very steep, and every third building seemed to have a sign outside advertising that it was a *chicheria*, or bar. There was noisy singing coming from some of the bars and plenty of drunks staggering around the streets, and it was also bitterly cold, so I retreated to the little hotel, where a well dressed man started a conversation in English. When he turned out to be a Baptist evangelist with pockets full of religious tracts, I excused myself, arranged to be called at 5:30 in the morning, bought the local newspaper, and retreated to my cold bedroom, where I curled up in the surprisingly comfortable bed. I was sure it was the warmest place in town.

When a boy woke me at 5:30, it was bitterly cold, and I had to wash my face in ice water and dry myself on the bed sheets. There was no time for breakfast. Along with silent men in boots and helmets with backpacks made of sacking, I stumbled through the twilight streets, feeling decidedly out of place.

At the mine entrance, the miners climbed onto rail cars and smiled and waved as I photographed them disappearing into the mouth of the tunnel. There was a statue of the Madonna in a niche over the entrance, where they all crossed themselves as they went in, leaving me standing and waiting. It was obvious that I was too early. I found a canteen, which was a bare, utilitarian place, and breakfasted on delicious hot cocoa and almost broke my teeth on an ancient bread roll. It was good to stand in the warm rays of the rising sun until, half an hour later, a man came up and said that he would find me a guide. Another half an hour later, a little man dashed up and hustled me into a dressing room where I was given a yellow jacket and belt and some uncomfortable boots. We hurried along to another room, where he found me a lamp and a battery and a helmet. It was then that I remembered that I had not brought my flash unit, so I left the camera in the dressing room.

Feeling very much like a tourist, I sat with the next batch of miners as the train plunged into the darkness of what seemed to be a long ride into the heart of the mountain. My headlamp picked out wide, dark, rock walls with electric wires overhead and numerous side tunnels. About half way along, the train slowed as we passed a small brick chapel with glass windows. As the men crossed themselves, I thought of Tio sitting quietly in Ramiro's lead mine.

The train emptied at a rail junction, and somebody showed me the safety office, where the supervisor gave me a detailed lecture on silicosis and health and safety, after which he found a young assistant to take me on the grand tour. Within a hundred yards of the safety office, we came across a crowd of men sitting on the railroad tracks chewing coca. "They are on strike," my guide explained. It seemed that on the previous day a miner had lost a hand and an eye when a fuse misfired. Now the blasters and drillers in that section of the mine were on strike for reliable Chilean-made fuses instead of the cheaper Peruvian ones. Further on, we came to drillers who were working. The noise was incredible. Crouching in the gloom, the narrow space illuminated only by their lamps, their legs tangled in hoses, and their boots slipping in a mixture of mud and broken rock, the drillers manhandled the heavy drills up against the ancient rock and stood in a shower of dust, stone chips, and icy water as the drills roared and rattled only inches from their ears. I did not envy them their jobs.

For the next four hours, my young and extremely energetic guide led me on a complicated and confusing journey through the bowels of the earth. To this day, I have not the faintest idea how he knew where he was going, as there did not appear to be any pattern to the arrangement of the tunnels and shafts. We scrambled over piles of debris, splashed through muddy water, picked our way over tangles of pipes and wires, walked along silent and empty tunnels, cracked our heads in mouse holes, stumbled down wicked ladders in the pitch dark, held our ears against the roaring of the drills, and hugged the tunnel walls as loaded rail cars hurried by. There were a few quiet areas, but mostly it was a scene of noisy, busy, organized confusion with scores of helmeted men hurrying about their business. It was a gigantic, underground bee hive.

I was soon covered in gray mud, and bits of rock clung to my helmet. At that altitude, climbing the slippery ladders was very hard work. There seemed to be water everywhere, dripping from the walls and puddling underfoot, and everywhere there was the smell of dynamite. Some of the tunnels were cold and drafty, while others were hot and steamy, but the air throughout was reasonably fresh. At one point, my guide took me into a small elevator that plunged a heart-stopping distance further down into the earth. He wanted to show me a good vein of ore, so we hunched down and scrambled over freshly dynamited rock to where a surprisingly light colored streak of mineral about as wide as his hand showed clearly against the darker rock in the light of my headlamp. I looked around at the men crouched in the gloom in their cramped holes and pits in the depths of the mountain and thought of the tailings pickers in the bright daylight outside.

It was an extraordinary experience. I was quite overwhelmed by the activity and the complexity of the mine, but my young guide assured me that I had seen only a fraction of it. He knew very little about the electrical system or the compressors that kept the drills running or the pumps that removed the water, and he had only a vague idea of the miles of rail line that we kept crossing and recrossing. He did know that there were four or five elevators, but he was not sure how deep they were, so we went into a hoist room to watch the machinery. Then he led me to the engineer's office, which was deep underground.

The chief engineer was an older man who knew most of the statistics. On a large table lay a great stack of maps covering about a dozen levels and numerous sub-levels and off-shoot areas. I looked through the top few, then gave up. It was like trying to map one of those giant African ant hills. When I asked the engineer if anybody had ever visited every tunnel in the maze, he snorted. "That would probably take a year! It's hard enough just keeping up with the tunnels and shafts that are in use. Many of these tunnels were abandoned years ago." He next explained that when the price of tin was good, there could be well over a thousand men working in the mine. He tapped the pile of maps and said, "This is a whole mountain of tin! The biggest in the world. Four or five generations of miners have worked it, and there is still plenty left." Then we walked over to some shelves and he showed me samples of tin in all colors and all shapes, some of it in river clay and some of it in hard rock.

Our next stop was at another safety office, where a line of men, most of them chewing coca, waited cheerfully for a male nurse to patch up various injuries, which seemed to range from smashed fingers to dust in the eye. They were a friendly bunch and smiled broadly as I walked by. I got the impression of that these were men who were extremely proud of their work and the giant mine in which they labored. Although the medic was busy, he took the time to explain the problem with the dynamite fuses. He was very angry that management was cutting corners by buying the less reliable fuses. The miners clustered around us took it more philosophically, as if unreliable fuses were just another little problem they had to put up with.

I left the mine just after midday, tired, dirty, and feeling decidedly grubby, but extremely glad that I had taken the tour. I paid the hotel and found the micro-bus where the driver recognized me and saved the front seat for me. Just as we were about to leave for Oruro, another bus pulled in and blocked our way. There was a rivalry between the bus lines, and just when it looked as if it would come to blows, two short, dark, very tough-looking policemen arrived and settled the problem.

As we bounced across the railroad tracks, my driver boasted that on a good day he could get to Oruro in only a few hours, but the ore train from the mine was so antiquated that it took the whole day and nobody was planning to modernize it, at least not as far as he knew. I said, "Well, it's far better now than when Simon Patiño started the mine. He had to use llamas to bring out the ore."

The driver was astonished. "I never thought of that. God! He must have had to use hundreds of llamas. It would have taken a week to get to Oruro."

It was hot in Llallagua, but as we climbed out of the valley it became quite cool and there were rain clouds over the *altiplano*. True to form, the heavens waited until we were nearly in Oruro before opening up.

Chapter 9: The Yungas

The Yungas are a series of valleys that plunge eastwards from the highest part of the Andes between Cuzco and La Paz to the Amazon lowlands, where they are just a few hundred feet above sea level. Both the Incas and the Spaniards valued these steep valleys for the gold that could be found in the river beds. The sands have been worked and reworked for hundreds of years and produced large quantities of gold. Today, the Yungas still produce gold, but the area is also valued for its tropical and semi-tropical fruits and vegetables and for the high quality coca that grows on the fertile slopes.

I was determined to take a trip down into the Yungas. I wanted to plunge, in just a few hours, more than 12,000 feet from the cold and treeless *altiplano* to the hot and humid Amazon rainforest. I was not deterred when Ramiro reminded me that the road to Coroico and Caranavi has the dubious title of "the most dangerous road in the world."

When I inquired in La Paz about buses to Caranavi, I was reminded that I would need a military pass. At the army headquarters, however, they were reluctant to give me a permit because of all the political unrest, and so I had to concoct a story about writing a book on agriculture in the Yungas. I even claimed to be a professor at UCLA. Finally, and reluctantly, they gave me the permit.

I was planning to leave next morning, but I woke up to find

trouble in the streets. Small groups of students were marching about with placards, and many of the shops had refused to open. Suddenly, a truckload of riot police wearing helmets and brown uniforms appeared. The officer in charge was carrying a tear-gas gun. When some shots were fired, the crowd broke up and ran in every direction. My hotel was on the route to the presidential palace, and this little drama occurred three or four times during the day as the students attempted to reach the palace.

I therefore spent most of that day standing at the window watching the police chasing students behind the hotel. Groups of police with long sticks ran past and truckloads of soldiers also sped past in both directions. Now and then a shot rang out, but it always sounded like a blank, and twice an ugly water-spraying truck went by, obviously looking for a target. As far as I could see, the students were far outnumbered by the police and the riot troops. By sunset, everything was back to normal. What I found humorous was the policeman on traffic duty. He stood on his little podium and, completely ignoring the turmoil around him, continued to direct traffic as if it was a normal day.

Breakfast the next morning was a cup of coffee from an Indian woman who had a primus stove perched on the curb near where the buses stopped. Although I got a comfortable seat behind the driver, the windows were filthy and there was no chance that I would get any good photos. We went north out of La Paz instead of west to El Alto, and after the obligatory stop for gasoline and oil, we sat shivering in a long line of vehicles at a checkpoint on a muddy stretch of road while an official checked each vehicle and stamped our passes. There was a group of English and French tourists in a hired car at the checkpoint, and it was obvious that nobody had told them that they would need a military permit. Their driver was negotiating with the official as we left.

As the road climbed up a wide valley, I saw small patches of ice and snow on the hillside that were melting rapidly in the bright sun. The road we were on was surprisingly busy, most of the vehicles being huge trucks crowded with Indians and loaded with fruit and vegetables wrapped in dry banana leaves. Our little bus slithered its way up through Arctic barrenness until I estimated we were about 15,000 feet above sea level, then it crested a hill and we found ourselves on the edge of a great valley that was quite bare of any vegetation. Far below us, the narrow road dropped down so steeply that the trucks below looked like toys. As we started down, we inched past an overloaded truck hugging the cliff face as it crept up. It was moving at a slow, walking pace, and behind it walked a man carrying a long pole with a big triangular wooden block on the end. This was obviously a wheel chock to be used in case the overloaded truck should start to slide backwards.

While the gravel surface was surprisingly good, the road was very narrow and had no guard rails of any kind to mark the edge, not even a few rocks. Here and there were slightly wider sections where two trucks might pass, but the edges were crumbling and looked suspiciously unstable. Up-hill traffic seemed to have priority and always hugged the cliff. Our driver was either in a hurry or just eager to show his skill. We raced down the open stretches and spun around the countless hairpin bends at what to me was a lunatic speed.

Within half an hour, we hit the rain forest, and the bare rocks gave way to thick vegetation dripping with water, The blue sky changed to fog and heavy clouds, and whenever the fog lifted we could look back and see the road winding in and out, looking more like a groove scratched along the mountainside than a major road. At a couple of spots, water poured off the cliff in a small waterfall onto the road, and the gravel was badly eroded. At other places, usually sharp bends, we had to splash through small streams which were also doing their best to wash out the road. Building bridges or digging tunnels in this terrain would have been fantastically expensive, so the road simply followed the contours of the land and went in and out of every side valley and around every mountain spur. It was an engineer's nightmare.

The road twisted and turned like a snake in agony for almost the entire distance, but the most dangerous spot was there in the rain forest. Somebody in La Paz told me that more than twenty trucks a year went over the edge. One year, a bus with 100 people had gone over at a particularly bad corner and the bodies had never been recovered. All the way down, I could see small white crosses at the edge of the road, sometimes in tight clusters, and at one point we passed three concrete memorials to some politicians executed during a revolution. I caught the word *Democracia* on them as we sped by.

I have been on quite a few bad roads in my travels, but this was so bad it was actually exhilarating. Photography was out of the question, so I clung to my seat with both hands, swaying with the vehicle, gasping at the horrifying drop over the edge, holding my breath as we scraped past other vehicles, and, rather like a child on a circus ride, enjoying every minute of it.

We came out of the rain forest rather suddenly and found ourselves in a region where the vegetation was not so dense and the road was dusty. It quickly became very warm, and I struggled out of my jacket and then my sweater and relaxed in the heat. As we dropped even lower, the vegetation became semi-tropical and I saw small farms on the steep hillsides and a number of narrow roads leading off the main road. At noon, when we stopped for twenty minutes at a corner where there were two cafes and three adobe houses, somebody pointed out the town of Coroico, perched on the edge of a little plateau high overhead, just glimpses of buildings hiding in the bright green brush.

As I stood in the shade sucking a huge, fresh orange, the carload of English and French tourists pulled up. They were a mixed bunch and knew very little about the geography or the history of Bolivia. The French girl disliked everything she was seeing, and one of the Englishmen kept demanding to see "real jungle," but the others were pleasant. They had rented the car and driver on a whim and had not the faintest idea where they were going. The road had really impressed them, and now they were wondering just how long it would take them to get back to La Paz. When they asked the driver, he just shrugged.

The man sitting next to me on the bus explained that it was possible to reach the Beni district in the Bolivian Amazon rain forest by this route. He had not been there himself, but he had friends who had. The route he described was by truck and riverboat and sounded like a great adventure, but I had decided to go no further than Caranavi, although I did intend to get into the Beni region before I left Bolivia.

CARANAVI

The last stretch of the road became very hot and humid, and Caranavi turned out to be just a little village scattered across the hillside and slumbering in the tropical heat. There was another military checkpoint where bored young soldiers with huge submachine guns and no ammunition, checked our passes. The hotel where the bus stopped was rather primitive, but it was clean and had good mosquito nets. The manager checked my passport very carefully and promised that he would turn on the water for the shower "soon". He had a pair of red squirrels in a cage, but he could not tell me much about them except that they were a local species.

While the little town had no building higher than one story, it had a pretty little plaza with jacaranda trees and flowering shrubs. Bananas and papaya trees grew everywhere, and every house had a lush, green, garden plot. Behind some of the houses I could see sugar cane and some coffee trees. There was a pioneer feel to the place. and the stores seemed to carry just the basic necessities with absolutely no luxuries. I estimated that there were no more than 2,000 people there, yet it had a rough but functional airstrip and a well kept football (soccer) field. The marketplace was empty except for a pamphlet rack outside the evangelical church.

In the plaza, I met an English tourist wearing a straw hat and a bright poncho that was much too warm for the tropical afternoon. We looked up at the surrounding hills and discussed the slash and burn farming that was slowly but surely destroying the forest. Many of the lower slopes were already clear and signs of erosion were already showing.

At sunset, the mosquitoes appeared and we retreated to the

hotel, where the water was still not running. I managed to trace the pipes to the turn-off valve and opened it. The shower water was tepid but refreshing, and the evening was nicely cool, so the Englishman and I made our way to a little restaurant for a good chicken dinner. We were sitting and talking on the patio when the lights flickered and the hotel generator was switched off. We took this as a sign to head back to our rooms through the warm darkness, and we went to bed by candlelight.

Three roosters right outside my window woke me at 4:00 in the morning. After a quick wash (still by candlelight), I went out to where the bus had pulled up in the dark. The hotel manager was dressed in his pajamas and a warm sweater, and a few sleepy people, including the Englishman in his poncho, drifted out and stood around the hurricane lamp, but the Englishman wandered off as we climbed onto the mini-bus, and so we left without him. We had hardly gone a few yards when we had to stop at the military checkpoint and everybody got off the bus with their passes. It would not have been an incident worth remembering except that the guard became very angry because I left his little wooden shack by the door marked *entrada* instead of the one marked *salida*. The two doors were side by side, and the tiny building was hardly bigger than a garden shed, but the signs were freshly painted and he was determined that everybody would use them properly. "What's wrong with these foreigners?" he demanded of the bus driver. "*¿No puden leer buen Castillano?* Can't they read perfectly good Spanish?"

The driver was not in a good mood that day. He leaned on the horn at every opportunity and threw the bus so violently around the curves that I had to hang on with both hands as he skimmed the edge of each corner, especially those with horrifying drops. Fortunately, the road was empty except for a couple of women carrying huge bundles. At last dawn touched the mountain tops and slid down the hillsides, and I could see bananas and papayas and other fruit growing semi-wild around little settlers' cabins high up on the hillsides. There were patches of mist in the hollows and wisps of smoke from burning fields.

COROICO

About 9:00, we stopped at a lonely cafe down by the river, where the sun had not yet reached, I retrieved my bag and had a coffee and sandwich while waiting for another bus to take me up to Coroico, which was only a few miles away but high on another mountain ridge. The cafe owner said she would tell me when something arrived but that it would probably be a long wait. Minutes later, a second bus appeared with the poncho-wearing Englishman, who was heading back to La Paz and then on to Cochabamba. He assured me that there was a decent hotel in Coroico and that the town was worth a visit, so I relaxed on the patio with a large black dog and a little monkey anchored to a chair and who kept trying to climb up my trouser leg. When the manager told me that there were two strangers catching butterflies near the garbage dump, I strolled down and walked into a great cloud of butterflies, thick as a swarm of bees. It was a gorgeous sight, with butterflies of every color and size flashing in the morning sun and flitting around my head. The "strangers" were two English students with a big net who had taken two hours to walk down from Coroico. They were very happily making what was going to be a very fine collection.

Nobody seemed to want to go up to Coroico, but eventually one of the big fruit trucks returning from La Paz offered to take people up for the very generous fare of one peso. By this time, quite a small crowd had gathered and all of us, including the butterfly collectors, piled in. We stood in the truck bed, hanging on to each other and ducking our heads under low tree branches as the truck slowly climbed up the mountain. My fellow passengers were almost all Indians who thought it was funny that three foreigners would ride in a truck.

We jumped out of the truck when it reached the market place of Coroico, and I carried my bag to the hotel, which was perched on the edge of a cliff. There I discovered one of the most beautiful views that I have ever seen. The genius who had built the hotel had chosen the perfect spot, which presented an almost uninterrupted panoramic view of at least fifty miles in every direction.

The hotel was big and fairly new and boasted a pool, a tennis court, and a comfortable lounge. Even though the grounds were neglected, there was no hot water, and the toilet did not flush properly, there were bowls of flowers everywhere and the staff were cheerful and attentive. The two English students and I were the only guests in a hotel that could have slept sixty or more.

The three of us sat down to a pleasant lunch in the large empty dining room, after which I went out onto the terrace, found a comfortable chair, and sat gazing out over the beautiful mountain scenery. The hotel and the whole town were perched on the end of a steep ridge at least 1,000 feet above the valley. Some clouds were forming in the deep blue sky far to the east. As I watched, a great bank of thunderheads rolled up from the jungle below and advanced up the valley. It was perfectly quiet and very relaxing, and I dozed off, only to be woken by a hair-raising flash of lightning and an enormous clap of thunder. For two hours, the rain came down in torrents accompanied by an icy wind. The hotel manager dashed around closing windows while a maid mopped the water off the floor. Then, in typical tropical rainstorm fashion, the downpour stopped, the sun came out, and the storm was forgotten.

After the storm, I wandered around the little town. It was obviously an old town, perhaps dating back to an Inca military defense point, and it had a relaxed, almost sleepy feel about it. There was very little traffic and in the plaza I met the students again, so we sat under a tree and discussed entomology. They were very serious students and were waiting for sunset so that they could study the insects that come out at night.

When the sun had set, as we watched the fireflies dancing under the trees, the students caught a couple of specimens and enthusiastically examined them. They also taught me a few things that I had never known about these delightful insects. Then we listened to the frog chorus and they tried to identify the various types by their sounds. Some honked, some beeped, others chirped like birds, and others simply groaned. It was all very interesting, and we continued our conversation over a fine supper and then relaxed on the patio under a sky that glowed with stars. That night, I fell asleep to the complete amphibian orchestra and chorus.

It was a bright morning when I awoke, and from the garden I could see the river far below. It was yellow with mud. Up the valley, the road was visible for twenty miles and there was traffic on it, which told me the rain had not washed it out. It was Saturday, and a few other guests had arrived, but the students were already off collecting insects.

In the town again, I passed an extraordinarily ugly church dated 1929 and noticed that many of the palm trees were heavy with parasitic ferns. Up a steep hill where small boys were playing soccer with bottle tops, I found a small chapel with confetti on the steps. The door was locked, however, and a herd of cows was tethered on the grounds. This was a good place to rest in the cool breeze and admire the view. I could see a village about ten miles away and narrow roads winding over the hills and down into the valleys. Far up the valley, I could glimpse the white tipped peaks of the Andes. Wandering up the road, I came to two small boys making bird cages out of sticks. They talked to me enthusiastically, naming the plants and the birds and pointing out the power station in the valley. They could count to 10 in English, had been to La Paz, and were very positive that they would never live on the *altiplano*, even though they were very proud of the magnificent view and pointed out four hawks that were hunting over the orange and banana groves.

The trail down the hill back into Coroico went through some farms where the soil looked black and fertile and everybody was cheerfully friendly. A boy carving a little flute from a length of cane pointed out the coca fields, and I slithered down a muddy trail accompanied by a large friendly dog and four or five children who had appeared like magic. They showed me some low coffee trees and pointed out which berries were ripe for picking, then guided me to a steep hillside plot where the coca plants were only six inches high. When I asked to see taller coca plants, they took me to another plot, where I was surprised that the mature plant was only waist high. I had been expecting something much bigger. The kids obviously considered me a little crazy, but they were very polite when I asked how anybody knew who owned each of the little oddly shaped plots scattered across the hillside. "But, sir," they said, "*todos sabe*. Everybody knows." I had to take that as an answer, but I was still puzzled at how land ownership was organized because the plots were of all sizes and shapes and there were no boundary markers that I could see.

At lunch back at the hotel, I talked with the entomology students again and asked them why they had chosen Coroico for their collecting.

"Well," said one, "it's easy to get to and it has a good hotel and no mosquitoes," said one.

"Oh," said the other, "this area is very popular with bug people. It has an extraordinary variety of insects. The conditions are pretty well perfect for every kind. Sometimes exotic types get blown up from the Amazon region."

The first student grinned and said, purely for my benefit, "We've caught a few pretty nasty stinging types in the bushes just down the hill. None of them are poisonous, of course."

I was glad to hear that and, in exchange, I pointed out the way to the coca plantations so that they could look for parasites on the plants.

By that time, a barbecue and dance was starting on the patio and the small band was playing enthusiastically. I went to check on the bus back to La Paz. There was no bus due, but the hotel's

Jeep station wagon was going to go all the way to La Paz next day. But first they had to fix the brakes. A cluster of men worked all that afternoon and well into the night fixing the brakes. Their way of testing them was unique. When they thought they had it right, somebody would speed the vehicle across the yard and slam on the brakes. At the edge of the yard there was a low stone wall, which hid a sheer drop of at least 200 feet. The brake testing was nerve wracking to watch, so I wandered around town again and found a cafe where the radio was playing Andean music, which I particularly like. I sat there and drank a beer and watched the fireflies. On the way back to the hotel, I met the party from the hotel heading for somebody's house. They were accompanied by the entire band, which now included an enormous drum. I could see it was going to be a long night for the neighbors.

I had left all the windows of my room open during the day, so before I went to bed, I carefully checked every corner of the room and squashed quite a nice variety of bugs. "None of them poisonous, of course."

Next morning, the hotel manager told me that the Jeep would not leave until noon, so I sat on the patio in the sun and discussed the tourist industry with three Bolivian businessmen. A stiff breeze was blowing huge white clouds up the valley and the bright sky was an extraordinary scene of ragged and twisted clouds clinging to mountain tops or drifting below us as foggy patches in the valley. I felt as if I was on the top of the world. Noon came, I had lunch, and then the Jeep appeared, already crowded with passengers. I made sure I was first in line and squeezed in behind the driver in a seat that had neither head nor leg room. The only view I had was over the driver's shoulder. The two entomology students and their specimens were squashed in somewhere in the back.

This driver was very young and very careful, but the Jeep was in bad shape. Strange noises came from the transmission, and we stopped two or three times to let it cool down. Halfway through the trip, part of the muffler fell off with a loud clatter, but we kept on going. We made good time and were soon up in the rain forest, where we stopped at a tiny village of stone huts and drank coffee in the wet mist. The clouds continued right up to the *cumbre*, the top of the pass, then suddenly we were in bright sunshine again. It was cold, the land was bleak and bare, and there was a small herd of llamas near the road.

From there, it was a fast drive down into La Paz, where I met the two young English students again in a restaurant. According to all the posters stuck on the walls, there was a circus in town, so we decided to see it. We found a huge crowd milling about the big tent and scores of venders selling cooked food, and there were also dozens of policemen, one of whom asked us very politely if we were going to "start a riot." I assured him that we had come only to see the circus. He smiled with relief and said, "This is a very good circus. It has come all the way from Colombia." It was a very good circus indeed, with elephants and clowns and a high wire act. It finished at midnight.

That night, after a very cold walk back to the hotel, I took all the blankets from the other bed and tried to think of sleeping under nothing but a mosquito net in Caranavi.

THE TRAIN TO ORURO

Just for fun, and because I like old trains, I took the regular train to Oruro. That is how I discovered just how old a train can be and still function perfectly well. I was on a long train with seventeen cars, which included some ancient wooden boxcars, five newish freight cars, two old mail cars, a sleeper car built in Argentina in 1939, and a kitchen car and diner built in 1920. The regular coaches were British and at least half a century old, with English leather seats and shiny brass fittings, very worn but still serviceable. There seemed to be no difference between first and second class, except for a few pesos in price. The train was more than crowded. It was packed, and so I sat in the restaurant car talking with a Canadian engineer who worked for the La Paz power company. Scores of venders swarmed up and down the train, pestering the foreign tourists and offering not just food and fruit, but also pens, bags, watches, and even lamp shades. The train started half an hour late and was so overloaded that it had to be taken up to El Alto in two sections where, fortunately, all the venders got off.

The waiters served us a very good, four-course lunch in the charming old dining car as we chugged slowly across the *altiplano*, which had suddenly turned bright green after the recent rain. There were many stops. At one village, the venders were offering whole sides of mutton, while at another the main offering was flowers in huge bunches. In Oruro, as the track ran for a few miles down the middle of a very crowded street, a swarm of small boys jumped onto the old train, hanging onto anything they could grasp and screaming with laughter.

THE ROAD RACE

Back in Oruro, Barbara and Ramiro listened to my travel tale. When Barbara said that they ought to go to Coroico one day, Ramiro said, "Not until they fix that road! You think I would risk my family on that road?" I had seen Ramiro handle worse roads with easy skill, but I said nothing. "Talking of roads," Ramiro said to change the subject, "there's a road race this week-end and my cousin is in it. He's driving a Jaguar."

We got up early the next morning to watch the cars go by, and while we waited for the race to start, Ramiro explained just how popular car racing is in Bolivia. A good, reliable vehicle is a necessity in Bolivia, and keeping your car running is the number one priority. In a land of deplorable roads and extraordinarily thin air, a great deal of time and money goes to adjusting the engine and the shocks and reinforcing vital parts, so most owners end up being skilled mechanics and, because of the mountain roads, skilled drivers, too.

This race would start in Potosí, then make a circle through Oruro, Cochabamba, Sucre, and back to Potosí. It was an enormous distance with changes in altitude of up to 6,000 feet and no service stations except in the larger towns. Most of the cars were either British Jaguars or American Mustangs.

From our perch on a high rock near the road, we watched the cars, starting with a great yellow cloud in the distance, growing rapidly, and then roaring past, leaving us choking in the dust. They were evenly spaced and were being followed closely by a brightly painted 1929 Ford which, we later learned, completed the circuit with no major problems. Ramiro spent the rest of the day glued to the radio, following every twist and turn of the extraordinary race. While he was thus occupied, I strolled around the town and found the zoo.

It was a sadly neglected place, with a pitiful collection of ducks and parrots in cages. But they did have four giant condors. They were magnificent birds, black with large, white ruffs and naked heads with huge, curved beaks. Their cage was small for so many large birds, and they stood there, silently eying the distant mountain peaks and completely ignoring me. When one of them stretched its wings, I estimated the wing spread to be at least eight feet. For food, somebody had tossed a dead dog into the cage.

Back at Ramiro's house, I was greeted with bad news. Somewhere on the long, empty road between Cochabamba and Sucre, Ramiro's cousin had crashed when a front tire blew out and the car flipped over. It had happened a long way from any telephone, and we sat around the house for hours waiting for further news, then suddenly a ham radio operator who had contacted another ham radio operator in the area phoned. The car had turned completely over and was a wreck, but Ramiro's cousin had only a couple cracked ribs and a cut on the head. His copilot had gotten only a cut on his head. Fortunately, the accident happened on a flat stretch of the road, rather than on a steep mountain stretch. Another race car had stopped and helped them, and a passing stranger had taken them to the hospital in Sucre for x-rays.

Everybody was quite relieved. Ramiro suggested we drive down to the plaza, then over to his father's house for a cup of tea. Oruro is proud of the trees in the main plaza because when they were first planted, all the experts said they would not do well and would never get more than five feet tall. They were sixty feet tall now and in excellent health. The plaza was crowded with large family groups and children playing happily on the bronze animals around the fountain and spending their pocket money at the ice cream venders. On the street corners were groups of tough-looking riot police with bags of tear gas bombs. "You know," Ramiro said, "while you've been traveling, we've had two presidents and two governments." He paused. "And I'll take bets that this one won't last more than a couple of weeks, either."

Ramiro's father was a very interesting gentleman who was an encyclopedia of information on mining. He had an excellent library and proudly showed me a copy of the *Arte de los Metales*, a very famous and extremely rare book first published in Potosí in the 17th century. "A lot of the information in this book is still used today," he said. He began talking about mining in the "old days" and about Simón Patiño. He mentioned that Patiño had built a large house in Oruro and that it was now the law school. During our conversation, he also told me that he had been in the Chaco war, but he did not talk about the war very much. When I told him where I had been, he was very interested and said, "Tarija. You have to visit Tarija. It's a bit hard to get to, but the climate is wonderful and the people are charming." I assured him that Tarija was on my list of places to see. It was also on my route to Salta in Argentina, so on our way home, Ramiro and I stopped at the railroad station.

For some reason, the passenger trains from Bolivia stop at Villazón, which is on the border with Argentina, but do not cross the border, despite the fact that the rail line is directly connected to the Argentine line. When we asked the station manager, he did not know why, but he assured us that there were plenty of buses from the border to Salta. I would have to wait another day, however, for a seat on the train to Villazón.

THE FIESTA IN ORURO

That extra day in Oruro was anything but boring. As soon as it was warm, I walked up the hill to the plaza in front of the miners' church, Nuestra Señora del Socavon, where there was a fair going on. The little plaza was packed with Indians in their very best clothes, the men wearing formal suits and the women wearing their full regalia of wide skirts and colored shawls and displaying a wide variety of regional hats, not just the tall, white hats of Cochabamba and the derby hat of the La Paz region, but also other, more interesting hats that I had never seen before. It was a wonderful display of color, contrasting with the gray and brown rock of the mountain. The church, a rather ugly building of cement blocks, was wide open to display a statue of the Virgin covered in yards of brand new silk. The other statues in the church had also been newly dressed in silk and colored tissue paper.

On the plaza, tables had been set up for every form of gambling, and women with their tiny portable kitchens were selling everything from hot dogs to food that I did not recognize. Many of the stalls had tall arches covered in silver objects ranging from old silver coins to pots and pans, similar to what Lily and I had seen in Potosí. There were bright new shawls for the women, candy for the children, an endless supply of beer, and at least three small bands in fierce competition. All I could do was sit on the crowded steps and soaked it all in while nibbling on a piece of barbecued guinea pig that was more bone than meat, but quite tasty.

That afternoon, we returned to Mr. Miranda's house and were having tea on his inside patio, a lovely oasis of flowers and shrubs, when a brass band passed the house and we took the children out to watch. The band, which was playing *altiplano* music, was followed by two rows of dancers in T-shirts, red hats, and sneakers, and behind them came a huge crowd of supporters, some of whom carried large religious banners. "Ah," Ramiro's father said, "they are practicing for the great *Diablada* parade."

It was still many weeks before the great parade, but at that altitude, it takes weeks of practice to build up the stamina to leap and whirl continuously over the long route taken twice a day for three days, and sometimes longer.

The dancers in the T-shirts must have been trainees, because behind the religious banners came a group of about a dozen dancers nearly all wearing the famous devil masks as well as bits and pieces of the costume. "Those are last year's masks," Ramiro said. "They make new masks every year." His father added, "They seem to get bigger and bigger every year. When I was a boy, they were just ugly faces with big staring eyes and a pair of horns. Now they're enormous things with many eyes and horns. But they certainly are much more colorful. Fantastic! Fantastic!"

Each group was led by a man in a mainly white costume wearing a helmet and carrying a sword. On his back he bore an enormous pair of wings. "That's San Miguel the Archangel," one of the children told me. Some of the St Michael angels were wearing only the wings and were obviously having trouble with the maze of supporting straps that kept the beautiful wings in position, but the experienced dancers with the huge, wonderfully grotesque masks seemed to be having no trouble at all. For the rest of the afternoon and late into the evening, we stood and watched as group after group, over two dozen of them, each with its own brass band and whirling archangel, danced its way down the hill.

Chapter 10: South to Argentina

The Ferro-bus left at midnight. This was a brand-new, Japanese-made, diesel train of four cars, including a buffet car. It was very smart and not crowded, and I had a seat to myself and my very own, rented, huge, neatly folded blanket. There was a quarter moon overhead, with stars as big as melons, but I fell asleep immediately and woke up only once when we stopped in Uyuni.

The sun came up very quickly when we reached Tupiza, a small mountain town of dusty streets and adobe houses surrounded by small irrigated farms. Where there was no irrigation, the land was brown and bare. The stewards brought breakfast, and the train worked its way out of the valley and onto a wide plateau that seemed to be a continuation of the *altiplano*. It was bone dry and there were a few cacti, but here and there a lucky farmer had found enough water to irrigate a small patch and protect his crops from predators with tall willows that glowed bright green.

Villazón was a small, uninteresting town on the wide plateau. I saw no signs in the station pointing the way to the Argentine border, so I hired a small boy with a wagon to carry my bag. He showed me where to get an exit stamp in my passport, then led me along the railroad track and through the town for over a mile to a police post for another stamp and to register my camera before entering La Quiaca, which is in Argentina. The two towns are separated by a wide open space and a trickle of a stream crossed by a modern bridge. My guide took me across, but the Argentine border guard refused to let him bring his wagon into the country, so he whistled up his big brother to take care of the wagon and we continued on. The Bolivian passport stampers had been an irritation, but they were polite and even friendly. The Argentine passport stampers were arrogant and rude and deliberately took their time. And there were three of them: the customs, the police, and a third who simply admired all the pages in my passport and handed it back.

It was hot, and I had walked nearly two miles by then, but my small guide was still cheerful. He took me to a *cambio* to change my money, then on to the bus station, where I found that there was a time difference and I had two hours to wait for the next bus to Salta. La Quiaca was smaller and even less interesting than Villazón, so I decided to spend the time eating a leisurely lunch.

When the bus arrived, it was big, comfortable, and uncrowded. The driver and his assistant were dark Andean Indians with serious faces, and the stewardess was a prim girl with a serious frown. She brought us coffee, then cookies, then hot dogs, then lemonade, then a pastry, then yet more coffee.

THE HUMAHUACA VALLEY

The countryside in Argentina was still wide open desert with a scattering of cactus and herds of goats and donkeys, but by late afternoon it had narrowed down to a wide canyon. We began to leave the high country. I had hopes of reaching Humahuaca before dark so I could get a photo or two, but just a few miles away from the town, we were flagged down by a truck with oil problems. It took nearly an hour for the two drivers to solve the problem, and the sun set in glorious Technicolor while we sat and waited.

Humahuaca has given its name to the valley that connects Argentina and Bolivia. It was down this valley that the Incas and the Spanish invaded the fertile land of Tucuman, and it was back up this valley that mules and wine and cotton flowed to Potosí and as far as Cuzco. During the wars for independence, armies marched up and down this dry and rocky valley, and after independence, Buenos Aires tried mightily—and successfully—to include it in the new Republic of Argentina. To this day, it is still the gateway from the pampas to the *altiplano* and the dividing line between the very European Argentine culture and the very Indian Andean culture.

As we arrived in Humahuaca at twilight, I could make out a statue of an Indian runner, a *chasqui*, on a high monument in the middle of the bustling little town. The dusty streets were full of people, mostly Andean Indians, and it looked quite prosperous with cattle yards and a fairly large rail yard. We stopped only for a few minutes, then drove on past farms dependent entirely on irrigation, almost all of them surrounded by shade trees. It was the trees that, for me, marked the transition from one world to another.

About fifty miles from Juyjuy, the next major town on my route to Salta, in the pitch dark, we were flagged down by another truck with oil problems. Its driver needed a piece of cardboard to make an oil filter gasket. A passenger produced what he wanted, but by then all his oil had leaked out and our spare oil was all used up. So we sat and waited in the dark until a pickup came along with a few spare cans of oil. But the time was not wasted. Across the aisle from me sat a gentleman with a compass and a briefcase full of maps. Using our flashlights, we studied the maps and discussed the history and geography of the region. He knew every dry river and dusty arroyo by name.

Chapter 11: The Tucuman Foothills

Setting off again and looking for oil, we stopped at half a dozen villages and made a side trip to the bus company's garage before we finally pulled in to Juyjuy at 10:00 that night. As I got off the bus to stretch my legs, I caught a glimpse of a large, spread-out city and a modern bus station. As we were sadly behind schedule, however, we stopped for only a few minutes. There were only a few passengers left on the bus, and now it was quite warm, so I fell asleep and did not wake up until we were in Salta. By that time, it was 1:30 in the morning and everything seemed deserted. I found a taxi and asked for a good hotel in the middle of the city, but the driver took me to what must have been the right place to be seen on a Friday night. There was a large crowd at the sidewalk tables, so I told him to find another place. He found an older hotel with patios. It was comfortable and the water was hot. When I went to bed, my ears popped being from the lower altitude.

I slept late and spent the day wandering around Salta. Although it is a large city and the provincial capital, I got the impression of a small town. In the center there were mainly low 19th and early 20th-century houses that looked very Spanish with their ornate front patios. Further out, there were bigger and more modern homes. The streets were wide and busy, and in the distance I could see a circle of hills. There was a very Moorish post office built in 1939, and the main plaza was full of trees and a wide variety of flowers. It was quite attractive. There were also children's swings and the

usual oversize bronze statue to some general. On one side of the
plaza sat rows of cafe tables under umbrellas crowded with family
groups. While the town boasted very few modern buildings, it
had a charmingly ornate cathedral and a Franciscan church so
overly ornate that it bordered on the grotesque. Inside there was a
wax "dead saint" under glass.

I had been wondering why the town seemed so different
from any I'd seen in Bolivia, and then it suddenly became
obvious—there were no Indians. Although it was nestled at the
foot of the Andes, Salta was not an Andean city. It was clearly a
Mediterranean European city, and the population, at least in the
city center, was European. After months in the Andes, this took a
little getting used to.

During the *paseo* at sunset in the plaza, young men walked
about in groups and pretended to ignore the young women who
were also walking about in groups and pretending to ignore them.
It was all very Spanish, and just as Spanish was the annoying habit
of not eating supper until nine or ten in the evening. I was the only
one in the restaurant at 8:00, and I had finished before anybody
else arrived.

Next morning, the hotel manager told me how to find the
monument to Martín Gűemes, the gaucho warlord who controlled
this region during the wars for independence. His bronze statue,
in a park on a hillside, was impressive, showing the hero on
horseback in gaucho clothing and on a typical saddle but with the
huge leather chaps that were designed not just to protect the rider's
legs but the horse as well. The way the leather wrapped around the
horse's chest, it looked as if the chaps were actually part of the

horse's tack. I thought this statue would have been an excellent thing for the local children to play on, but it was perched on top of a high stone pillar. I scrambled up the hill behind the park to get a photo of the city, but it clouded over and some raindrops began to fall, so instead I visited a museum in a 17th-century building near the plaza. It had a surprisingly interesting collection, ranging from old coins to colonial maps and everything in between. The custodian was not happy with the North American influence on Latin American culture, but while he was talking I noticed a very American looking *supermercado* right across the street. It seemed to be very popular.

At the tourist office, the lady suggested that a bus to the Bolivian border at Yacuiba was probably the best way to return to Bolivia. When I told her about my travels in Bolivia and Chile, she was horrified. "But those are Indian countries," she said, "and they are such poor countries." Then she admitted that she had never actually been to either country. "But I know people who have," she insisted, "and they say they are very poor countries." I didn't argue with her.

Munching on huge red and yellow Argentine apples and enormous oranges, I wandered around Salta and found plazas dedicated to France and to Italy. I started thinking about the Indians in Argentina. They migrate in from Bolivia and Paraguay to work on the farms and pick up menial jobs, usually for poor wages. Their labor is essential to the economy, but nobody wants them to actually live in Argentina, so they migrate back home each winter or live illegally in slums on the edges of the cities, where they are often rounded up and deported. The apple I was eating, in fact, had probably been picked by a migrant laborer. It reminded me of California.

Next morning, it took nearly an hour for the bank to, very reluctantly, change a few travelers checks for me. Then I made my way to the bus station, where I found that the only bus to Yacuiba did not leave until ten in the evening. Perhaps I could catch an earlier bus in Juyjuy. I took a bus back to that city. This took two hours, and what did I learn? There was no bus to Yacuiba. The lady in the travel office then suggested that there might be a bus from San Pedro, but I would have to wait two hours for a bus to San Pedro. To my surprise, the nearest restaurant was closed for lunch! I sat in the bus station and wondered how a restaurant could close for lunch.

When the bus arrived from Salta, it was packed. The driver let people on by the numbers on their tickets, and those last in line had to stand all the way to San Pedro. Many of the passengers were overweight, and it struck me that I had not seen an overweight person for many weeks. When the bus stopped at a cemetery crowded with tiled monuments in bright colors—blue, green, yellow, and even pink—and there seemed to be a picnic in the cemetery and people with huge bunches of lilies got off, I grabbed the first vacated seat.

The hills in this region were still dry and sprinkled with tall cacti that looked rather like saguaros, but down in the valley there were new spring flowers by the road and blossoms on the trees. In the gardens surrounding most of the houses we passed there were brilliant yellow bushes and blue or orange colored trees and the gardens were turning green. Men were planting seedlings in the tobacco fields, and I also saw stacks of cordwood and tree roots to be used as fuel in the drying sheds. This was obviously an important agricultural region, but here and there in the scrub I saw small coal mines, slag heaps, kilns, and what looked like coke ovens and cooling towers.

SAN PEDRO

San Pedro de Juyjuy, a small agricultural market town surrounded by sugar cane fields, was a dirty, scruffy place. The only color came from the roses and other flowers in the plaza. I checked at the railroad station, but the train to the Bolivian border had left early in the morning. On the wall was a public notice pleading for "faith" in the railway system. From what I could see of the run-down station, with weeds growing between the tracks and a general air of abandonment, they needed faith. Back at the bus station, I learned that the bus to Yacuiba, the Bolivian border town, would arrive at 11:30 in the evening and that it was the same bus that I would have caught in Salta. I was furious with myself.

I looked around for a clean-looking restaurant, but when I discovered one, the waiters insisted that they could serve no meals until eight in the evening. I had a sandwich and a coffee in the bus station and then wandered around the town. There were quite a few Indians in San Pedro, most of them men, and I guessed that the majority were migrant laborers and farm hands. The stores were full of cheap goods, and each store seemed to have its own loudspeaker blaring music or advertising. A couple of loudspeaker vans added to the din. There was even a giant TV screen fastened to the church steeple. Since large rain clouds were gathering, I retreated to the bus station.

THE GAUCHOS

There were other passengers waiting, so I hardly looked up when a man and his daughter entered. Then I took another look. I was looking at a real, live gaucho. He was a tall man and was wearing the complete outfit, all in sand brown. He had the soft boots, the wide baggy trousers, the loose shirt, the shallow hat with the narrow brim turned up in front, and even a sash with a long knife tucked in the back. He was straight out of the picture books I had read as a boy. I couldn't help it. I sat and stared. (His daughter was wearing a mini skirt and high heels.) When they left, I thought that he would be the only gaucho I would ever see, but then another came through the door. He was obviously an old timer, and his clothing was well worn and gray. This gaucho had a stubbled chin and a drooping mustache and looked like the grand-daddy of all gauchos. After seeing these two men, I felt that my wait in San Pedro had not been entirely wasted.

Chapter 12: The Pilcomayo River

It was dark and the bus was full when it arrived, but I soon found a seat. It had started to rain heavily and was suddenly very humid and the road was terrible, so even though I needed some rest, it was hard for me to get to sleep. I finally dosed off and had a very uncomfortable night.

YACUIBA

While I slept, most of the passengers had got off the bus, and by the time we reached the end of the line, there were only three or four passengers left. I awoke at five in the morning to find it was still drizzling. When I got off the bus, I couldn't see anything in the dark except a row of houses all locked up. Some porters with carts appeared, and I chose a gray-whiskered character who said he knew what to do, so we splashed off into the dark and the rain. Behind the houses, at a small table under a tree, stood a policeman with a large flashlight. He stamped my passport and brushed aside any talk about customs. The border here seemed to be just a muddy gully in the brush. My guide led me around some more buildings to a little wooden hut with no sign on it. He said this was Bolivian customs, but there was nobody there. When we peered through the window, we could just make out a man fast asleep on a bunk. We let him sleep and made our way through the dawn to a group of buildings in front of which a couple of taxis were waiting. My guide explained that we had crossed from Argentina into Bolivia and that we were now in Yacuiba. I had a deep suspicion that we had by-passed the usual formalities of border crossing, but I was grateful and tipped my guide well. Later, when I thought about the back-alley route and the trail through the bushes and across the river at a shallow part, it dawned on me that I had been brought into Bolivia by a smuggler. I had crossed many borders in my travels, but I had never before used the services of a real, live smuggler. I had to admit, though, that it was a lot less of a nuisance than going through all the formalities.

Yacuiba was not on my list of places to visit, but there, waiting for me, was a bus to Tarija. The girl who sold the tickets said there was only one bus a week and I was lucky because it was leaving immediately.

The citizens of La Paz may boast that their road down to Caranavi in the Yungas is the *most dangerous* road in Bolivia, and it certainly is, but the *worst* road in Bolivia is the road from Yacuiba to Tarija. It is not a busy road, which is fortunate, because it is a narrow road with a deplorable surface cluttered with fallen rocks, and in many places it is washed away. It winds its way up from the Chaco lowlands to the Andean heights through winding valleys, zigzagging over mountain passes and along alarmingly steep hillsides with sheer drops that encourage serious and very rapid prayer.

The bus was a typical "gondola" with twenty seats, plus five illegal seats that blocked the aisle. It was a six-cylinder Toyota and in reasonable condition, but the seats were hard and painfully narrow, and there was very little leg room. The passengers were the usual mixed bunch, and the driver was a young man accompanied by his mother, who "assisted" him verbally. I got the impression that this was his maiden voyage over this route.

Unfortunately, I had been so eager to get a seat that I had not asked how long the trip would take. There was not much traffic, so we made good time through fairly empty brush and thorn scrub under a gray sky If was obvious that we were on a secondary road that was badly maintained and washed out in places. Soon we entered a canyon and began to climb. It was a hair-raising ride, and as we climbed higher and higher up the wall of the canyon, I began to think that my luck had run out. There was barely room to navigate the countless bends, and every drop seemed to be at least 500 feet. Even the little bunch of drunks in the back seat fell silent. I suspect they were praying as the bus slithered over the wet rocks and skidded away from the badly eroded edge.

Two perilous hours later, we left the canyon and found ourselves in a region of dry scrub and mixed forest overlooking range upon range of wooded hills and colorful rock formations. The land here was almost uninhabited, with just an occasional settler's hut on an irrigated patch. Except for a rare truck, there was no other traffic. That was good because passing on this very narrow road was a major problem. There were a few bridges, but mostly we splashed across fords when we came to the occasional river. It seemed that not one mile of this road was either straight or flat. It was up and down and bends all the way.

We stopped for lunch at a cabin at the crest of a hill, but I was not hungry, so I had a coffee and a slice of bread, and the lady gave me my change in cigarettes. While I stood beside the road, stretching my legs, I watched a mule train passing by. It was carrying wine in oval barrels. Then I watched new passengers. One was a man who boarded the bus with what seemed to be a ton of luggage that included a folding iron bedstead. Another new passenger was a large Indian who took a seat behind me. He immediately fell asleep and snored very loudly, but we had hardly started off when the snoring man woke up and was violently sick.

Ahead of us, we could see the road for at least thirty miles, winding its way up a mountain range. In the valleys, there were weirdly shaped cacti, some brilliant yellow, plus flowering trees and wild jacarandas in bloom. I also saw hawks in flocks and an eagle with white on its wings and a white tail that floated gracefully over the trees below us.

Surprisingly, there was only one military checkpoint. It consisted of a double bunk with no mattress and protected from the weather by four sheets of corrugated iron. This checkpoint was manned by boy soldiers wearing ragged uniforms and sandals. One boy was wearing an old German helmet, another, a brand new American issue helmet. Their officer looked younger than his men. They were in charge of a long stretch of road that had been "improved" by a bulldozer. It was wider here, but the surface of jagged rocks was even worse than it had been. I worried about the punishment the tires on the bus were taking.

Inevitably, there was engine trouble. We stopped at Entre Rios, a small town in the middle of a wide, fertile valley. It was a good site on a low hill, and the town had a small plaza with lots of trees, numerous stores, and a church. It looked like a prosperous little farm town. It took an hour to fix the bus's broken oil pipe, and when the driver finished the repair, the dip stick showed empty. If it had been my vehicle I would not have moved it an inch, but the driver and his mother talked it over and decided to drive on to Tarija. So we all boarded the bus again.

Now came a long climb up a pass, at the summit of which the bus stopped again and the driver tinkered with the oil line. It got quite cold, fog settled over the mountains, and then it got dark. When the snoring man behind me decided to get noisily sick again, somebody shoved his head out of the window, but the cold fog drifted into the bus, and somebody else closed the window. Eventually, we drove off, but we soon made two more stops to try to buy oil from passing truckers or from houses hidden in the woods. The third try was successful.

TARIJA

We reached Tarija at almost midnight, after more than twenty-four hours on buses. I was sore and dirty and ready to flop onto a bed in any hotel, no matter how primitive, just as long as it had a shower and hot water. The streets of the town were dark and deserted, but a swarm of boys with wagons were waiting at the bus station. When a cab driver suggested a hotel, I chose a boy and walked beside him the three blocks to the main plaza to stretch my aching legs. I was pleasantly surprised to find a brand-new, first-class hotel of about thirty rooms and a very friendly night clerk who insisted on sending up coffee and bread and marmalade for a bedtime snack. The plumbing in my room was modern, the water was hot, the bed was firm and new, and everything was spotlessly clean. I ate, then stood in the shower for ten minutes. After ordering breakfast in bed at nine a.m., I dropped into the wonderfully comfortable bed. It was a very nice ending to a very tedious couple of days.

I awoke to a beautiful sunny morning, and after my leisurely breakfast in bed, I strolled to the post office to send off a letter. Both Lily and I had learned early on that the first thing one does in a new town is to find the way out, so I went back to the bus station, where I found out that, unless I wanted to go back to Oruro and La Paz, the only other way was back over that terrible road to Villa Montes. Further, there was only one bus that week, and it left on Friday. I immediately bought a ticket. Ramiro's father had warned me that Tarija was a hard place to get to.

It had a very relaxed feel. Nobody seemed to be in a hurry, and even the traffic seemed to be slower. The people were friendly and smiled a lot. At 6,000 feet above sea level, it was lower and dryer than Cochabamba, and its plazas were covered in trees and flowering bushes. Near my hotel was a charmingly tiled plaza with about twenty huge palm trees in it. There was also a beautiful boulevard lined with eucalyptus trees that led down to the river, where the water was very low. I sat beside the river and watched some women washing clothes in the ancient way, then strolled up to the next bridge, where children were swimming in the river at the foot of a hill with an enormous metal Christ standing on top. Somebody told me that the river was named the Guadalquivir and this part of Bolivia is indeed very much like Andalusia. Also like southern Spain, the inhabitants of Tarija love a long siesta. The whole town closed down at noon.

In the marketplace there was a good selection of vegetables and fruit, some of it obviously trucked up from the lowlands, but as I wandered about I did not see any bales of coca leaves for sale, and nobody was chewing coca. Many of the market women wore the traditional clothing, but they wore small, flat-topped hats and light, silk fringed shawls instead of heavy blanket shawls. Everywhere else in the Andes, the women carry bundles on their backs, but the women of Tarija were different: they carried their bundles on their heads. This seemed to improve their posture, making them look slightly taller than their *altiplano* cousins. The Indians here were also lighter skinned and lacked the dark, sun burned faces of most high mountain dwellers. Instead of the knitted wool caps with long ear flaps, the men wore wide brimmed straw hats.

Later, I chatted with the owner of the hotel, a young man who had lived in Mexico, the United States, and Canada. He told me that he had built the hotel in the North American style to attract tourists. "You can't rely on Latin Americans," he explained. "They travel to visit relatives and they stay with their relatives, not in a hotel." Then we spent a while comparing other hotels we had experienced, both good and bad. For dinner, the manager suggested the social club on the main plaza. It was an old, dark, paneled room with very few guests and ancient waiters, but the food and service were excellent and the local beer was quite good. After supper, the plazas were crowded with family groups and swarms of children out to enjoy the cool evening.

Next day, I sat in the plaza talking with a university student who explained Tarija's "predicament," which was that "it was too isolated." A major problem, he said, was selling its agricultural products and importing what it needed. Since the town offered a limited market and had no minerals of any importance, there were few factories or industries, and without enough employment many of the men left to seek their fortunes in other Bolivian cities or in Argentina. "Unless the government does something for us," he said a trifle dramatically, "Tarija will die." When I remarked that the city seemed rather quiet, he laughed. "Quiet? It's empty!" He told me that all the students in his class had made up their minds to leave Tarija after they had graduated.

Back at the hotel again, I learned that the girl at the desk spoke perfect English. She told me about spending a year in Iowa on a Mormon church scholarship. It was fun to spend half an hour comparing Bolivia with Iowa.

I met an American agricultural expert who had come to Tarija a number of times. He liked the relaxed atmosphere there and the way the region proudly showed its independence whenever it could. "La Paz never tells Tarija what to do," he said. "It makes a suggestion and Tarija *thinks about it.*" Then he pointed to the traffic lights around the plaza. "Somebody in La Paz insisted that they needed traffic lights right here," he said. "So traffic lights were installed." He laughed. "But nobody wanted them, so they were never switched on." I looked more closely. Sure enough, the lights were not working. Instead, there was a policeman standing on a little podium who blew his whistle energetically at anybody on a bicycle. The cyclists, all good citizens of Tarija, completely ignored him. I think he would have been surprised if they had paid attention to him.

In the evening, a loudspeaker car drove around advertising a *cabildo abierto*, or citizen's meeting, near the university. By sunset, a good crowd had gathered. There was a band playing folk music and trying to compete with popular music being blasted from a loudspeaker. A big, open truck inched through the crowd and became a grandstand with microphones and banners protesting the central government's neglect of Tarija. The national anthem was sung and was quickly followed by popular regional songs, which were sung much more loudly by everybody, including the little children. There seemed to be a good cross section of the community on the truck, and everybody spoke passionately. Each speaker stressed the same point. The central government in far away La Paz had to do something quickly before Tarija died or seceded and joined Argentina. The American expert whispered to me, "Tarija has been pulling that trick for years. Argentina has always claimed this part of Bolivia and would love to have it. But don't worry. Tarija detests Argentina more than it dislikes La Paz."

Despite the big crowd, the banners, the noisy university students, and the angry speeches, there were no riot police. In fact, I did not see any policemen! I also noticed that although there were some local politicians, there was nobody from the central government in La Paz. The meeting ended with a giant march around the Plaza.

It rained during the night, and when I went to the bus stop at 6:30, it was cold and gray clouds covered the mountains. The bus I boarded was packed, and with the windows closed, it soon became uncomfortably stuffy. I was sure it was going to be a miserable trip, and it was.

The valley of Tarija was a sad sight. The land has been overgrazed for centuries, and almost all the trees have been cut down for fuel, leaving the soil exposed to the elements. Erosion has produced a moon-like surface with deep cracks and gullies and great patches of barren land and strange rock formations. I was not able to see much, however, because the fog and mist hid the view for most of the way. Having made this trip once, I was not quite so terrified the second time. The heavy mist blocked my view of almost everything, making sight seeing and photography from the bus impossible. Taking a nap was also impossible, so I concentrated on trying not to get too badly bruised. To add to the misery of all the passengers, eight people were sick, and when we ran out of plastic bags those who got sick next had to stick their heads out the windows. This brought in some fresh air, but it was cold, damp air, and the windows were soon slammed shut.

At Entre Rios, the young bus driver, whose mother was nowhere in sight, recognized me and proudly showed me the extra cases of oil that he had stashed behind his seat. The bus had only gone a couple of miles when a girl in the back seat who had dined rather too well was sick all over the floor. Whenever anybody was sick inside the bus, those nearest him scrambled to find old newspapers or any other bits of paper to clean up as best they could. Some passengers had the foresight to bring plastic bags. The whole mess was then dumped out the window.

The driver, eager to get out of the mountains before darkness fell, threw his bus around the bends and raced down every slope. We barely survived two near collisions with trucks in the fog, but he managed to shave half an hour off the trip. The afternoon sun came out as we left the final canyon and raced across flat land to the bridge over the Rio Pilcomayo and into Villa Montes.

Chapter 13: The Eastern Lowlands

A t the bus station, a soldier told me to take my passport to army headquarters in the plaza, but he did not tell me when to do this, so I looked for a hotel first. There was not much to choose from, as I could only find two and they were both third class. I chose the one where the people were most friendly and there was a huge bougainvillea in the patio. But there were flies everywhere, the doors had no locks, and the bathroom was "across the patio" and had no running water. After a maid brought me some water from the well, I shaved and cleaned up before walking over to army headquarters.

VILLA MONTES

The officer, who spoke good English, was very friendly. As he looked at every stamp in my overcrowded passport, he showed great interest in my travels. "Are you one of those people who come to see where Che Guevara was killed?" he asked me. I had quite forgotten that Che Guevara had died in Vallegrande, a little town in the Bolivian foothills near Santa Cruz and that the citizens had erected a small monument to his memory (and also to attract tourists to the town). I told him that I was more interested in the Chaco War than in Che, and he was relieved. He told me that there might be truck transport across the Chaco to

Asuncion from Boyube. "One million of American dollars would not persuade me to make that journey." With that, he smiled, stamped my passport and wished me luck.

To me, Villa Montes looked like a town waiting to get started. It had been well laid out with wide avenues, it had two bridges, and it was on the rail line between Argentina and Santa Cruz, but its population was only about 3,000. The avenues were rutted and potholed, and bush and scrub was reclaiming the land. The electricity did not come on until half an hour after sunset, and it was clear that many houses only used kerosene lamps. Apart from the military base, the only industry there seemed to be cattle ranching. At one of the bridges, I talked to a man who said, "There's plenty of water in the river for irrigation, but those damn Argentinos won't let us dam it." He spat into the river and added, "They say it's an international river." When I asked about fishing, he assured me that there were plenty of big ones in the river, though he could not think of a restaurant or cafe in town that served fish.

When the hotel manager suggested that I take the train to Santa Cruz, I dropped any vague idea I had about crossing the "green hell" of the *chaco* to Asuncion. So I took a taxi to the railroad station to buy a ticket. All the taxis were Japanese jeeps or Land Rovers, and the drivers drove them like wild horses down the pot-holed streets.

I dined that night in a *chaco cantina* with a brick floor and a tin roof. The furniture was handmade, and the mud walls were decorated with old calendars. I expected a tough steak, but despite the great herds of cows surrounding the town, supper was canned soup and mashed potatoes with an egg, all washed down with warm beer. Afterward, I strolled around town for a bit, then joined some men sitting on chairs outside the hotel. Two of the men were sipping *yerba mate* from their *bombas*, and the rest of us smoked to keep the mosquitoes away while we chatted with passers-by until the lights went out at 10:30. One of the beds in my room looked as if it had never been changed. The other was a thin mattress on wooden planks; a good salesman would have called it "extra firm." It did not cool down during the night and was so hot, in fact, that I tossed off the sheet and woke up next morning with quite a few bad mosquito bites. Fortunately, Lily had packed a little tube of ointment in my bag for just such an occasion before we parted, and the ointment worked.

Breakfast was a cup of black coffee with a slab of dry bread, after which I took a jeep taxi to the station, where the train was waiting. The train was a fairly new, single-car, German-made diesel with a cheerful bunch of people, mostly business men. I got a good seat to myself. Up front there was a man with a large bald head who was lavishing his attention on a pretty teenager. He soon let everybody know that he was the Argentine consul. He got off the train at a whistle stop about thirty miles from Santa Cruz and was left behind. Every single passenger roared with laughter.

The steward served a good lunch with soft drinks and beer as the train moved on a level track paralleling the foothills of the Andes. The train route between the Rio Pilcomayo and Santa Cruz roughly marked the limit of the Paraguayan advance after its army had captured almost all of the *chaco*. The Chaco War (1932–35) was a ghastly one fought with modern weapons in primitive conditions in which more men died from thirst and illness than from bombs and bullets. The *chaco* is so huge an area that in the beginning the Bolivians suffered from very poor supply lines. By the time the utter stupidity of the German-trained officer corps allowed the Paraguayans to capture almost the entire region, however, the Paraguayan army also found itself overextended. By 1935, there was a stalemate which became an armistice which eventually became a treaty. It has been estimated that a man died for every one of the 115,000 square miles of useless wilderness.

The engineer did not mind my standing up and looking out over his shoulder as we raced through the miles of low, gray and green scrub, but he never took his eyes off the track ahead because every now and then we would approach a herd of cows or a flock of goats wandering along the track. The goats moved away quickly, but the cows needed several loud blasts on the air horn before they slowly ambled away.

I spotted bottle shaped trees with cotton-ball flowers here and there and cacti in flower, their blossoms vivid orange or yellow. There were also patches of blue wild flowers, their color startling against the dull thorn bushes. At one point, I watched two foxes racing across the tracks as we came around a bend. We crossed a number of good bridges over wide, empty river beds leading down from a line of red hills to the west. There was also a thin oil pipe line resting on the ground alongside the track.

Although we stopped for a few minutes at two or three towns, we raced past numerous lonely settlements consisting of three or four wood and clay houses, where the women stood at their doors and watched us go by. In the front yards were wooden platforms holding round clay ovens, identical to ovens I had seen in Mexico and Guatemala. All the isolated cabins also had carts with huge, solid, wooden wheels.

SANTA CRUZ

About mid-afternoon, we passed a large grove of palm trees and several small farms. The small farms soon became large farms, and these were soon replaced by huge fields of sugar cane, and then we passed two large sugar refineries. We soon arrived in Santa Cruz de la Sierra.

The station there was crowded and noisy, and the customs clerk simply waved me through. At the ticket window I was told that the fast diesel to Corumba, in Brazil, was full and that I might have to take the slow train, but the clerk was not positive about this. I hailed a taxi and let the driver choose a hotel for me. He took me to a brand-new place that was very modern. But it lacked hot water. There was an almost useless Brazilian-made electric gadget on the shower, but in the tropical heat I quite relished the tepid water.

The main plaza in Santa Cruz was crowded and noisy. The stores were crowded with shoppers eager to buy, and pretty girls dressed in the latest fashions smiled openly at whistling boys as they strolled along the covered sidewalks. Jeep taxis dashed through the heavy traffic, radios blared, and there was a definite, if tropical, Wild West boom town atmosphere to the city. Wandering in and out of the stores, I was astonished at the number of Brazilian goods on sale. There were also Argentine products and expensive

American imports, but there was nothing Bolivian except what was produced locally.

After a gorgeous sunset, I dined on steak and french-fries American style with real ketchup and then followed the music to a pop music festival near the hotel. It could have been Los Angeles or Chicago with all the teenagers happily whistling and clapping and cheering every performer, even the mediocre ones. At midnight I went to bed.

Sunday is a good day to look a town over. For a couple hundred years, Santa Cruz has been regarded as a sleepy, little, backwoods town famous only for its immense herds of semi-wild cattle, not to mention the depth of the mud in its streets during the rainy season. Within a few minutes, however, it was clear to me that those days are long gone. The discovery of oil and gas had changed everything. The city had been planned in a series of circles with four or five major ring roads radiating out from the center. In the heart of the city, almost all of the buildings had colonnaded façades, often two stories high, to protect pedestrians from sun and rain, and many old houses with moss-covered, tiled roofs and covered sidewalks remained, but there was also new construction everywhere. I wondered if the old, historic part of the city would soon disappear. Further out from the center, there were some expensive new houses, but the roads had massive holes in them, many of them half full of water. With the high rainfall and tropical humidity, there were flowering bushes and trees everywhere. I noticed small cacti growing on the tiled roofs and orchids growing on the sides of palm trees. The cathedral, which stands on a pretty plaza with plenty of trees, has an attractive exterior but an extremely dull interior. I also noticed that the First National Bank had a tough, riot proof front.

One thing was clear. Santa Cruz was going to shake off the stigma of being the "muddiest city in Bolivia," the city where only the high-wheeled ox wagon could navigate in the rainy season. Everywhere I went, the roads where being repaved, most of them with octagonal stone blocks, which gave them an attractive tiled look. Even the plazas and sidewalks were getting this treatment. From what I could see of the old sand-covered roads, the new surfaces would be very much appreciated.

After siesta, I was sitting outside a Chinese cafe drinking expensive tepid beer and watching the crowds going to the afternoon movies—probably to take advantage of the air conditioning—when a sound truck followed by four trucks loaded with workers and their wives drove into the central plaza. From the first truck came a long, loud speech in support of the national government, but nobody seemed to be listening and the few "*Vivas*" that followed were very half-hearted. Pasted to the wall of a building was an official notice explaining how the income from the oil and gas was being spent, but somebody had painted over it a slogan declaring that the oil revenue belonged to solely to Santa Cruz. La Paz and the *altiplano* seemed very far away, and it struck me then that I had seen very few tourists. The foreigners were mostly businessmen.

There was another gorgeous sunset that evening. As the sun went down, I could make out the Andean foothills in the far distance. Near the university, I saw groups of students studying for their final exams, hunched over their books like ancient monks and straining their eyes in the gloom.

THE TRAIN TO CORUMBA

I had learned the day before at the bus station that there were a great many buses, but none to Corumba. In fact, one clerk even doubted that there was a road to Corumba. Early in the morning, therefore, I dashed to the railway station and managed to get a ticket that had just been cancelled for the next train. I had an excellent, tilt-back, window seat, and my neighbors on this train included a Spaniard who spoke all the Romance languages, including Catalan; his friend, who had a beautiful Konica camera with all the possible lenses and did not take a single photo the whole trip; and a Bolivian man who worked in Brazil and was taking a five gallon bottle of *chicha* to his foreman. He assured me that it was the best Cochabamba-brewed *chicha* available. They were all friendly and asked me a lot of questions about California. They also pointed out that the line to Santa Cruz from Brazil had been built by the Brazilians, the line from Argentina, by the Argentines. "They all think they will get their hands on our oil," said the Bolivian man, "but we are watching them!" And he winked his eye. "Yes," said the Spaniard, "and they are both carefully watching each other!" Everybody laughed.

The lunch on the train was good, and although it was warm as we raced through the brush that had turned surprisingly green in the recent rains, it was not uncomfortable. The railroad skirts the northern edge of the *chaco* near a range of low hills, and there are a number of old Jesuit missions strung along the route, though we could see none of these historic, Indian-built churches from the train. Here and there, however, we glimpsed a new mission school staffed by what were obviously North American padres. We stopped at a few lonely little towns, where the entire population gathered around the train to sell cooked food, homemade drinks, and fresh fruit as the women waved off the flies with big chicken feathers. Once we also pulled onto a siding to make way for an old wood-burner pulling a long string of Brazilian freight cars.

This was cattle country, though there were a few small patches of bright red earth under cultivation, and we saw cowboys carrying shotguns and wearing huge gaucho-style leather chaps that looked like wings. Now and then we also saw palm groves and flowers like huge snowdrops, plus numerous wooden wheeled carts and the usual cows and goats on the tracks. A couple of cows had to be bumped out of the way, and at least one chicken was turned into chickenburger. I also saw a small deer near the track, herds of semi-wild burros, and an armadillo, and whenever we slowed down I saw numerous lizards, some quite large, baking in the sun. Where the vegetation was thick, there were flocks of parrots flashing green in the sun and dozens of hawks.

At one point, the line cut through a low range of flat-topped mountains that is part of the Brazilian shield, the remains of an ancient Precambrian mountain chain that had once covered the area. There was also a black volcanic pipe sticking up out of the red rock, but we saw no rivers, just a small pool here and there. All the way, we were accompanied by two lonely phone lines on their tilted and warped poles, the only link to civilization. It is a wild and lonely land. I found it hard to believe that our little train traveled in a mere twelve hours what used to take three months, at the very least, by horse and wagon.

Chapter 14: The Paraguay River

We reached Puerto Suarez, which is near Bolivia's border with Brazil, in the dark. It took half an hour for the porters to get all the baggage off the train, five minutes to check it, and half an hour to get it all back on the train. Meanwhile we passengers stood around, sweating and swatting mosquitoes and some of the biggest night insects in South America. After we retrieved our passports and boarded the train again, the train went on for another half an hour, moths swarming like snow in the headlights, until we pulled into a modern station in Corumba, Brazil, where a spotty youth checked our passports again and deliberately kept the Europeans and North Americans waiting until last.

I shared a taxi with two Italians and discovered that the Brazilian driver did not speak a word of Spanish. He took us to a hotel where nobody at the desk spoke a word of Spanish. The Italians, who also spoke English, were horrified. "But this is a border town!" they said. "Don't they understand tourism?" I suggested that tourism was not exactly big business in Corumba.

I took a room in the hotel where, strangely, the clerk understood a little English. Upstairs, the bathroom was down the hall from my room, but there was no hot water. The town seemed to be slightly less hot than Puerto Suarez, but there was a fan in the room. I only had to kill two large beetles in the shower, and there were no mosquitoes in my room. Next morning, my breakfast was bread and cheese and a large slice of papaya. It was hot and humid by 9:00.

Corumba, which is on the western edge of Brazil, is built on the bluffs overlooking the Rio Paraguay and has a grand view across the plains to some low hills shimmering in the distance. The river was flowing steadily and looked wide enough for year-round river traffic. When I reached the small docks, I saw cattle boats, a small oil tanker, and a grain barge from Argentina, plus a sign warning that the passenger ferry across the river was not running. I asked a few people in the port authority office about passenger boats down to Asunción, the capital of Paraguay, but nobody was interested in talking to me, and when I spoke to someone in the shipping department, I was told that the water was too low. Nobody was friendly. Everybody showed a provincial dislike of strangers who carry cameras. This was quite the opposite of my experience in Bolivia. I gave up any idea of going to Asunción.

To this day, I am not quite sure why I wanted to go to Asunción, either across the *chaco* or down the Rio Paraguay. Lily and I had been there on our travels, and I thought that a couple of days in that river city were quite enough to see everything. Anyway, I had come to study Bolivia, and especially Puerto Suarez, which I hoped to make my next stop.

Corumba, a large, old city with a few modern buildings, looked fairly prosperous to me, with half a dozen banks but only one would handle traveler's checks. There were numerous unfinished buildings and unfinished roads, and there was little of interest to me in the stores, where pearl-handled revolvers and hammocks seemed to be the big sellers. Many of the stores were

Syrian or Arabic owned and had names like Casa Siria or Casa
Cairo. Everybody I saw wore loose clothing and sandals, and the
women wore their hair tied back from their faces and no make up.
The women and the children of Corumba were definitely the least
attractive I had seen in all my travels. Everybody spoke rapidly
in a heavily accented Portuguese unlike any I had heard before,
very few had any English, and almost nobody in this border city
understood a word of Spanish.

I ate lunch in the Grand Hotel Corumba, an old building with
a new coat of paint. There were cans of Argentine olive oil on each
table, and the meat and potatoes were soaking in grease, but the
hearts of palm salad was huge and delicious. The chairs had cotton
covers on the backs to soak up the perspiration of the diners.

After a three-hour siesta that I spent lying in front of the fan
turned on maximum, I wandered around and found a park on the
bluffs. It had tall palms, a fine view of the river, and a slight breeze.
From this viewpoint, I could make out factories, a flour mill, and
the Paraguay River, which was yellow with mud and swirling
slowly in the humid heat. It was so hot that it was easier to walk
around town than to sit in a sweltering bus on plastic seats. I could
find no bookstores or any kind of map of the city or even of the
state. Even the railroad station had no map of the rail system or
a schedule, and the clerk was quite surprised that anybody would
want one. For supper I tried fish caught in the river, but it was soft,
tasteless, and served in a pool of grease. However, the Brazilian
beer was very good and served nice and cold.

Checking at the bus and railroad stations, I learned that I
would need a re-entry visa to get back into Bolivia, but when I

tracked down the Bolivian consul, I found that the clerk could not speak Spanish. Nevertheless, I got the visa.

PUERTO SUAREZ

In the relative cool of dawn the next day, I caught the bus to Puerto Suarez, which was only a few miles away. Before boarding, however, I had to stand around for two hours while soldiers and minor officials looked at passports and baggage. The road was fairly good, and we soon splashed across the little stream that constituted the official border, passed the railroad station, and drove into what at first glance seemed to be just a tiny settlement of about 2,000 people and an army barracks. Here and there were new homes and some slash-and-burn farms with tiny mud huts on them. This was Puerto Suarez.

The center of the town was laid out in avenues, and somebody had planted tiny trees along them that were protected from the goats by sticks. The low houses, built of adobe, were shaded by palms or banana trees and bougainvillea. There were a few stores and one hotel, which was full. The manager was sympathetic and suggested that I go to a *pension* just around the corner. It was very simple, but clean and tidy, and the family that ran it was cheerful and talkative, that is, except for the chicken that was brooding eggs in the toilet. She was very hostile.

One member of the family was a young man who had some English. He showed me the way through the brush and weeds to the "port. It was a sad sight. In 1867, when Brazil grabbed a huge chunk of the western bank of the Rio Paraguay from a sadly weakened Bolivia, it allowed Bolivia to retain "access" to the international river through Lake Caceres. On paper, this looked like a good deal, or at least it was better than nothing. But the great muddy Paraguay River twists and turns and almost every rainy season it changes its course and silts up its meanders. Lake Caceres, which is in Bolivia, is big, but it is extremely shallow and dredging a channel to the main river would be a never-ending and impossibly expensive business. I stood beside the lake and looked at a few rotting dock piles, a muddy patch of water, a dug-out canoe lying in the mud, and a vast expanse of matted water weeds. There were some children swimming in the water nearby and the driver of an ox cart collecting water in huge drums. "Some months it dries up almost completely," said my guide. "They say that one day they will dredge it and make a real port." He sounded like he believed it.

On the main street of the town, the Syrian owner of a bar was selling Brazilian beer to jeep taxi drivers and army officers as fast as he could open the bottles. This made me think that all a man needed was a kerosene fridge and some chairs to make a fortune out here.

As I strolled past the scattering of military buildings I came across one building with a neat sign indicating that it was the headquarters of a detachment of the Bolivian navy, but I saw no sailors. I soon retreated to the *pension* to chat in the shade with the family. The father had to go by the railroad station, so he offered to put my name down for the next train.

Even under a palm-thatched roof and drinking tepid soft drinks, I was exhausted by the heat and humidity. But I had come to see the town, and when I mentioned orchids, one of the children took me behind the house and showed me a tree that was entirely covered in pale blue orchids. There must have been 200 of the beautiful plants. The boy also showed me where some engineers were drilling for water and warned me not to drink the local water, as it was too salty. It was wonderfully quiet there, and the wide sky was a perfect blue, but the moist heat weighed on me like a blanket, and I soon flopped down on my bed to perspire for two hours. There was no chance of a cooling shower, and the salt on my skin sparkled in the light.

Puerto Suarez was not a dead town. On the contrary, I saw new houses and a few new stores, and everybody I spoke with was optimistic about the future. Many of the men had found work at El Mutún in the iron mines across the border in Brazil, where geologists had discovered what they claimed to be the largest iron and manganese deposits in the world. The men I met described a new floating dock on the river and barges of ore that went downstream to Argentina, and somebody claimed that a small town was beginning to take shape on the Bolivian side of the border. Sadly, the valuable iron ore deposits were on the west side of the river on land in western Brazil that had once been part of Bolivia. When I asked if there was any way that I could visit the iron mine, everybody agreed that it would be very difficult and probably impossible. We discussed it for a while, but it seemed that the Brazilian authorities were very strict about who went near their iron mine.

At sunset, the town woke up. The insects woke up, too! Puerto Suarez is on the southern edge of South America's largest swamp, the famous Pantanal in the Brazilian state of Mato Grosso do Sul and known to the early Spanish explorers as the marsh of Xarayez. In Puerto Suarez, I was treated to visits by the largest and friendliest collection of flying and crawling insects that I had seen in many years. The *pension* manager's wife immediately began dashing around with an old pump spray, sending a cloud of chemicals into every room. It seemed to work on the mosquitoes, but the larger insect visitors ignored it, and the chickens took the spraying as a signal to go and roost in an orange tree. We humans dined on rice and eggs outdoors under a tiled patio roof because it was too hot indoors. As we ate, we discussed international politics while three large frogs hopped around our feet and various large insects tried to join the conversation. The *pension* had its own generator, but it stopped suddenly, and so we dined by the yellow light of oil lamps.

Despite the insects, women and girls in sleeveless blouses and miniskirts strolled up and down in the dark and young men in hot jackets strolled, too, while children ran and played in the cloying heat. In the plaza, a band started to play as fruit and soft drink peddlers pushed their carts around. The band moved on to the officers' club, where there was a dance. All the windows and doors were wide open. The dances were nearly all very lively dances of the *altiplano*, and the officers in their tight uniforms danced as energetically as they would have in the chilly barracks in Oruro or La Paz.

I tried to write my notes later by candle light, but so many insects wanted to commit suicide in my candle that it became impossible to write, so I went to bed. Lightning was flashing on the horizon, but the temperature did not drop, and all I could do was lie on the bare bed and feel the sweat dripping off me. At one point, I thought of putting a towel over my forehead to soak up the sweat, but it was too hot even to move. I must have fallen asleep because I was woken by a gust of wind when the skies opened and the rain came thundering down.

THE TRAIN BACK TO SANTA CRUZ

It was overcast and damp the next morning, and the temperature had dropped a tiny fraction. When the train arrived, it was almost full. I met a few tourists, including some French and Americans, in the coach. There was also a German back-packer with a long, blond pony tail that fascinated the Bolivians. I sat next to a drug salesman from Santa Cruz who explained all the strange tropical fruits that were on sale at the stations and which we sampled.

Although it was sticky and uncomfortable, as we went along there was a cool breeze coming through the windows. I looked out on great puddles in a wet and muddy land that was rapidly becoming green after a long drought. I saw a toucan in a tree, more flocks of green parrots, and some vultures, and we only killed one cow that stubbornly refused to get off the tracks. After a good lunch, my neighbor and I had a huge *cherimoya* for desert. At one of the mission towns, I noticed the padre, a blond German-looking priest wearing a gray robe with baby blue sandals, riding a pink motorbike. At Robore, we waited while the regular train went by. This was a steam train pulling a mixed collection that included a sleeping coach and a *comedor*, or dining car, through whose windows we could see two tourists enjoying a leisurely trip that would take at least two days. They waved as they passed us. At the end of the train was a flat car crowded with Indians who had paid much less than the tourists for the trip.

We crossed the extremely long bridge over the Rio Grande and arrived back in Santa Cruz, where a little man in plain clothes politely asked to see my passport. I took a jeep taxi to the same hotel where I'd stayed before and headed straight for the shower, then I went to bed and slept like a log.

Chapter 15: Santa Cruz to Oruro

Next day, I decided to take a rest from my nonstop traveling. After a leisurely breakfast, I splurged on the laundry and dry cleaning service, which was as good as any in North America and gave four-hour service complete with plastic bags. When I strolled around town, it was hot, but not as humid as on the Rio Paraguay. I browsed in some bookshops, picked up a map of the city, and even found a news magazine in English. After siesta, I worked my way to the botanical gardens through streets torn up for water and drain pipes and along wide avenues still in the sandy planning stage. The gardens had not been kept up and looked more like virgin bush. The little zoo nearby had little more than a wild pig and some tortoises. Along the Rio Piray there were families picnicking on the banks of that almost empty river. I passed an oil pipeline slung across the river, then caught a bus back to the city center. Its ceiling was so low that I had to stand stooped over. That evening I dined in solitary splendor in the hotel and read my magazine from cover to cover on the patio, where I was bitten three times by mosquitoes and ran out of Lily's ointment.

Next morning, I bought a bus ticket for Cochabamba for the following morning, then took a long bus ride out to the small town of Montero. It was nearly two hours' north, but it was the center of an ambitious repopulation program. The *altiplano* has an ever increasing population and an ever decreasing amount of agricultural land, but the plains around Santa Cruz were still almost empty. For some years, the Bolivian government had been offering free land, tools, basic food supplies, and free transport to anybody who would move down to the lowlands. It took time and patience, but gradually the idea caught on and many thousands of highland dwellers took up the offer of free land and settled around Santa Cruz.

The bus drove toward Montero through flat, newly opened country where there were large fields of sugar cane, cotton, and other crops. There were plenty of small holdings, but it was mostly large farms. It seemed that as soon as the government built a few properly paved roads, the big planters moved in. We passed cotton gins and sugar factories, and the roads were busy with trucks loaded with sugar cane. In the distance, I could see smoke from burning fields. Now and then we stopped at a small settlement of grass thatched huts with outside ovens where banana and papaya trees seemed to grow wild.

Montero was a scruffy and very dusty little town, but it had a prosperous look about it, and there were plenty of bright plastic goods in the stores. Scores of young people were buzzing about on new motorbikes, and in the market there was an excellent variety of good-quality fruits and vegetables, as well as piles of fresh meat covered in flies. One lady was selling magnetized earth, but she could not explain to me what it was used for. The population seemed to be mainly Andean Indians who had exchanged their distinctive hats for straw hats, though the women still wore their heavy skirts and blanket shawls, whereas the younger generation seemed to favor blue jeans and T-shirts.

I took a cab for a short distance in town, and the driver assured me cheerfully that the place was booming and expanding further north and east at a fast pace. Back in the center of town, I tried a glass of raw cane juice. It was a muddy, dark green, but very tasty.

After supper, back in Santa Cruz, I sat on the patio talking with the owner of the hotel, a Brazilian from São Paulo who saw great opportunity in Santa Cruz and had imported almost the whole hotel from Brazil, from the tiles to the bathroom fixtures. He was well traveled and spoke good English, but he had never been up on the *altiplano* and his Spanish was worse than mine.

BUS TO COCHABAMBA

I was at the bus station in Santa Cruz before dawn and climbed aboard a big Spanish-made bus that was not quite full. Since 1956, when the Corumba-Santa Cruz Railroad was eventually finished, there has been a rail line stretching across Brazil from Rio de Janeiro on the Atlantic Ocean through São Paulo to Corumba and into Bolivia. There are also rail lines from Cochabamba to Oruro and down to the Pacific Ocean. Constructing the missing link in this transcontinental railroad, the short stretch between Santa Cruz and Cochabamba, has been discussed numerous times, but it was never started and probably will never be built. Everything between these two cities therefore goes by road or by air.

The road was a paved one, and the bus climbed quickly into the foothills through a dry area where the only vegetation was cacti, but this area soon gave way to a rain forest area with heavy fog and moss on the trees. It was refreshingly cool. Then we crested a hill and dropped down into another valley. We seemed to be going from valley to valley, but we were climbing all the time and the scenery was spectacular. At one stop, I bought a candy bar for lunch and noticed two girl tourists who didn't eat or talk and looked quite sick. When I tried to talk to them, they did not respond, so I left them alone. The bus was so comfortable that, despite the wonderful scenery, I dozed off and slept past the Inca ruins at Samaipata.

As the road twisted and turned ever higher, we entered a foggy patch and it got cold. I was still wearing the light clothing I'd worn in Brazil, and my sweater and jacket were in my bag on the roof of the bus. The cool breeze from the open windows was now an icy draft. Fortunately, we were close to our destination and soon dropped down into the Cochabamba valley with its green fields and trees. There was a small refinery in the valley and an oil pipeline running alongside the road, and there were also a new cement plant and other signs of industry in the valley that I had not noticed before.

It was cold and cloudy again when we pulled into the bus station. I got my bag as soon as I could and hurried to the hotel to dig out my sweater and jacket, all the time thinking about the heat of Santa Cruz, only hours behind me. That evening, I dined at the same Chinese restaurant that Lily and I had visited. Across the room sat four English ladies in short haircuts, tweed skirts, and sensible shoes. They sounded like school teachers and looked exactly like characters in an Agatha Christie story.

That night I slept under two blankets, and the next morning I slept so late that it was almost noon before I got to the railroad station to book a ticket to Oruro. It was a fairly modern station and on display was an old steam engine, a lovely old 19th-century antique good enough to have been in a museum. It looked tiny in comparison to the later small coal-burners, yet it had once scaled these enormous mountains and chugged across the vast *altiplano*. Those early pioneer railroad builders were extraordinary people who combined brilliant engineering with absolute confidence in their abilities.

BY TRAIN TO ORURO

Although the sky was cloudy the next day, it was quite warm as I took my seat on the half-empty diesel train to Oruro. The driver was a short, dark Indian who looked very serious in his tight uniform jacket and dark tie. The conductor was a more cheerful fat man who told me that most people traveled between Oruro and Cochabamba by bus because it was cheaper, so the company was thinking of canceling the service and just carrying freight.

The line ran through a beautiful avenue of eucalyptus trees and irrigated fields then it zigzagged out of the valley into some dry hills where the jacarandas were in full bloom and weeping willows shone bright green. For hours, while I nibbled sandwiches and sipped coffee, we climbed further and further into rugged mountains with spectacular views and past tiny villages with irrigated fields. Then suddenly, we were out on the *altiplano*. It was bleak and cold, but now I had my jacket.

At one sharp bend, the train hit a cow. Up to then we had seen few cows on the track, but villagers used the track as a convenient road and always waited until the last minute to step aside when a train came along. We pulled into a little town called Paria so that the crew could wash the blood and guts from the dead cow off the front of the train.

Juan de Saavedra, one of the first Europeans to set foot in this land, stopped at Paria in 1535 to gather provisions for Diego de Almagro's great expedition to Chile in that year. It was an expedition that became a tragic disaster when the Inca guides led the Spanish host into the Puna of Atacama, the worst possible part of the Andes. Hundreds of Indians and many Spaniards, as well as 170 horses, died of cold, thirst, and starvation before the expedition finally reached the Pacific coast. While he was waiting for the other conquistadors, Saavedra ordered a small house to be constructed in Paria. His little adobe cabin vanished long ago, but today the tiny Indian village of adobe houses claims to be the oldest European settlement in the Republic of Bolivia.

ORURO

When the train was clean, we resumed the journey and raced across the plains. Soon we were in Oruro, where I found that while I had been wandering through Bolivia's eastern plains there had been serious political trouble on the *altiplano*. Oruro has always been a volatile city, ready to riot at the drop of a hat. The latest episode involved students attacking the army barracks with dynamite and the army retaliating with heavy machine guns. Twenty people were killed. During this small war, Ramiro's family had spent a couple of days in the middle bedroom of their house, away from the windows.

It was quiet when I arrived, but heavily armed police still cruised the streets and the city's central plaza was empty.

That afternoon, Ramiro and his family and I sat around a table with a map of Bolivia and checked off all the places I had visited. Ramiro's father was eager to hear about Tarija and Salta, but Ramiro was more interested in the iron ore deposits in Corumba and was as disappointed as I was that I had not been able to visit the mines there. "Well," he said, "now you've seen everything except the Beni." He pointed to the Amazon rain forest north of Santa Cruz.

"Yes," said his father, "you have to see the Beni. It is a very important part of Bolivia. But getting there could be a problem."

At this point in my travels, I was beginning to run out of both time and money, but the idea of flying into the Beni and flying out again seemed all wrong. I had come to see the whole country, not just airports and hotels. Also, like millions of other people, I had always dreamed of taking a boat trip down one of the mighty tributaries of the Amazon, so we decided that I would go to the Beni region by riverboat down the Rio Mamoré.

"About how long should it take?" I asked.

Nobody knew. Then Ramiro's father said, "Going downstream, it should not take more than a couple of weeks at the very most. And you can fly back."

It all sounded so easy.

Chapter 16: The Riverboat Trip

To get to the Rio Mamoré, I would first have to go back to Cochabamba and find transport over the mountains to the Rio Chapore, where most of the riverboats started their long journeys north. So two days later, I boarded a bus back to Cochabamba. It would have been an uneventful ride, but high on a mountain road, our bus was overtaken by another bus, and we were very nearly driven off the road and over the cliff. Our driver took the actions of the other driver as a personal insult and immediately tried to overtake the other bus. For about twelve miles we raced along the narrow mountain road and swung around hairpin bends, sometimes alongside but more often right behind the other bus and completely enveloped in a huge cloud of yellow dust. Eventually, thank goodness, our driver gave up and stopped to relieve himself while the dust settled and his passengers began to breathe again.

All the people I spoke to in Cochabamba were helpful, but nobody knew exactly how to find a riverboat. In the marketplace, when I spotted produce and lumber that had come in from the Beni, I struck up conversations with the truck drivers who assured me that San Francisco, a village near Villa Tunari in Bolivia's Chapare Province, was the place to start. They also said that there were always boats leaving for the Beni. I next went to the local travel agency, where the lady (who insisted that I would need a mosquito net) gave me the phone number of a boat owner, who turned out also to be the owner of the bus that went to Villa Tunari. Next I went to a bookshop, whose German owner and his wife both spoke excellent English, were very interested in my travels, and had many good suggestions. They claimed that their shop had a better collection of books than the local university and found me some books I was looking for. They also told me to get a mosquito net.

Back at my hotel, I spoke with the clerk, who was learning English and had many questions about Canada. He was especially fascinated by my description of a Canadian winter and admitted that the only snow he had ever seen was the top of Andean peaks many miles away. He also mentioned that the police had dropped by and wanted to see my passport.

The next day was Friday the 13th. First thing in the morning, I presented myself at the police station, where, after a long look at my passport, they sent me to Immigration. At Immigration, the clerk took a long look at my passport and sent me to the chief of police. The chief looked at every stamp in my passport and asked me why I had no stamp from the time I returned from Tacna. I replied that there had been no stop at the border and nobody boarded the train to check passports.

"But you should have gone to Immigration in La Paz and gotten a stamp." he said.

I pointed out politely that nobody had told me to do so and, anyway, I had an entry stamp from Argentina and one from Brazil. This did not satisfy him. He kept me waiting for an hour, then sent me to the army headquarters.

The officer at the army headquarters was a short, cheerful, little man who listened to my story, then snorted and made a rude remark in Spanish about the chief of police. "But you are here now," he said. "Does he want you to go back to La Paz just to get a silly stamp?" He signed a permit and gave me back my passport. "Tell those idiots I said you can go to the Beni," he said as he shook my hand and wished me good luck.

Back at Immigration, I told the clerk that I had been given a permit to go into the Beni. The clerk scowled, slipped my passport to the bottom of a pile of documents, and went off for lunch. For hours, I sat there on an uncomfortable chair and watched the clerk slowly write in a huge ledger then slowly stamp a document and slowly pick up and read another document. I gritted my teeth and stared at the ceiling and told myself to have patience, that I would sit there all night if necessary. By late afternoon, the clerk got tired of seeing my face, so he found my passport and stamped it, then wrote in his huge ledger. Without a word, he gave me back my passport.

My next problem was to find the corner where the bus for Villa Tunari would stop and what time it would leave. A friendly truck driver told me there was no office and no tickets; the bus just stopped in the street at six a.m. Then he showed me where to wait. While I was buying more film I thought it would be wise to pick up extra toilet paper and a can of mosquito repellent, too.

At 6:00 next morning, I went to the right corner. The bus was there. The driver said, "We will leave at 9:30 when the bus is full," so I went back to the hotel for breakfast. While there, I met a bearded Englishman who also wanted to go into the Beni, so I explained how to go about it.

Back to the bus. The bus driver was talkative and said that there was a Canadian doctor at Villa Tunari. The driver also had a lot of questions about Canada. I was getting the distinct impression that somebody had spread the word in Cochabamba that Canada has a permanent winter with snow six feet deep and that polar bears wander the streets of Vancouver and Toronto.

The bus was full, and there were people squatting in the aisles, too, but the driver had saved me a seat. All the other passengers had huge parcels of things they had bought in Cochabamba, and one lady had a little green parrot, too. We set off. The road was fairly new and had been well engineered, but the surface was terrible. It was also dangerously narrow, and there seemed to be an overloaded truck around every hair-raising bend. After we left the valley, we entered the dry and treeless hills, then climbed high into the mountains. Our lunch stop was at a cluster of stone huts with thatched roofs where Indian women in battered felt hats sold greasy fried meat and potatoes. I thought that we had reached the top of the mountain range there, but we climbed even higher into bare grassy hills that soon became just bare rocks.

Then we entered a cloud bank, and it became quite cold. For half an hour, we crept through the chilly fog until suddenly we were in a cold rain forest where the bushes dripped water. There were streams everywhere, and small waterfalls worked at washing the road away. The low bushes quickly became tall trees, and then we were in an extraordinary rain forest filled with a tangled mass of plants and trees, many with flowers, and huge ferns bigger than the small bus. I also saw odd-looking trees that I could not identify. Everything was bright green and wisps of fog swirled among the branches of the trees and drifted across the road.

Astonished at the sudden contrast between arid mountain top and lush hillside, I sat with my nose glued to the window. Almost as suddenly, we slipped out of the clouds, and there, in the distance, was an enormous flat green blanket stretching off to the far horizon. This was the Amazon rain forest.

As we descended, it got warmer. Eventually, we stopped at a village of thatched bamboo houses, where an officious soldier checked everyone's permits. While we waited to be processed, we nibbled on bananas and corn on the cob. Bananas seemed to be growing wild there, and there were also mango trees and tall papayas, while, behind the houses, dead trees lay scattered over newly cleared fields already green with fast growing weeds. There was also a field of rice growing in the soft damp ground. A mile further on, we reached a newly surfaced road where road crews were working with machines. Then we crossed a concrete bridge and entered Villa Tunari.

THE RIO CHAPARE

Villa Tunari was only a village, and it seemed to have more bars than houses. Almost every little thatched hut had a white flag outside, the signal that a new brew of *chicha* was ready for sale. I could see the familiar huge brown jars just inside the doors. There were also small houses and some open-front shops, but there was no hotel. The driver stopped suddenly and pointed to a building half hidden in the dense vegetation. It was a hospital. "I think this is the best place for you." he said, "The doctor is Canadian." I got off the bus and he drove away.

The hospital was actually a small clinic, very neat and clean, with some religious tracts in Quechua on the waiting room table. The doctor was a woman who was very pleased to see a visitor. As soon as she had finished with her patient, we went up to her house to meet her husband, who was a Baptist missionary. They were Hungarians from Toronto and spoke English perfectly as well as other European languages. They had been in Villa Tunari for six years and had built everything themselves from scratch. Their home was a little bit of civilization in the wilderness and as modern as they could manage. They even had a small swimming pool. The house sat in the middle of a large, neatly manicured lawn. This was because, as they explained, "snakes don't like wide open spaces." They showed me a fine collection of pickled snakes in bottles, all caught in the bushes surrounding their house. They also had three dogs and a baby wild cat. Because of the seasonal flooding, the house stood on a small hill. We went down to the creek to admire their water pump, which was a large, round gadget that worked entirely by water pressure and needed no fuel. I was intrigued, but I never did understand just how it worked.

The doctor and the missionary were a very interesting couple. Chatting with them, I soon learned that working on the frontier was hard work with many problems and frustrations, but they were happy and eager to talk about their work. They insisted that I stay the night, and over supper we discussed the seventy percent child mortality rate and its various causes, yellow fever, coca, alcohol, and hook worm and intestinal parasites, the ever-present tuberculosis, and snake-bites. "Almost everybody on the *altiplano* has TB," the doctor explained, "but it's so cold and dry that it doesn't show. When they come down here into the warmth and humidity, the TB takes off rapidly. We have the medicine to cure it, but the Indians take the medicine only until the symptoms go away. Then they stop, and the TB starts up all over again."

Late in the evening, we had visitors, a group of European students that included two Dutchmen, one with a huge red beard. The students were studying a band of Yura Indians who lived two days' hike into the jungle. The Yura are a very shy and primitive people who still hunt with bows and arrows, make their own cloth from bark, and trade with beads.

They were all horrified that I had neither hammock nor mosquito net. "Never sleep on the ground or even on the floor in the jungle," they told me. When he heard this, my host left and came back with a hammock and mosquito net and gave me the address of a friend in Cochabamba where I could leave them when I returned. That night, I slept in a proper bed with the screened windows wide open to the night breeze. It was to be many weeks before I slept in a proper bed again.

After breakfast, the missionary and I set off for the *boca*, or port. The river at Villa Tunari was almost dry, so we were going further downstream to Todos Santos, where the Rio Chapare was still deep enough to float smaller boats. We drove for what seemed like miles past small-holdings hacked out of the forest. They were simple bamboo structures with steep thatched roofs surrounded by fruit trees and tiny patches of vegetables. Each one had a huge green blanket of coca drying in the front yard.

"It's the only cash crop they have." explained the missionary. "They can grow their own food, but they need cash for everything else—salt, flour, clothing, kerosene." Then he added, "The best coca comes from the Yungas. This stuff has bigger leaves, but they say it's not so good. Everybody knows it's going to the cocaine dealers, but nobody wants to do anything about it."

We stopped for a few minutes at a tiny chapel where the service was in Quechua and Spanish. On a bench under a huge avocado tree nearby, a row of children were learning their catechism.

Then we drove down to the port, which was a muddy creek in the forest where there was enough water to float a couple of long barges and half a dozen motor launches. There were also half a dozen high-roofed thatched huts and one shop. "Buy a big bag of sugar candy," said the missionary. "You'll want it." I did.

We asked around about a boat to Trinidad, an important town on the Mamoré that is often confused with Trinidad in the Caribbean, and got estimates of between three and eight days. That sounded about right, and by sheer good luck one of the motorized barges was about to leave. The missionary bargained a good price for me, and I scrambled aboard with my bag, my mosquito net, and my hammock. Just then, a Bolivian naval officer appeared and everything stopped while I went back on shore to his "office," a tiny thatched hut, where I presented my passport and military pass. A few minutes later, we cast off and drifted into the main river where the barge's brand-new, Mercedes Benz diesel engine was started. We were off to the Beni.

THE FIRST RIVERBOAT

The barge was painted red and white and had a simple tin roof and a miniscule cabin in the stern where the captain's wife cooked. The barge carried general goods, ranging from furniture to sacks of flour, and there was an open barge lashed alongside filled with sacks of beer. The captain sat behind the wheel on a high chair far up in the bow, and there was a huge Bolivian flag flying from the stern

The Rio Chapare was dark brown. Huge trees lay in the water, and there were massive sand bars and mud flats everywhere. The river twisted and turned like a snake and the boat zigzagged back and forth across it, making what seemed to me to be good speed. The captain, both hands on the wheel, never once took his eyes off the water ahead. He also kept up a steady flow of commands to the crew through an assistant who stood by his shoulder. Now and then, a man with a long pole took soundings off the bow, and once or twice we bumped over a submerged log. There were no rocks, just layers of silt and sand that had over the centuries washed down from the Andes.

With me on the barge were a half dozen crew members and a half dozen teenagers from Cochabamba who were going to Riberalta, the largest town in the Beni region, situated at the junction of the Beni and Madre de Dios rivers. They were a lively bunch, and most of them had studied English, so they practiced on me and asked a lot of questions. One of the students explained that the Rio Chapare was very low and less than 300 feet wide, but it would be ten feet higher in the rainy season, when it often overflowed its banks. The high river banks were covered in bushes and cane, with occasional giant trees overhanging the water. When the water undercut these trees, they fell into the water to produce yet another snag. Occasionally a huge red and orange butterfly flew out to inspect us. It became very hot, but while we were moving there were few other, more troublesome, insects.

At sunset, we all sat dangling our toes in the water as we ate a supper of rice and meat soup with a cup of coffee. When it was dark, we sat on the tin roof of the barge, enjoying the breeze and chatting while the captain continued down the river, going much more slowly and using a searchlight to pick out landmarks that only he recognized. At 7:30, we saw a cluster of lights in the distance and soon came alongside five or six riverboats nosed into the bank unloading and loading cargo, mostly lumber. There were two big boats. We pulled alongside the larger, then all the passengers dragged their gear in the dark and clambered aboard the bigger boat for the trip to Guayaramerín on the Rio Mamoré in the Beni.

SLOW BOAT DOWN THE RIO MAMORÉ

This larger boat, which was painted red, white, and blue, was one of three riverboats owned by a shipping company. She was about 150 tons and had a pilot house, two decks, and seven cabins for first-class passengers. The crew and second class passengers slept on the deck. The captain told me later that she could do twenty-five miles an hour downstream, but coming upstream in the rainy season she could only do fifteen. I was shown to a tiny cabin that was about seven feet long. There was absolutely nothing in it except the bare floor. It was hot that night, and I was dying for something to drink, but the water in the stone jug sitting near pilot house had a bad taste so I talked the captain's son into sharing the stick of sugar cane he was peeling. It was delicious. I checked the cabin for mosquitoes a bit later, then closed the door and lay down on the mosquito net and used the hammock as pillow. The floor was hard but cool, and I slept well until about 4:00 in the morning, when it got quite cold, I slipped on a sweater and went back to sleep.

I awoke at sunrise about an hour later to find the crew already working on the engine, a new Japanese 350 HP. It looked as if this would take all day. After a breakfast of corn mush and purple *api*, the crew backed the boat up to the river bank, where they stood waist-deep in the muddy water, slipping and laughing as they put the new propeller on the boat.

By ten, it was very hot so I climbed up the bank to a large, open warehouse standing among the scattering of shacks. The walls of this warehouse were six large tree trunks that were fastened entirely by vines and held up a roof made of palm leaves that were woven in two different patterns and interlocked to form an attractive, waterproof cover for the simple building. It was a work of art.

In the warehouse were men sitting and talking on the piles of tropical hardwood planks. They were short, square, lowland Indians, barefoot and wearing the minimal clothing. It did not take me long to understand that the Rio Mamoré was their entire world. None of them had been further than Santa Cruz and they had no interest in the *altiplano*. They knew very little about the outside world and had no interest in railroads, but they knew the value of the freight that was traded at their little riverside village and could argue for hours over which was the best outboard engine for their dugout canoes, one group preferring a tiny Swedish import, the other favoring small American Johnsons. One of these men asked me how many days it would take to sail the riverboat all the way to the U.S.A.

My main problem was that I was thirsty again. The only drinking water available was from the river, and even though everybody else was drinking it, I shuddered at drinking that muddy, and probably polluted, water. When the captain's son took the stone jug to refill it, I followed and watched him dip a bucket of water from the river. He dropped the jug in a hole in the floor in a little room next to the kitchen at the rear of the boat. This room was the communal bathroom, and the hole was the toilet! In time, however, I learned to ignore where the water came from and drank it like everybody else.

In the boat's kitchen, there were a small table and some benches where we lunched on rice, fried bananas, and a meat stew. After lunch, I went back to the big warehouse to nap on the wooden planks while the teenagers went off to swim and the crew transferred a mixed cargo that included sheets of corrugated iron and more beer from a smaller boat.

After my siesta, when it was a tiny fraction cooler, I walked down a trail past little plots of yucca and corn growing tall in the rich soil to the nearby village, which consisted of half a dozen houses surrounded by banana and mango trees. One of these houses was mud stuccoed and painted blue, another was a tiny store where I was able to find a bottle of warm soda water to quench my thirst. While I stood in the shade sipping my drink, five little barefoot girls dragging a baby appeared and seated themselves in a line to stare silently at the strange foreigner. Behind the village, a group of boys were playing an energetic game of soccer in the heat.

When he learned that my wife and I were teachers, the owner of the village store said, "You must come and see our new school." He led me to an open field behind the little village. There on a raised spot in the middle of the field stood one classroom built from four huge logs that supported a high-pitched, palm-thatched roof resting on massive cross beams. The classroom, which was open on three sides, had a mud floor and one wall made of adobe brick and smoothly finished. Inside, there were four rows of wooden benches made from split and smoothed logs and set into the floor on shorter logs as legs. Although this school had absolutely no equipment, it was very well made. The people of the village had obviously worked very hard on it. The store keeper was very proud of it. When I asked, "When does the teacher arrive?" his face fell. "There is the problem," he replied. "We told the man from the government that we would build a school and provide a new house for a teacher." He shrugged his shoulders. "But they have not sent us a teacher yet. Perhaps after Christmas."

Back at the river, I saw that the teenagers had produced a guitar and a tape player and were having a lively party. Freight was vastly more important, and more profitable, than passengers, so we waited at that lonely spot on the river for four days until every inch of cargo space was full and the crew began to fill a barge that was lashed alongside. I watched a steady stream of small boats delivering goods. The crew was also still tinkering with the new engine, so everybody was quite busy. Except the passengers, who endured forced idleness. I soon became bored and a little anxious about the time. I had to be back in Los Angeles by a fixed date and had not reached my destination. I was also concerned that if the rains came early I might have trouble finding transportation out of the rain forest.

Right across the river was a large cleared patch of forest that was quickly being covered by new vegetation. On the riverbank I saw that a farmer had left one huge tree that was just too big to cut down. It was a tall tree with a white trunk and a mass of lilac-colored flowers. I spent a long time watching the tree and its inhabitants, an extraordinary collection of birds. Since this tree stood in the middle of a wide open space, it must have been free of snakes and other predators, thus making it safe for the birds. All day long, parakeets of every color came and went and squawked in its branches. In the morning, the larger parrots left in flocks, to return at sunset, clouds of color in the sky. A parrot sitting in a cage is a miserable, awkward-looking thing, but a parrot flying free is surprisingly beautiful and graceful. A pair of very large macaws with very long tails were nesting near the top of the tree. They were brightly colored, a beautiful sight as they set off each morning, sailing smoothly and gracefully into the rising sun. One day a strange pair of parrots arrived and tried to set up home in the tree. They were large birds, too, but that made no difference to the residents who, when they returned at sunset and saw the intruders, dived straight in to attack. The noise was extraordinary. All the smaller birds came out of hiding and flew around shrieking while the main combatants dived and spun and swooped and slashed at each other and added to the noise with even louder cries. All work on the boat stopped as crew and passengers alike watched as the intruders gradually gave way and eventually fled for the safety of the forest. The victors then spent ten minutes flying around the tree and over the river, boasting of their victory and challenging all comers. It was dark before the tree settled down.

At 6:00 the next morning, I jumped into the river and washed and shaved as best I could. It was refreshing, and I was dry within minutes, just as the engine started up and we swung out into the river.

"We will just try her out today," the captain explained to us. "We have to see that the engine is working properly. Tomorrow we should be able to leave."

Breakfast was the usual eggs with pickled meat and corn mush and a cup of *api* (which is very tasty stuff), but as a special favor, I was invited to have a cup of coffee with the captain, who was interested in my constant note-taking. I visited him in the pilot house, where he had a bell that he used often, but he talked without ever taking his hands off the wheel or his eyes off the river.

The captain was an educated man from Santa Cruz who had traveled a little. His only interest was the Rio Mamoré and the boats on it. However, there was one more thing he dearly wanted. "I would like an American house with air conditioning." he said to me. "Do you have an air conditioned house?" I replied that I just had a small window unit in the bedroom of my house in California. He smiled. "An air conditioned bedroom. That would be quite enough."

The Mamoré was very busy that day. We passed a cattle boat going upstream, an anchored riverboat, dugouts with outboard engines, and a few more dugouts being paddled with curious round paddles. Then we pulled up alongside a barge at a cattle station made up of two huts and a big corral. Nearby were solid wheeled carts, three dogs, a herd of hairy pigs, and some long horned oxen wallowing in the river where a small boy was washing his clothes in a dugout canoe. A pair of gold and blue parrots passed overhead.

We were there to transfer the cargo from their barge to our larger barge. The captain was particular about how he wanted everything loaded, so the sun set before it was done, and they continued working into the night, using candles stuck in whiskey bottles and set under palm trees outlined against a star-filled sky.

"It takes six months for something ordered from North America to reach this point," the captain said, and indeed I thought it odd to see Christmas goods being loaded in the heat of an Amazon night in November. The captain used his searchlight to help the work along, and soon we were finished and heading back up the river.

A new man now joined us on the bridge, the river pilot who took command of the wheel and, in the moonlight and using the searchlight only now and then, skillfully took us past the countless snags and through narrow gaps (some of them barely 100 yards wide) between sandbars. We were going back to where we had been the night before. I found two hooks on the walls of my cabin, but I could not sleep in the hammock so I went up on deck and watched the moon rise. After a while, I also began to smell smoke from a fire in the forest. Eventually it got cold, the river misted over, and I retreated to the cabin. I bundled up in my sweater and slept on the floor.

Next morning we set off again, but now we were heading upstream to pick up yet more cargo. It had rained during the night, so the water was higher. We cruised for about an hour, then the boat made a sudden sharp U-turn and all the crew ran to the rails. There was a man overboard. It seemed that he vanished just after breakfast, but nobody had seen or heard anything. The water looked gray and ugly, and we cruised slowly downstream, with everybody on board quietly scanning the dense jungle along the banks as well the sand bars. Another boat came by, but they said that they had seen nobody. There are no piranhas in this section of the river, but there are always whirlpools and underwater snags, and so everybody was anxious. After an hour, a crew member standing on the roof of the barge gave a yell and the whole crew started laughing. There, sitting on a log on a mud bank was a lone figure who looked very unhappy. Somebody threw him a line, and he was soon hauled aboard, purple with embarrassment. One of his shipmates explained to me that sailors do not fall off their boats. Nobody was angry. We were all just very relieved.

It took all day to finish our trip upstream, take aboard a small load of cargo at an unmarked landing, and get back to our original base. Unfortunately, it was a wet, muggy day that brought out the mosquitoes. Two of the teenagers on our barge were girls, and they were very badly bitten. We used up the whole can of bug spray that I had brought. By now, everybody was impatient to be off, so the teenage boys on the barge helped the crew to load even more cargo that had just arrived. It was too humid for me to work, however, so I slipped into the river and sat there with only my head out of the water. I nearly got hit by a little boat with an overhanging roof of palm branches being paddled by some children selling bananas and corn.

After supper, the crew and the local population gathered on the bank and sat around discussing boats and telling stories and making jokes. Everybody held a bit of cloth or a small towel to swat away the insects, everybody except the sailors, that is, who seemed to be immune to any biting insect. My Spanish was not good enough to get most of the jokes or any of the puns, so I found a place on deck where I could hang my hammock. Then I fastened the mosquito net to the hammock. It worked quite well, except that it was damp on deck and by 3:00 in the morning I was quite cold. I retreated to my cabin and as before put on my sweater and slept on the floor.

I heard the engine starting up at 5:30 next morning. When I went on deck, I saw the crew loading big drums of oil and a huge cargo of pure alcohol in cans from Argentina. It was obvious that we were not going to move just yet, so one of the teenagers suggested that we go fishing for piranhas, so four of us collected bits of chicken from the kitchen and somebody found some lines with hooks attached. Then we set off into the forest. After a while, we came to a big, swampy, ox-bow lake with dark, almost black water. It looked evil enough to have piranhas in it, so we dangled our bloody chicken parts in the water and waited. Nothing happened. We tried other parts of the lake. All we caught were some nasty insect bites,

"I don't think there are any fish in this lake," somebody said. "Let's find some running water." So we scrambled through the forest in the general direction of the river. We had gone about half a mile when we came to a small clearing where two men were squatting around a fire. They were wearing shirts and ragged blue jeans and were darker and much shorter than the local population. I saw that they were both barefoot. They were Indians, but I could not see any bows or arrows or a blowpipe. They remained squatting as we approached, and one of them poked at what they were cooking.

Lying in the hot ashes was the carcass of a small monkey. It looked horribly like a cooked human baby. A couple members of our fishing party drew back in disgust as one of the Indians reached into the ashes and tore off a bit of meat and offered it to us. I was closest, so I took the offering and tasted it. The monkey had been roasted in its fur and there were still a few hairs clinging to the meat along with ashes, but it was well done and tasted quite good, closer to pork than to beef. I rather liked it. A couple of the other fishermen joined me, and we squatted down with the Indians and nibbled on roast monkey. The youngest member of our group stood well back and looked as if he were going to be sick.

The Indians, who didn't talk much, refused to say how they had caught the monkey, so I guessed that they had a gun hidden in the undergrowth. As it was obviously their lunch that we were eating, we didn't stay long. It had been a nice snack, and we thanked them politely and headed back to the riverboat.

On the way, we passed a sailor carrying two huge slabs of fish back to the ship. They were as big as sides of beef. He looked at our empty lines and laughed and said, "Don't worry. You will eat fish for supper today."

We did indeed have fish for supper, as much as we could eat, and it was delicious. The captain knew the name for this monster fish and explained that the locals cut it into long strips and sun dried it with lots of salt to make *charqui*, or jerky. "Then it looks old and black and tough," he said. "But it will last forever. Just don't make sandals out of it or the piranhas will get you." He laughed loudly at his own joke.

As I visited the village on the riverbank again and drank another warm soft drink, I met a man who had just finished building his own house out of poles and palm fronds. Now he was half way through making a solid-wheeled ox-cart. Almost all his tools were handmade out of bits of scrap metal and local hardwood but they looked very functional. He showed me the pieces of rock-hard wood with almost no grain that he had chosen for the big wheels and explained how he would fasten them together and shape them with an adze. One problem he mentioned was keeping his tools sharp. There was no rock in that region, just sandy soil and clay, and all stone had to be imported, especially the right kind of stone for sharpening his tools. Just before I left, he took me up to some trees and showed me a spider that was at least eight inches across. "Watch out for spiders." he said, and then he winked and laughed.

I have seen solid wheeled carts in a number of countries. They are very practical. A wagon wheel with spokes is obviously much lighter, but it is a very complicated thing to build, needing precise measurements and great skill. It also needs an iron rim and is more fragile than a solid wooden wheel. Far from civilization, any man with muscles and simple tools can produce a solid wooden wheel, and long after the trade of wheelwright has disappeared, wagons with solid wooden wheels will still be trundling slowly along dirt roads.

We had tea with our supper that night, and it was very welcome as tea and coffee are considered luxuries and are reserved for special occasions. Afterward, the captain and one of the teenagers brought out their guitars and everybody sang popular Bolivian songs. I tried to join in the chorus. The music of the Beni is similar to that of the *altiplano* except it is faster and sounds almost Brazilian. The party lasted almost until midnight, when the captain announced, "We will, perhaps, leave tomorrow."

After our breakfast of the usual corn mush and *api*, we sat around impatiently waiting for a boat to arrive with one last load. Nobody could explain to me just how everybody knew exactly when a boat was arriving or leaving because there was no telephone or radio. There was certainly no fixed timetable, as we passengers had learned. Along with the cargo, this last boat also brought the bearded Englishman I had met in Cochabamba. Now he was on his way to Manaus in Brazil. He quickly made a deal with the captain to go as far as Guayaramerín.

At noon, the entire village came to see us off. As soon as we were in the river, there was a slight breeze and the mosquitoes went away. It was delightful to relax in the shade and watch the scenery as the afternoon wore on, but at sunset things changed. Because the boat was very heavily loaded and already riding low in the water, the pilot refused to continue in the dark. The captain agreed with him, and I had to admit to myself that it was probably a very wise decision. So we pulled into the bank and tied up to some trees. The jungle at that spot was dense and overhung the deck, and the girls, who were worried about snakes, persuaded a crewman to use his machete to hack off some branches. While that solved the snake problem, it did nothing to solve the insect problem. The mosquitoes descended on us in black swarms. We seemed to have stopped in the very worst spot on the entire river.

Although the teenagers fled as soon as they had gulped down their rice supper, the Englishman produced a battered pack of locally made cigarettes and we stayed on deck, making as much smoke as possible and talking with the crew, who simply ignored the insects. They said that quite a few foreigners passed that way, mainly French and German, but also Americans and English. Quite recently, one party had made the entire trip in a large canoe. The sailors thought this was absolutely crazy.

Suddenly we heard the sound of an engine, and within minutes a searchlight came cutting through the night. These preceded a strange sight—a large and very battered riverboat, dirty and stained and looking like a floating gypsy camp with a tattered palm-frond roof and a tent pitched in the middle. The crew and some women were lounging around half naked and gleaming with sweat, while two evil-looking men played dice at a green kitchen table under one of the two kerosene lamps. To complete the scene, a large, very black African man wearing a scarlet bandana, and not much else, stood next to a pole from which hung two cow's heads still dripping blood. As this barge pulled alongside us, we could see a pile of gray and red meat dumped on a hide on the floor. It was a floating butcher's shop.

I just stood and stared, and the Englishman said, "Hollywood couldn't have done it better. Straight out of one of those old pirate movies." I had to agree. As we watched, our captain boarded the barge, stepped daintily over bones and offal, and bent down to inspect the pile of meat. The piratical crew, actually a friendly and cheerful bunch, produced a set of bar scales and dragged the cuts of meat around to show off their best qualities. There was a lot of good natured haggling, then a great pile of meat, about fifty pounds of it, was passed back to our boat. Our captain then invited the other captain and his wife over for a cup of coffee. As a final gesture, our captain received one of the cow heads and the African chopped it open with a wicked looking axe.

While the guests sipped their coffee, our crew went right to work, tearing the meat into strips and hanging it to dry on long poles in the bows. When the other captain and his wife went back to their boat, that floating shambles with its ferocious looking crew headed off into the dark, its searchlight probing the banks for another customer.

We were on the move before dawn the next day, our departure disturbing flocks of parrots, a pair of herons, and a little herd of capybara that had come down to the river to drink. It was a pleasure to lie in the hammock and watch the world go by. I saw groves of palms, then open patches here and there where the river had changed its course, then some false banana trees or a cane brake or a giant tree peering over the bushes. Somewhere in the green tangle were snakes and monkeys and other wildlife, but all we could see from the boat were birds and butterflies.

The water seemed to be a little higher now, and we were making good speed. We soon arrived at a cattle station where another, smaller, boat waited. There was cargo to be unloaded and yet more to be loaded, and the crew worked all evening and late into the night. There was not much to see because the main ranch was miles inland, and here there was only a big corral holding a healthy-looking herd of mixed European and Brahma bulls. There were also millions of cattle flies. The girls bought some yellow fruit from a child, but half of the strange things had worms in them.

The Englishman had brought a clever looking nylon net hammock in a bag, which we helped him rig up that night, but it was useless as the nylon cut into the bare skin, so he slept on the cabin floor and used it as a pillow. At four in the morning, a storm broke and the rain thundered down, but it cleared the air of insects.

We had taken over a week to travel two days down the river, and I was getting anxious and frustrated. Next morning, I saw that there was a second boat lashed alongside us so that our floating island consisted of the riverboat with a large barge lashed tightly on its left side and a smaller barge lashed to the right side. There were also three or four smaller boats either lashed to the barges or trailing behind us on short lines. There was also a small family camped on one of the barges. We must have been quite a sight. We passed small settlements beside the river where children stood to watch us. One place with exactly three buildings had a large name board nailed to a tree proclaiming itself San Pablo. A bit later, we passed a large canoe traveling upstream and hugging the riverbank. In it was a family. The mother, who looked about sixteen, was paddling in the bow, her young child was paddling in the middle, and the husband was steering in the rear. Two more tiny heads peered over the side and waved as we passed. A couple in another canoe came out from the far bank, both man and woman paddling toward us. They had a letter that they wanted posted. Then two women in a canoe selling pineapples and scented soap arrived and I bought some soap. That night, we tied up a little past the mouth of the Rio Secure River. We were not even half way to Guayaramerín, 500 miles downstream.

That evening, as I was standing at the rail watching the stars glistening on the water, there was a large splash and a dark shape broke the surface. I could see that it was not an alligator, and it was too big to be a fish. As I looked closer, I saw that it was one of about half a dozen creatures swimming near the surface. One of them surfaced again. It looked like a dolphin! I had always thought that the dolphin is a salt water mammal. I had seen many on my travels, but now I could not puzzle out what a school of dolphins was doing thousands of river miles from the Atlantic Ocean. It was a few days later when one of the crew members understood what I was talking about. "Yes sir," he said, "we have dolphins in the rivers. We leave them alone. They are good luck." Then he smiled and added, "This means we will have a safe trip with no problems."

We set off again at dawn and were doing quite nicely until, just before noon, we came to a sudden stop in the middle of a wide stretch of the river. It was clear that we had hit a sand bar. If the water level in the river had been dropping, we would have been in serious trouble, but it was slowly rising as rain fell in the hills upstream, so nobody was particularly worried. The largest barge was allowed to drift away and was tied to a tree. Then everybody, passengers included, jumped into the water and started to push the overloaded riverboat while the cook was sent off in a canoe with a long pole to find the channel. There was a stiff current, but the water on the sand bar was only three or four feet deep and everybody pushed vigorously at the sides of the riverboat.

All our efforts were useless, however. The boat refused to budge, so we went back on board and had lunch and then tried again. Finally, after more than six hours of pushing, we got the boat off the sand bar. Meanwhile, the rope holding the barge had snapped, so we all clambered aboard and the riverboat gave chase. Capturing the barge was easy, but we ended up with the boat facing the wrong way. The captain had to steer slowly downstream until we came to a spot wide enough to turn around.

No soon were we all relaxing and congratulating ourselves on our success with the sand bar when the engine suddenly made some strange noises and stopped. The captain remained calm, but the pilot said a few things in Spanish that I could not translate and managed to steer us to the river bank, where we tied up to some trees. While the captain inspected the engine, the teenagers scrambled ashore and found some wild mango trees. They brought back a welcome dessert to go with our rice and spaghetti supper. Just before sunset, the captain and a crewman set off in a canoe to look for help.

Next morning, I awoke to find that the captain had returned during the night and had fixed the engine just enough to get us a few miles downstream to a logging mill owned by a German settler who happened to be building a large boat on the riverbank. His house and all the other buildings were Indian-style huts, and his two boys looked exactly like the Indian children they were playing with except for their shockingly blond hair. One of them explained that their main house was further inland. This was, he said, because the water could rise as much as thirty feet and flood all the land near the river. The saw blade was run by an old automobile engine, and everything was on skids with a tractor ready to pull it back to safety when the floods arrived.

Meanwhile, the German mill owner and the boat's crew set about repairing the engine, and the teenagers set out to find more mango trees. At the same time, the captain's dog barked at a herd of goats on the shore. They took up the challenge, scrambled down the riverbank, and charged across the barge, onto the riverboat, and began running all over the cargo. This was fun to watch, but the cook did not think so and locked the dog in the toilet. By noon, the captain said he was satisfied with the engine repairs, and so we set off again. At four in the afternoon we arrived at the port of Trinidad on the Mamoré River.

TRINIDAD

Technically, we were now in the Beni, but actually we were in the Moxos, a 50,000-square-mile region of savanna between the Brazilian border and the Chaco of Bolivia. The Moxos is a mixture of open plains with scattered brush and heavy vegetation along the rivers. Since colonial days, it has been famous for its great herds of semi-wild cattle that were slaughtered only for their hides, but it is also famous for its extraordinary wet season, when the parched savanna suddenly becomes an enormous inland sea and all activity comes to a stop for four months.

There was no port here, just a section of riverbank where half a dozen riverboats and dozens of smaller boats were lined up with their bows beached in the mud. Some children were swimming on a sand bar, and everybody stopped to watch as we came in. It was obviously a time to show off, and the pilot brought us in smoothly alongside a big, gray, military-looking vessel that was loading drums of gasoline. On the high bank above us were a flag pole and half a dozen bamboo huts, all of them cafes.

The captain, dressed in his very best, was first off the boat. He was immediately surrounded by a crowd of women, and it was obvious that he was very popular in Trinidad. The Englishman and I went ashore together and headed for the cafes in search of a beer, or at least a soft drink. In the largest cafe we met two New Zealand backpackers who introduced us to another New Zealander, an extremely attractive, statuesque blonde. They told us that they were heading for Manaus but had been stuck in Trinidad for ten days waiting for a boat. They also reported that there were up to twenty others looking for a ride. The New Zealanders then scrambled down the bank to talk to somebody on the riverboat. As the Englishman was happy to sit in the shade, I hitched a lift on a truck going into Trinidad.

The truck driver was talkative and very knowledgeable about the local history and geography, and we chatted during the whole ten mile drive over a good but very bumpy road. "Trinidad is growing," he said proudly. "Soon we will have a big city here. Maybe as big as Santa Cruz." Then he added, "As soon as La Paz builds us some more roads." About half way along, we had to cross a river at the grandly named Puerto Almacén. There was very little there except a hand-operated cable ferry, a couple of tiny cafes, and an open walled church. I helped the driver haul on the ferry rope, and we crossed the river. The road, which was raised above flood level, ran perfectly straight for about five miles through the bush and across the grasslands to the city.

Trinidad did not strike me as a future metropolis. It was a worn and squalid place, and it smelled. The truck driver let me off in the main plaza, a dusty square bordered by some huge trees loaded with scarlet blossoms and half a dozen coconut trees. I thought it odd to see coconut trees so far from the ocean. The road around the square was not completely paved, but most of the streets of the city were wide and had fluorescent lights hanging from wires across them. There were also a church and some old buildings, many of which had roofs on pillars and, like those in Santa Cruz, sheltered the sidewalks from the bright sun. Others were two stories tall, and there were also three movie houses. I worked out where the bad smell was coming from when I saw that all the streets were edged with open drains. Some of these were covered by cement slabs, but down the side streets they were open. There were food stalls near every corner, and it was obvious that the city had no street cleaning service. Perhaps they waited for the annual rains to do the job.

At the post office, the girl could not find the key to the stamp drawer, so I gave her the money and a letter to Lily and hoped for the best. As I was leaving, the postmaster asked me if I would do him a favor and take a look at the "lost mail" that was accumulating on his desk. We spent an interesting hour looking at letters with astonishingly useless or completely undecipherable addresses. The problem was that too many postal clerks somewhere along the line were confusing Trinidad in Bolivia with Trinidad in the West Indies. I eventually helped the postmaster sort them into a West Indian pile, an undecipherable pile, and a little pile that looked important enough to go back to La Paz and let somebody else work it out. The postmaster was extremely grateful for my help and pointed out the way to the telegraph office, where I sent Lily a cable to assure her that I was safe and sound.

It was hot and sticky, and there were plenty of flying bugs of various sizes, so I took refuge in a cafe with a new Brazilian fan, where I had some papaya juice, then some delicious cream cakes and a glass of milk, a nice change from the simple food on the riverboat. There seemed to be quite a few foreigners in town. The Germans with their blond children stood out clearly from the local population. The other foreigners seemed to be mostly French tourists. Late in the evening, crowds of citizens began the nightly *paseo* in the plaza as the local youths entertained themselves by racing their little Japanese motorbikes round and round the square. There were no taxis or buses, though I noticed that some of the motorbikes were hiring out as taxis. It was quite a sight to see a large woman with a full shopping basket balancing side saddle on the back of a little motorbike driven by youth intent on winning the Grand Prix.

I had no intention of staying overnight in Trinidad, so I asked some of the motorbike taxi drivers if they would drive me back to the riverboat. Nobody was interested, however, so I set off to walk back. I remembered the wooden bridge across the river that bisects the town, so I knew I was heading in the right direction, but with only starlight to see by, it was a long tiring walk on the rough road. Every time I stopped for a rest, the bugs attacked, so I kept up a steady pace. I estimated the distance at about ten miles and only one car passed me in three hours and a few motorbikes came from the river. Otherwise, it was a quiet night broken only by the croaking of thousands of frogs and the flash of countless fireflies in the trees.

After a few miles, I saw something on the road ahead and soon came up to an ox cart being pulled by two long-horned oxen. The driver sat hunched up, almost asleep, but woke up in surprise when I appeared out of the starlight. He patted the edge of the cart and offered me a lift. I could walk faster than the oxen, but it was a friendly gesture, so I perched next to him. There was no conversation. He simply went back to sleep and I sat there staring at the rear ends of the oxen. I had seen this type of cart in other countries and had often wondered why oxen had a huge wooden yoke instead of the leather collar around the chest that is used with horses. Sometimes the yoke is on the neck behind the horns and sometimes it is on the forehead in front of the horns, but this pair had a very light yoke tied directly to the horns. After about a mile, my pondering of this deep philosophical problem was halted when the oxen, who knew their way home, turned off the road and bumped across the ditch. As the driver woke up, I jumped down from my perch, thanked him, wished him a good night and set off again up the empty road. I had ridden on many a strange vehicle in my travels, but that was the first time I had ridden an oxcart.

At Puerto Almacén, I rested for a while and watched a couple of men playing dice by the light of a hurricane lamp. Then one of them showed me how to work the ferry, and I pulled myself across the river. The next stretch of road was narrower, and the bush was thicker, so I walked carefully under the faint starlight, trying to look for snakes on the road and listening to very strange noises in the forest. More than once I stopped dead and cautiously detoured around something lying in the road that might have been a snake or might have been a dead branch. It was quite a relief to come to the riverbank and scramble down it. Two of the crew were still awake when I boarded the boat. They were astonished when I said I had walked all the way in the dark. "Not me," said one, and the other nodded and said, "I would have found a *chicheria* and a pretty girl. That's a better way to get some exercise." Actually, that long walk was the first real exercise that I had had for a week and after I had changed my sweat-soaked clothes, I rolled into my hammock. But I was too tired to sleep.

Next day, people started to come on board. The cook had predicted that because of engine trouble we would not leave that day, but the new passengers poured onto the ship nevertheless. Along with the three New Zealanders with their enormous backpacks there came an old Austrian man married to a local girl who seemed to have brought all her female relatives along. There were also two Bolivian youths who spoke to nobody, a family with various children and all their furniture (including the kitchen table), and a lot of second-class passengers with swarms of children. These latter passengers made themselves comfortable on the barges that were lashed alongside us. Tied to our stern were three or four small boats floating on the ends of long ropes. Some of these boats also had people in them. One boat was quite pretty. It was a little houseboat with a palm frond roof, a swinging hammock, and a tiny wood stove with a huge old black pot on it. There were a bicycle and a chicken cage on the roof, and a stem of bananas hung over the side. The father was lounging in the hammock while mother tended to whatever was cooking in the black pot, and three little heads peeked over the edge of the boat and stared at me.

When I pointed this out to one of the New Zealanders, he also admired it, but added that he thought that the whole thing, which was simply a large dugout canoe, was "bloody unstable." I agreed, but then I thought back to when I was about thirteen and we lived in Guiana for two or three years. My brothers and I were very adventurous, and on holidays or with the Boy Scouts we often paddled dugout canoes. Dugouts are carved from a single log and sit very low in the water, but they are remarkably stable and almost impossible to sink, even by a bunch of lively little boys. These canoes are quite different from the traditional Canadian canoe that gave me so many dunkings in icy-cold northern lakes that to this day, I usually decline any offer of a ride in one.

MORE DELAYS ON THE RIVER

The cook was wrong. We actually started moving at midday. One of the New Zealanders had gone swimming and barely made it back in time, but she need not have worried because our overloaded ark got stuck in the mud just a few hundred yards offshore. Everybody jumped into the water and helped push, and soon she was going again. But not for long. A couple of hours downstream, we had to stop again as a sudden windstorm began producing waves that swamped the deck and threatened the cargo, which included sacks of flour. The crew produced sheets of purple plastic to protect the flour, but the captain still was not happy. Two hours later, the storm ended, we set off again and kept up a steady pace until dark, when the captain used his searchlight to find a mooring near a corral on the riverbank. Supper was served in three shifts, and then there was a lot of fuss to get everybody settled. The New Zealanders chose to sleep on the roof, little tents sprang up all over the deck, and the crew slept wherever they could find space. There were bodies everywhere. The captain wandered around with a flashlight, checking everything. The Englishman had slung his nylon hammock in our cabin, so there was no room for my hammock and I slept on the floor to the tune of mooing cows and snoring people. And I slept quite well.

At seven the next morning, the captain appeared on the riverbank with a bevy of females that he introduced as his nieces, who joined us for breakfast at the wooden table near the kitchen, but went back ashore before we left. We had bread and tea for breakfast. It was the first bread I had tasted for many days, and I savored every last crumb. There was a brilliant sky with no sign of a cloud as we set off, but there was also a high wind and waves smashing against the boat and sending spray as high as the roof.. The vessel shook with the pounding waves and three or four times we had to stop to allow the gusts to die down, The Rio Mamoré was wide here, but it meandered all over the place and the pilot was having difficulty keeping to the channel, so he had a man standing in the bow taking soundings with a long pole. He also sent a couple men out ahead in a canoe taking soundings with another long pole.

The strips of meat we'd bought from the floating butcher had cured well, and now piles of *charqui* lay on the roof in the sun.

Everybody on the ship seemed to be eating *charqui* and mangoes. At noon, when we stopped to drop off a family, I counted nine barefoot children standing on the riverbank, two of them with the pot bellies of malnutrition and one in a straw hat holding a shotgun. Part of the luggage passed ashore was a large can of 90 percent alcohol.

We saw no animals that afternoon as we sailed on, but there was a wide selection of birds, including herons and vultures, and there were big, open stretches of dry, yellow grassland quivering in the heat. The wind also brought the smell of brush fires from far off across the savanna. That night it was too stuffy to sleep in the cabin, so I just lay on the roof watching the stars and enjoying the warm night until about 3:00, when it became cold and I retreated to my cabin. Many other passengers were doing the same.

Next morning, we woke to such a bright sun that I had to find my sunglasses. We had another surprise for breakfast: fresh milk and cane juice. I decided the cook was working miracles. The wind was just as bad as yesterday, so the captain had all the flour sacks moved to a drier spot on the deck. At mid-morning, when we stopped at another ranch to put off another family, everybody scrambled ashore to buy pineapples and steal mangoes. The mangoes were as sweet and juicy as ever, but the pineapples were quite tasteless. Even with the wind, it was quite hot that afternoon, and I was getting a little sunburned, so I sat in the shade. Some children showed me how to play cards and make faces out of mango stones. It was a very lazy afternoon. I spent hours just sitting behind the pilot watching him work. His eyes never left the water, and his hands never stopped turning the wheel back and forth.

Given the slightest opportunity, a river will meander. Rivers seem to have an ancient fear of straight lines and consequently spend all their time attempting to change course. As the Grand Canyon shows us, only a wall of solid rock will keep a river in its course, but even rock will wear away in time. The great rivers of the Amazon Basin have nothing to restrain them, so they constantly change course, especially during the annual rainy season. The end result is an unbelievably complicated series of loops, bends, and cut-offs, with oxbow lakes and dead end channels as well as innumerable sand bars and mud flats with wide, shallow areas and sudden deep holes and even the occasional whirlpool. The constantly eroding riverbanks produce thousands of fallen trees that drift until they catch in the mud to form deadly snags that are often half hidden by the water and usually capable of impaling an unlucky boat.

Mark Twain revered the pilots on the Mississippi who guide the riverboats through every twist and turn of that mighty North American river. But the meanders of the Mississippi are as nothing, compared to the wild contortions of the Chapare and Mamoré rivers of South America. Since the riverbanks had few distinguishing features, the best way to see the turns and twists was to sit and watch the sun. Never did it stay where it belonged for more than a minute, but swung constantly backwards and forwards, sometimes just a few feet, but often in great swoops from side to side and often right around as the boat followed the snake-like river. We were very rarely sailing due north as the map said we were. Sometimes in fact, we were heading south on our way north, and I estimated that for every mile of actual progress we traveled five or even more extra miles.

When we tied up for the night, it was too hot to sleep, so I sat on the roof watching an electrical storm on the horizon far to the east. At one point in the night, a boat heading upstream hailed us to ask if we had any salt to spare. We had none, and so they went on their way. The teenagers set up their tape player and started to dance on the roof by the light of one bare bulb. The Englishman danced with the New Zealand girl and fell off the roof into the water and had to be fished out. Then a youth who was at least a foot shorter than her danced with her and everybody laughed and cheered. The families on the barge sat and enjoyed themselves watching us as if they were at the movies. By midnight, it turned cool and everybody went to bed.

Next morning we woke to gray sky and cold weather. Everybody scrambled to get things under cover. Soon the rains came, hard, cold, and windy, and everything became wet and clammy. When the storm got too violent for the pilot to be able to see, we pulled up and waited for an hour. At noon, we reached Exaltation, a tiny spot on a bend in the river where the water was so shallow the passengers getting off there had to use a canoe to reach the shore and the crew had to cut steps in the clay banks. It took two hours to unload four families and all their luggage while the crew tried to protect the women and children from the pouring rain with bright plastic sheets.

There must have been a village far back from the river because the captain's son went ashore and then appeared with his arms full of watermelons. He was followed by crew members carrying round cheeses. One of the crew slipped and slid all the way down the mud bank on his rear, but he saved the cheese. Everybody cheered.

The rain finally stopped, and we went on at a good pace to a cattle ranch set near the river but on high ground. There was time now to stretch our legs, so all of us foreigners walked to the ranch, where we watched the cheese making. A worker picked some palm fronds and with a few clever twists turned them into a sturdy basket for carrying cheese. They sold quite a few of their hard, rubbery, white cheese. While this was going on, I wandered into the stables, where I saw that all the saddles and almost every piece of equipment was made by hand from leather or very hard wood. In the yard outside was a baby rhea, an ostrich-like bird that I had thought was only found on the Argentine pampas.

Next morning, after a cold night at a lonely hacienda near the river, there was a brisk wind. The rain had stopped, and the sun crept from behind the clouds and began to dry everything. Things went smoothly all morning, and we had just finished delivering a family to a farm when we ran onto a sand bar. We were in the water trying to push the boat for an hour, but our pushing was useless, so we climbed back into the boat and sat down for lunch, Suddenly the boat swung sideways and slipped off the sand bar all by itself. There was a general sigh of relief. Within minutes we reached Puerto Siles.

PUERTO SILES

Puerto Siles surprised me because it actually looked like a river port. There were about a dozen boats of various sizes nosed up to the bank and a real wooden staircase led up a steep cliff to a row of about twenty buildings high above, most of which were plastered. One, the navy office, was painted white and had a flag pole in front of it.

The other thing that surprised me was the rock. The port sat on a rocky outcrop, and there was another big outcrop on the other side of the river. I could see outcrops of red and black layered rock all along the riverbank here. But that rock was not supposed to be there. All my geography and geology texts had insisted that the Beni and the Chaco regions consisted of extremely deep layers of fine silt, sand, and clays washed down over millions of years from the Andes. The hard rock of the Brazilian shield was many miles to the east. Yet here was a rocky area that was obviously an exposed spur of the Andes, which were far to the west. My first reaction was to walk along the beach and pick up a couple of small samples of the crumbly red and black layered conglomerate to show Ramiro.

Up on the cliff top, I saw two soldiers were building a house using little more than their machetes. There was also a little church with four bells, two of which were real bells, but the other two were old liquid gas cylinders with the bottoms cut off. I also saw palm trees and a few papayas and some boys playing soccer in the heat. At a little café, I sat sipping a *refresco* as I chatted with the owner about the rocks in the river. "Oh, yes, sir," he assured me, "those rocks are all around here, but nowhere else. When the water is very low, they can be a problem for some of the bigger boats." Then he added, doubtfully, "I think that's why the port is here."

While we were talking, a powerful motorboat arrived. It was more of a houseboat, and with its chrome and polished teak, it stood out clearly from all the other craft. Across the front was painted the slogan *Mensajero del rey*, "The King's Messenger." I knew that it was a missionary boat. The captain was a large man who was chewing gum, and his wife was a thin woman in a very dowdy dress that reached almost to the ground. They were delivering a family that included a girl about eight years old with blonde curls. I found out later that she was a child evangelist and held lively Baptist services that drew large crowds. The places these messengers visited had no other form of entertainment.

I saw quite a few missionary boats in the Beni, and at times it seemed to me that the tiny population would be swamped by missionaries in boats that were all big and expensive. Quite a few of the missionaries also had private planes, and the quiet of the vast land was often broken by the roar of a float plane coming in to land at some mission in the forest. Invariably, there was an air-conditioned house alongside the white-painted church. These missionaries lived very well.

Fortunately, the young evangelist and her family did not try to hold a service on the boat. They carefully ignored the various foreigners on board and sat quietly in a corner until we reached their mission and then they left us. When I asked a sailor about the various missionaries that were working in the area, he just shrugged and said, "I don't understand what they say, but it is fun to go. There is music, and sometimes they give us things."

We did not stay long in Puerto Siles. We were soon off again, and the day passed quietly. I saw a herd of capybara swimming across the river and saw some turtles sunning themselves on a bank. A huge toucan flew out to inspect us, but there were very few parrots there, and the vegetation was changing. We were seeing less savanna, and the trees were bigger with a greater variety. It was very beautiful and there was a gorgeous sunset as we pulled in to tie up for the night at a cattle ranch.

Next morning, we awoke to a cheerfully sunny day. We were now within two or three days of Gayaramerin, and I was eager to be off the boat. But it was not to be. When I happened to look down into the engine room, I saw the long driveshaft lying on the floor and some crew members huddled nearby in a discussion group. When I inquired, one of them explained that they needed a washer-gasket for the driveshaft and, as there was no metal lathe within many hundreds of miles, they were making one out of wood. "It is very hard wood." he assured me. "With plenty of grease, it will work just like metal."

The men worked all morning with chisels and files, patiently turning a block of yellow wood into the sleeve-like object they needed. It was fascinating to watch. I kept thinking of engineers in Japan with their precision instruments and million dollar tools and I wondered what they would have thought of this small manufactury.

The ranch where we were still halted was very modern and had a tiled roof, a water pump, and barbed wire fences. The owner, an American Baptist missionary of German descent, had a swarm of blond-haired children who galloped around on horses with imported American saddles. This was a horse breeding ranch, but they also had a nice herd of milk cows. I wandered through the cheese-making plant, then out to where they were branding the animals. They did it the traditional way with branding irons in a fire and the animals held by half a dozen cowboys, all wearing American ten-gallon hats and tight blue jeans.

The handmade engine part was installed by lunchtime. It worked smoothly, and so we were off again by noon. The land alongside the river was more populated now, and we stopped in at three or four little places and picked up as many passengers as we let off. At one place, where the captain was well known, we were presented with a basket of melons, and soon the deck was littered with melon seeds. The vegetation on the high banks became thicker and more like jungle than it had been, and soon it became much hotter. To make up for lost time, the pilot carried on after sunset, but inevitably, or so it seemed, we struck a sandbar right in the middle of the river, much too far to throw a rope around a tree and winch ourselves free. While we all stood around looking glum, the current swung the riverboat and its barge and all the attached small boats around in a circle, and soon the whole, overloaded, floating village drifted free.

Instead of mosquitoes, some new visitors arrived. These were huge yellow and black horseflies with an astonishing capacity for human blood. Fortunately, there were not many of them, and so we all armed ourselves with scraps of cloth or plastic to swat the beasts away. After a delicious supper of fresh eggs, fresh milk, newly baked bread, and soft white cheese, I sat in the starlight discussing the Suarez family and the rubber industry with a passenger whose family had lived in the area for generations.

It was the first of December now, and I had to be home before Christmas. I was gratified therefore to hear the engines start well before dawn. We passed two fishing rafts on their way to market with the live fish in submerged cages, then we reached the mouth of the Rio Guaporé, which the Bolivians call the Iténez.

It flows from the east, rising in Mato Grosso, and forms Bolivia's northern border with Brazil for most of its length. The Guaporé is noticeably cleaner than the muddy Mamoré, and there is a distinct line between the waters for miles downstream. We had to stop at the junction to let the captain take his manifest to the customs post, which was little more than a store and a cabin on the steep bank and a dugout canoe with an outboard engine lying on the riverbank. The formalities took an hour, during which we bought sugar cane and bananas and I watched a woman working at a huge clay oven in the sweltering heat. To the north, I could see a range of hills on the Brazilian side of the river. A canoe came across the river to deliver a large, dark, ball of rubber. This was the first time that most of us tourists had seen rubber in its raw state.

The pilot decided that the river was now wide enough and deep enough to allow us to travel at night, but the weather decided otherwise. Huge storm clouds appeared out of nowhere, and when visibility in the heavy rain was reduced to zero, we pulled up alongside a riverboat with two barges and waited for an hour. This happened two more times, but the captain pressed on, and after sunset we continued by the light of the vivid lightning flashes and the searchlight By midnight, however, the storm was so bad that we stopped for the night. The captain said that anybody who wanted to could sleep on the boat when we arrived at Gyaramerin, as it would be tied up for at least ten days.

GUAYARAMERÍN AT LAST

The storm drifted off during the night, leaving a cool, gray day. We started early. After one passenger was put off in a canoe, we picked up an "escort" of a very tattered pair of soldiers who had no guns (and one had no boots). I suspected that they were there just to watch out for smuggling. As we approached Guayaramerín, there was more traffic on the water. There were also islands of waterweed caught up around the snags in the wide river. As we went along, we passed a large, modern looking saw mill that somebody said was American-owned and sent its hardwood only to the States. In the early afternoon, we saw a line of buildings on a bluff, then an island blocked off our view of the Brazilian side of the river, and we passed a flight of concrete steps and a row of motor launches. When it started to rain again, the small crowd of onlookers who had gathered on the bank to watch our arrival hurried to a small, round shelter with a sign on it stating the altitude as 128 meters, or about 420 feet above sea level. Nearby was a Bolivian navy launch manned by some very smartly turned out officers in white shoes and some very ragged sailors in bare feet.

When we arrived in Guayaramerín, our crew hacked some steps in the mud bank, then threw out a plank, and we all hurried ashore into the heat and the rain. I left everything except my wallet and passport in my cabin as the Englishman and I headed for the nearest café, where we sat at a sidewalk table under a shelter and sipped nice cold beers while I reviewed my plans.

Although it seemed to me that the riverboat trip that had been estimated to take between a week and ten days had dragged on for weeks, my notes showed that it had actually taken only a bit over two weeks. It had been a great adventure, packed with new experiences for me, and I had seen the country and its people close up, closer than most foreigners ever could. Thinking back on it, I was very glad indeed that I had not simply taken a plane.

There were two things that I dearly wanted to see. First was the historic and tragic "railway to nowhere," as the Madeira-Mamoré Railroad between the Brazilian cities of Guajara-mirim and Porto Velho was called. The other was the home and business center of the Rubber King, Nicholas Suarez, at Cachuela Esperanza on the Madre de Dios River. I also hoped to see something of the rubber industry and to go to Riberalta where the Rio Beni joins the Madre de Dios. My problem was that I would have to move quickly if I wanted to see everything and get out before the rains came. I also had to get home before Christmas, and it was already December.

The Bolivian town of Guayaramerín, which is across the Rio Guaporé (called the Rio Itenez in Brazil) from the Brazilian town of Guajara-mirim, was a small, sleepy little river town with a solidly Victorian bank and a large customs building on the main square, but not much else of note. The plaza had the same lovely red-flowered trees I had seen in Santa Cruz, and there were a few brick buildings, but the majority were adobe and most had roofs of tin or thatch. There were a small church and a few stores on the wide, red-mud streets where the only traffic was a few jeeps and motorbike taxis. The whole town, in fact, seemed to me to be taking a very long siesta. I strolled to the airport, which was just a strip of red clay almost in the middle of the town, and was told by a sleepy clerk that no plane was due in for at least three days. Then I walked to a relatively busy corner and was told that there was no bus station in town, and, anyway, there would be no bus to Riberalta until the road dried out. By then it was getting late, so I had supper in a cafe and went back to the boat and slept in my hammock under a mosquito net.

It rained all night but it stopped at dawn, leaving a gray sky. After breakfast on the plaza, I found the immigration building. After I learned that no permit was needed to cross the river for a couple of hours, I went to the bank to get some Brazilian money, but there I was told that only the manager could cash traveler's checks and he would not be in until noon. I left the bank and continued exploring the town. Down at the river, a small crowd of boatmen offered to change my money for me, though at a fat profit. I met up with the New Zealanders and the teenagers from Cochabamba, who had rented motorbikes and were dashing around on them. The New Zealanders went back to the bank with me. The manager had arrived by then, and so we cashed our checks and went back to the river. There we were told that the standard fare was two pesos, so we crossed the wide river in a motorboat. But when we tried to pay the man, he demanded five pesos each. We told him to go to hell. He called out to some soldiers, but they agreed that the price was two pesos. The boatman then found a Brazilian army officer and had a little quiet chat with him. The officer told us to pay ten pesos each. We were not even out of sight when the boatman paid the officer his cut.

What a waste of time and money that trip was. Guajara-mirim was not much bigger than Guayaramerín, and although most of its streets were paved, it had no decent restaurants and there was nothing to see. We went back to Bolivia for lunch.

Back at the immigration office in Guayaramerín, we met up with the Englishman and a friendly clerk who told us that the exit fees didn't even cover the cost of his pen and ink as he had so little business. "All the Americans and most of the Europeans go by plane," he said. He leaned back in his chair and sighed, "Twenty years ago, this was a very busy place. Lots of visitors. But not today."

Chapter 17: The Historic Jungle Railway

I fetched my hammock, mosquito net, and toothbrush from the boat, and then the three New Zealanders, the Englishman, and I went back across the river to Guajara-mirim. We found a Brazilian customs officer who very politely directed us to the police station, where the bored Brazilian officer tried to make life difficult for us. He spoke Spanish with a very bad accent and demanded photos and gave us forms to fill in that were all in Portuguese. None of us spoke Portuguese, but the tall, blonde, New Zealand girl kept smiling at the poor man until he eventually smiled back at her, stamped our passports, and let us go. At the old railroad station, we bought tickets for the train that was due to leave very early the next morning and left our packs with a lonely clerk, who directed us to a little restaurant. After lunch, we wandered along a street and came to a little movie theater, where the manager came out to talk to us and invited us in for a free showing. The audience was mostly children with their mothers, and we were the center of attention. The movie was a terrible Italian cowboy movie with scratchy sound and Portuguese subtitles, but we enjoyed it, and the kids enjoyed staring at us.

Back at the railroad station, we chatted with the guard and tried to settle down for the night. There was nowhere to sling my hammock, so I tried sleeping on a seat in an old, wooden passenger coach parked at the station, but it was too hot inside, so I moved outside to a stone bench. That was much cooler, but the bugs found me. When I caught two rather large ones crawling up my trouser legs, I tucked my trousers into my socks and wrapped myself in the mosquito net. I managed to get a few hours of sleep.

Where the Mamoré and Madre de Dios rivers meet to form the Rio Madeira, which forms part of the border between Bolivia and Brazil, there is a long section of dangerous rapids that completely block any form of river travel. Suggestions were put forth as early as 1867 to build a railroad around the rapids, but it was not until the great rubber boom of 1880 to 1912 that anything was actually done. Quite a few books have chronicled the various attempts to build a railroad in the heart of the Amazon jungle, a thousand miles from the sea. It was called the Madeira-Mamoré Railroad, and it soon became notorious as the loneliest railroad in the world. It was also the most expensive in human lives. Of the thousands of laborers who were tempted into the jungle by high wages, three out of every five died there. And it was all in vain. The railroad was officially opened in 1912 when rubber was selling at three dollars per pound, but rubber plantations in Malaya were already beginning to produce rubber. By 1913, the price dropped to only seventy cents per pound. The Amazon rubber boom collapsed overnight. The railway never made a profit.

Some years after my trip, I read that the Brazilian government had built a road using the solidly-built iron bridges as part of the road. The rail tracks may or may not still lie there in the jungle, but the ancient steam engines and rolling stock are now rusting away in Porto Velho. The tragic railroad is no more. Nobody will ever know exactly how many thousands of men died to build that useless railroad. I like to think that our little group was probably among the last paying passengers to ride the historic train.

After my uncomfortable night on the stone bench outside the station, I was awakened at 4:30 in the morning by the guard and the arrival of the train, which was made up of one passenger coach, two freight cars, and a baggage car. It was already puffing back and forth with lots of noise and sparks. My fellow travelers and I clambered aboard, and then the train slowly made its way through the outskirts of the sleeping town and into thick brush alongside the river. For years, no attempt had been made to cut back the forest, and so the tropical vegetation growing between the tracks brushed against the underside of the passenger coach as we passed.

The engine, a 1936 German-built wood burner, was rusty but in good condition. It picked up four more wagons and left a load of firewood for an ancient 1908 American-built engine that seemed to still be in running condition. "Put a coat of paint on that, and she'd look nice in any museum," the Englishman remarked, as we stood admiring the tiny thing. Our coach, which was painted baby blue outside and yellow inside, was quite plain, with swing-back wooden seats and no interior lights. A few windows and an entrance step were also missing, and the toilet was simply a hole in the floor with a four legged seat over it, but everything else was very clean. I later noticed that the catwalks on the roofs of the freight wagon were all badly burned by cinders coming from the wood-burning engine and that the passenger coach had no air brakes.

Dawn broke hot and humid, and at about 8:00 we stopped

for breakfast at Villa Murtinho, a tiny Brazilian town with a siding near the river. It was little more than a square of grass with a blue painted church, and a few huts. We bought coffee and bread and butter at one of the buildings and watched men unloading boxes of Brazil nuts from Bolivia from a launch and loading them onto the train. We guessed that they were destined for the Christmas market in North America or perhaps Europe. It is hard to think about Christmas, however, when one is dripping with sweat in the middle of the Amazon jungle.

After a family with a lot of babies and sacks of fruit and nuts joined us, the train chugged gamely into the green tangle of vegetation. Unfortunately, the forest was so thick that I never got even a glimpse of the terrible rapids that were the reason for the railroad. In fact, it was difficult to see anything except the monotonous forest, although there was the occasional huge tree towering over all the others and now and then a brilliantly flowering shrub. We passed a few cattle ranches with shacks raised on stilts, some isolated settlers' cabins, and quite a few open-sided school rooms sitting near the inevitable football fields. We also crossed numerous dark brown streams on sturdy-looking bridges made of riveted iron. Blanketing everything was the smell of rain forest and decaying leaves.

The train went at a walking pace and stopped for everything and everyone. As we picked up small loads of bananas and yucca and dropped off passengers at various small openings in the forest, it became obvious that although the line was obsolete, the settlers in the forest along the river found it very useful. At one point, the track crossed a brand-new road that was wide and surfaced in red gravel and had deep ditches on both sides. This road was a jarring reminder of the modern age that is transforming the ancient rain forest.

It was a very hot and humid day, and whenever the train stopped it became almost unbearable in the passenger coach, even with the missing windows. There was hardly any breeze. The back door was jammed shut, but we could sit on the steps and feel the weeds brushing against our legs and pretend that the slight draft was a real, cooling breeze. Now and then a puff of wood smoke mixed with steam would blow back into our faces. At one stop, we saw two men lazily hacking at the weeds with their machetes. "Now there's a lifetime job if ever I saw one," said one of the New Zealanders.

It was exciting to be riding on the historic train, but at the same time it was an extremely slow and uncomfortable trip. To make it even slower, we stopped for the night at four in the afternoon at Abuna. The conductor said that we would leave at two in the morning and that we should sleep in the passenger coach. The first thing we did was to go down to the river to wash. At this point, the Madeira becomes very narrow although it is still the only drainage for almost all the mighty rivers of northern Bolivia. The yellow river was moving dangerously fast, but we found a safe spot and splashed like children in the tepid but very refreshing water.

The town of Abuna was little more than a dilapidated railroad shed and one row of stores and houses facing the river. After our swim, we discovered that they had moved the engine up to a water tower, so we strolled along until we found a little cafe that served hot soup with bread and rather good coffee. All the prices were twice as high as in Bolivia, so we bought more bread and corned beef and retired back to the railway passenger coach. It was a steamy hot and very boring evening, with not a sound except for the insects and the distant roar of the river as it rushed toward the Amazon and the sea. At sunset, we closed the windows to keep out some of the mosquitoes, but that made the inside of the passenger coach even hotter. I found a place to hang my hammock, but even floating in the air, it was too hot to sleep. Next I tried sitting on the steps or walking about in the dark, swatting insects until I was tired enough to get back into the hammock. At last I covered my head with the mosquito net and fell asleep.

As promised, the train set off again promptly at two in the morning. As we traveled on toward Porto Velho, the ancient track got worse than it had been. Soon my hammock was swinging too crazily to be safe, so I moved to a seat. And a window immediately fell on my head. Fortunately, neither the window nor my head were broken. Every time the train stopped or started, there was a violent chain reaction of jerks, and it seemed that the engine had to stop for water every ten miles or so, so the windows—and much else in the train—were loose and dangerous. At sunrise, when we stopped to load more wood, the engineer dropped by to ask the blond New Zealand girl if she would like to ride in the engine compartment. None of us males was invited.

For breakfast, we tried a green, pimpled fruit as big as a football, which tasted faintly like a sweet onion. We bought it from a lady who also had Brazil nuts for sale, but we had absolutely nothing to crack them open with.

At another stop, they loaded a horse into one of the old wooden freight wagons, and at another we saw wild mango trees with slightly over-ripe, but very juicy fruit lying around. A farmer came over to admire the tall blond New Zealand girl and give her an armful of large avocados. (It was very useful to have an attractive girl along.) That section of the line also seemed to have the largest ants, locusts, and beetles in South America. Even the butterflies were as big as pigeons. The bug collectors whom I had met in the Yungas would have felt as if they were in paradise.

When we came to some rocky hills, a slight upgrade, and a bridge, the train had trouble making the grade. The bad scars on the bridge and the wreckage in the ditch below, clearly showed that other trains had had the same difficulty.

PORTO VELHO

We puffed into the station at Porto Velho with lots of rusty whistle-blowing, but even though the rail yard at Porto Velho was quite big, there was nobody there to admire our arrival. Across the yard sat rows of old railroad stock, including many engines, some built in the late 19th century and all showing signs of having been cannibalized for spare parts. In bright contrast, the yard was also being used to store road-building machinery. There were a score or more bright yellow bulldozers, scrapers, and heavy trucks.

We left our packs with a bored clerk in the station lobby, which was decorated with a model of an early train and a plaque to Colonel G. E. Church, the American who first attempted to build the railroad in about 1867, and wandered uptown in search of a cold drink. Porto Velho was a very old town situated high on a bluff. The roads were all paved, but the town was very run down. Some of its buildings date back to 1914, though there were also some new ones. "It looks just like an old Humphrey Bogart movie," the Englishman said.

The Englishman was anxious to get to Manaus, so we walked down to the river port, which consisted of some fishing boats and three or four floating cafes and stores, and made inquiries. The regular passenger boat was not due for several days, but one captain said he was just about to leave for Manaus. We looked his boat over. It was a small, fairly new boat with a large cabin and very big engine, which, he claimed, would get them to Manaus in three days. I very much doubted this boast, but my pal was excited and quickly made a deal for a "food included" trip. Then he dashed back to the rail yard to get his belongings. There were no mosquitoes at the docks, and there was even a slight breeze, so I lounged about with the New Zealanders and watched the sun set. They had decided to wait for the regular passenger boat. The blond girl had talked the local police into letting her use their shower.

That evening, we went back to the train station, but a Brazilian soldier refused to let us sleep in the passenger coach, so I went looking for a hotel while my friends wandered off into the dark. The taxi drivers I asked were pessimistic about the quality of any of the hotels, but I was hot and sticky, so I chose a hotel that they described as a "luxury hotel." It was one of those large buildings from the days of "grand" hotels, and although it still looked very swank, it was badly run down and not very clean. But the price was reasonable. Also, because I was less persuasive than the blonde New Zealand girl had been with the local constabulary, I needed the hotel's running water, which was nearly hot. Even though there were cockroaches in the shower, there were no flying insects anywhere, and it was a pleasure to shower and shave and rinse out a few clothes. That night, I had an ice cream on the patio and went to sleep in the first real bed I had slept in for nearly three weeks.

The next day was a Sunday. Although I was up and waiting outside the bus office by 6:00, nobody was there and there was no sign of a bus. When the office eventually opened, about 9:00, the clerk said there would not be a bus until noon. It required additional conversation, but he eventually admitted that there was another bus line just down the road. Hearing this, I smiled nicely and said in English that I hoped he would catch the pox, and then I hurried to the other bus line just in time to catch their daily bus to Guajara-mirim. The bus was not crowded, and I hoped there would be no problems because I had only enough Brazilian money to pay the ferry back to Bolivia.

The road was wide and new and straight, but it was also a sea of bright red mud and the ditches along the sides were full of water. A couple of the bridges were unfinished, but the road was raised above the surrounding land, and the driver made good time. The road builders had cut right through virgin forest, and I saw cabins in tiny clearings scattered through the tangle of vegetation. We stopped anywhere for anybody, and soon the floor of the bus was thick with mud. It was stifling in the bus, and only the little breeze coming through the windows made life bearable. I began to dread the constant stops as, true to form, the bus overheated and the driver had to stop a couple of times to fill the radiator with muddy water from the ditch.

Chapter18: The Rubber Forest

We arrived back in Guayaramerín in the middle of the afternoon. In six hours, the bus had traveled what had taken two days on the train. No matter. I was very happy that I had taken that historical train. Now I made straight for the ferry and the sleepy little town of Guayaramerín, back in Bolivia. It looked quite attractive after Porto Velho. A pile of balls of rubber on the river bank reminded me of my next task, getting to Cachuela Esperanza, the home of Nicholas Suarez, Bolivia's most famous rubber baron.

The boat on which I had sailed down the Rio Chaparé was now empty and deserted, so I moved my things to a little hotel off the plaza. After a couple of glasses of the local *chicha*, which is rather sweet and almost non-alcoholic, I started asking about buses to Riberalta. I could hardly believe my luck when the wife of the manager of the hotel, who was sitting in the shade, said, "You know, you might like to visit Cachuela Esperanza while you are here. My husband is going there in his truck tomorrow." I celebrated this invitation by dining on good barbecue with yucca and a banana dessert washed down with glasses of fruit punch. Then I sat in the plaza and watched the Sunday *paseo*, where all the town seemed to be present, and all the women in their Sunday best. Even the boys were all dressed up, despite the sticky heat. I saw a carnival huckster selling something, children crowding into the little movie theater, people reading public notices on a bulletin board in the middle of the road, the flickering yellow light cast by the old glass oil lamps, huge moths and flying ants, and gracefully balanced female passengers riding sidesaddle on motorcycle taxis. It was a pleasant evening.

CACHUELA ESPERANZA

I was up bright and early the next morning and walked to the corner where the pickup truck I had been told about was waiting. It was loaded with sacks of rice, but when I climbed up onto the cargo to sit beside half a dozen other passengers, the driver invited me to sit in the cab. We set off, and on the edge of town we picked up an American wearing shorts who turned out to be a Maryknoll priest who was on his way to Cachuela to try to persuade the farmers to set up an agricultural co-operative. As we talked, I got the impression that he was bracing himself for an uphill struggle.

Even though the road had been repaired recently, the rain had already washed out sections of it, including a bridge a group of soldiers were trying to fix. But the driver was cheerful. "Before the road was built," he said, "it used to take six hours to go just forty kilometers to Cachuela." Twice we hit stretches so bad that everybody had to get out and push. About halfway along, there was a pontoon ferry across a small river of dark, clear water, and here and there in the forest I saw very tall trees in flower with a clear space around the base. The priest pointed to one and said, "Brazil nut tree. Most Brazil nuts come from Bolivia," he added with a smile, "just like Panama hats come from Ecuador." Then he said,

"That's why they haven't been cut down by the loggers. This region often earns more money from nuts than from rubber".

There were one or two open patches as we went along, but mostly the road ran through thick rain forest. I saw no game and few birds, but we came upon two or three snakes at the side of the road, and the driver swerved to try and crush them. "That's a nasty one," he said in Spanish, and he told me what it was, but I no longer remember the name.

Then, quite suddenly, we were out of the forest and in another very small town. It was, at last, Cachuela Esperanza. When we stopped at a store, the priest pointed to some large sheds and said, "You'd be bored stiff at my meeting. Go over to the nut factory and take a look around. They'll be glad to see you. They don't get many visitors."

The Brazil nut factory was a complete surprise. I had come to visit the remains, and perhaps the ruins, of a town built in the heart of the jungle by a famous rubber baron. Instead, I found a modern, efficient factory producing nuts for export. It was quite a large operation, and I was impressed. Down the middle of the room were rows of benches where local women, eager to earn some money, were expertly cracking the hard nuts with small presses. "They must not damage the nuts," my guide explained. When I tried my hand, I quickly learned that it was not as easy as it looked. The perfect nuts went into one tray, the damaged ones, into another, and the shells went onto the red-tiled floor, where some men carefully swept them up. It was airy and relatively cool in the shed.

My guide next took me to the furnace room, where the shells

were used as fuel for the ovens that baked the nuts. "Otherwise," said my guide, "they go moldy very quickly." Next, he took me to the sorting room, where the nuts were graded into half a dozen sizes by the sorting machine, weighed, and packed in plastic bags as sharp-eyed women picked out damaged or defective nuts. "Nothing is wasted here," I was told. Then we went to a room where the rejected nuts were being pressed for their oil and the residue was being sacked for cattle food. All through the building there was the semi-sweet smell of crushed nuts. Before we left the main building, my guide took me to a storage room and lifted up a loose floorboard. "Take a look," he said, and I kneeled down and peered under the raised floor. In the faint light, I could see a forest of little green plants. It was hundreds of baby Brazil nut trees growing from nuts that had fallen between the floorboards, all trying valiantly to grow in the soft, damp earth. "Don't worry," my guide said. "Nut trees like the sun. That's why they grow so tall. These will all die off before they can grow big enough to lift the factory very high into the sky."

The plastic bags of nuts were packed into cardboard cartons, which then went into wooden boxes made from a local hardwood. I gathered that the nut packing plant had a contract with a nearby sawmill for a steady supply of the boxes, which were made of thin but strong wood, neatly cut and finished and quite attractive.

The hotel was a row of low buildings with verandas facing the river. Just across the dirt road, I could see the tangle of rocks and the boiling, muddy waters of the rapids where the huge river narrows and where in 1881 Nicholas Suarez created a portage point and the headquarters for a rubber empire that at one time covered 16,000,000 acres of prime rubber forest. The far side of the river was still virgin rain forest.

The hotel had not had a customer for a long time, and nobody could find a key to the padlock on my room, so the manager finally just took a crowbar and tore it off. The room contained an antique iron bedstead with four posts and iron rails to hold a mosquito net. There was an ancient oil lamp next to the plastic water jug, and high up on the walls was a row of large hooks for hanging hammocks. The manager produced clean sheets and a towel and fresh water from the well, "The river water is too muddy to drink," he explained. He also told me how to find the town's only restaurant. Everybody in Cachuela Esperanza was very friendly and curious about this Canadian who was interested in their little town.

At the little restaurant, I had a steak for lunch. Soon the priest dropped in to chat, followed by a small crowd of curious children. One bunch of small boys was particularly polite and eager to show me around. They proved to know more about the town than many of the adults. They also asked me a lot of questions. The priest was quietly proud of the Brazil nut factory and told me more about the trees. "They're widely scattered," he said, "and collecting the nuts is hard work. It's also very dangerous." He reached out to a shelf nearby and picked up a large black ball lying on it. "This is the nut," he said. "When it drops, it breaks open and all the Brazil nuts fall out. Only thing is, one of these things hitting you on the head can kill you. The locals call it the 'widow maker,' but the pickers still refuse to wear hard hats." He shook his head. "Also, lots of animals like to eat the nuts, so they hang out around the trees, and snakes like to eat the animals, so they hang around the trees, too. All in all, picking nuts is more dangerous than collecting rubber."

After this conversation, the boys began their tour of Cachuela Esperanza. First, they took me to the river bank, where a row of mango trees had dropped dozens of juicy fruits. Some cows were eating them and spitting out the big seeds, which was fun to watch until a sailor riding bareback on a horse chased them back to their corral. In the middle of town was a short concrete sidewalk with iron benches that led to the General Pando Theater. The theater was locked and boarded up, but the boys assured me that on some weekends movies were shown there. There were old office buildings, now used by the military, and at a store I bought some hand-rolled cigarettes made from local tobacco and stuffed into an old Brazilian packet. The town was very quiet and the air was filled with the smell of mangos and rain-soaked vegetation. We next walked to a large, rather elegant building with a sign that said *Casino*. It was now a tumble-down, weed-covered army barracks, where the boys threw sticks at birds' nests hanging from a tree.

Then we walked over an exposed slab of rock to the school that had once claimed to be the finest school in Bolivia, with twenty classrooms and imported teachers. The stone walls were still solid looking, and the woodwork had been carefully restored, but there were generations of scribbles on the walls and the building was tightly locked and shuttered. There were iron gates to the overgrown school yard, but no fence. Nearby was the hospital which in the 1930s had claimed to be the best hospital in Bolivia, with English and French doctors who specialized in tropical diseases. It was now an army barracks where two soldiers were trying to milk a very unwilling cow but soon gave up. Here and there, we could see evidence that somebody had attacked the encroaching jungle with a machete.

This little company town, which had been carefully laid out by Nicholas Suarez in the very heart of the South American rain forest, once housed more than 2,000 employees. It was situated on a stony outcrop above the flood waters of the Rio Beni, and the buildings had been well constructed with solid timbers and corrugated iron roofs on a stone or concrete base, and the major buildings were stuccoed brick. Many of the roofs had once had Victorian trim in lead or tin and red-tiled verandas, and the wood had been painted white or blue-gray. They had been built to last, but the forest was gradually creeping back.

Our next stop was a white marble bust of Suarez, the richest and most powerful of all the rubber barons, with his huge mustaches. He looked lonely in the scorching sun. We also went to the tomb where he and his second wife and two children are buried. There was a fence with an iron gate, and it was very picturesque but badly overgrown. The boys warned me that there was a large hornets' nest in the weeds. On a small knoll nearby there was a tiny chapel, square and cool and quite elaborate, with the date 1909 on one of the crosses. This was the only place we saw that was not overgrown with weeds.

THE GHOST TRAIN

Upstream from the town's theater was a row of abandoned offices and a small bridge that divided the factories from the offices and living area. There were corner seats on the bridge and an arch proclaiming "Welcome." Looking more closely at the bridge, I saw that it was a railroad bridge. It was well known that Suarez had built a short railroad at Cachuela Esperanza years before the Mamoré railroad was finished, so I looked around for the rails. But I found nothing, and the boys knew nothing about a railroad track. There were large sheds, all tightly padlocked, and when we peeked through the crack between the doors, we could see rusting machinery and dust covered work benches inside. The river road ended at a cabin labeled *Customs*, but it, too, was locked.

After we ate some juicy mangos, the boys became bored and dashed off to swim in the river, but not before they had dragged their little brothers into the crowd and asked me to take a group photo of them. The kids swam in the pools between the rocks, where some women were washing clothes, and I continued my hunt for the missing railroad. At the other end of the road along the river, below the rapids, there was a small cove where I watched some men loading boxes of nuts onto a launch. It could have been the same launch I had seen in Brazil unloading nuts onto the train. There was a shallow beach, but the surf from the rapids was quite high and the men had to walk through it to carry the wooden boxes out to the launch. To keep the boxes dry, they were carrying them on their heads.

The town ended right there, and it looked to me like a logical place for a railroad terminus, so I started to poke into the weeds and encroaching forest. It took about an hour, but eventually I found traces of old wooden railroad ties and followed them up river through a little cutting and an embankment and onto the road. The track must have run right past my hotel room, between the buildings and the river, I followed it across the bridge with its "Welcome" arch all the way up to the old customs post, which was near a small cove above the rapids. All together, the little railroad would have been a little more than a mile long.

Having found the track, I was now eager to find traces of the engine that rode on those rails. But nobody seemed to know anything about a steam engine. Then a lady in the store suddenly said, "But of course! It's in the last shed." Joined by two of the boys, I hurried back to the shed, and while the boys poked hopelessly at the big padlock, I strained to peer through the filthy windows. There, sitting alone in the middle of the gloomy building, was the ghost of a very small and very old steam engine.

I had seen enough now for one day, and so I went back to my room to change my sweat-soaked shirt and wash my face. Feeling cleaner, I walked over to the riverside monument to Esperanza, the first wife of Nicholas Suarez. This monument was only a simple, broken marble column, symbolizing a life cut short. It was set above the "Rapids of Hope" (the English meaning of Cachuela Esperanza) and surrounded by an iron fence, but I could see no names or dates, as creeping vines had covered the base and I did not dare go closer for fear of snakes in the heavy weeds. I thought it was very beautiful and yet very sad.

At the fly infested bar behind the nut factory, where I went for a well-deserved *chicha*, I met a young man and his wife. He was of

Yugoslav descent and was a mining engineer studying the alluvial deposits up and down the great rivers that have for thousands of years been eroding the mighty Andes. He insisted that there was plenty of tin in the river as well as a great variety of other valuable minerals. They were a very interesting couple, and we moved to their house, where we snacked on corn pancakes and our discussion turned to the wide variety of poisonous snakes that like to hide along the edges of rivers where he had to work. He insisted that the *sucuru*, or bushmaster, was the worst of the lot and said there were plenty of them around Cachuela. He also warned me that there was a little black demon that liked to live among the houses, and his wife listed all the local children that had been bitten while playing around the village.

By the time I was ready to leave them, I was more than a little anxious about walking back to my room in the dark, so they loaned me a flashlight. It helped immensely as I hurried back to my room, crouched over and suspicious of every twig or branch lying on the path and ready to run at the slightest movement in the undergrowth. When I got there, the large room looked dangerous in the dark, so I walked around shining the flashlight on all the gaps in the floor boards and all the knot holes in the woodwork and thinking of the open space under the building, a space choked with vegetation. I decided I would have supper before going to bed.

The lady at the restaurant was glad to see me, as her son had caught two fish that afternoon and she had prepared one just for me. The baked fish, along with rice and fried banana, was delicious. I took my time eating it and washed it down with a very refreshing drink made from palm nuts. I still was not in the mood to go to bed, so I engaged my hostess in conversation. We talked about floods and the weather until she had to close the restaurant and I had to pick up the flash light and leave. On the veranda of the hotel, I met the manager, who was in the mood to talk. He was very up to date about things going on in La Paz, and we discussed world politics until he too decided to go to bed.

Back in my room again, I checked every nook and corner and even shone the light under the bed sheets, where I found the mattress cover was made from old Pillsbury flour sacks. Then I turned the lamp up high, kept my boots on, and spent several hours catching up on my notes. At one point, I thought that I heard slithering at the door but decided that it was only rats in the walls. A bit later, I was horribly startled when there were a couple of loud thumps on the roof. I decided that it was mangoes falling from the tree. A tropical night can be noisy, and this night every little sound set my hair on end. Eventually, of course, I had to get some sleep. I slept with the flashlight beside my pillow and my boots on the floor alongside the bed, where I could grab them in a hurry. A passing storm had cooled the air nicely, and the moment my head touched the pillow I was fast asleep.

When I awoke next morning, without any snakes in my bed or in my boots, the first thing I saw was the row of hammock hooks on the wall. I could have hung the hammock and slept suspended above and away from visiting snakes or anything else! The one time the hammock would really have been useful, I had forgotten to use it. To make matters worse, in my foolish worry about snakes, I had also forgotten to hang the mosquito net.

The river had risen during the night. I could hear the dark

waters crashing loudly over the rapids, carrying uprooted trees and clumps of vegetation. While I was eating breakfast, my young friends turned up with marvelous news. One of them had obtained the key to the locomotive shed from the son of the military commander. We went there immediately.

The little, four-wheeled engine, sitting all alone in the middle of the shed, seemed to be in good condition. It had a huge spark-catcher chimney, and somebody had stuck an extra pipe from the chimney to a hole in the roof of the shed to vent the smoke. A brass panel had the date 1900 on it, but the maker's name was worn away. The ashes in the firebox were relatively new, and one boy reported that his father had said, "A few years ago, somebody rigged it up to turn an electrical generator, and we had lights all over the place for hours until the generator blew up."

I was very excited to have actually seen this engine that the great rubber baron had brought across the Atlantic and up the Amazon and the Madeira rivers, where it had to be dragged around the rapids, then floated up the Madre de Dios to this spot in the jungle, just to spend its life running back and forth one short mile carrying balls of rubber.

I treated all the boys to soft drinks in the café, and while we were celebrating, the teenage son of the commander turned up with a message from his father that I could join him for a visit to the house that Suarez had built and he could practice his English at the same time. His English was fairly good. While we walked, he explained that the casino had originally been the house built for Suarez's first wife. He built another house for his second wife.

Standing in the overgrown garden, I saw a large, but not

ostentatiously large, house of two stories with five iron balconies. It seemed to have a lot of rooms. It was very run down now, but it had been well built with stone and brick and cement stucco. "They say that everything was brought from Europe or America," my guide explained. "Even the bricks and the cement. Even the nails and the paint." The house had a fancy staircase at the entrance, and the walls had once been painted in pastel colors. The woodwork was fine quality and mostly still there, as were the heavy paneled doors with their solid brass knobs.

The door was not locked, so we went in. By modern standards the rooms of this grand house were small, but there were a lot of them and they were all wired for electric lighting. The wiring was the old, exposed, two-wire system on ceramic insulators with bulky, heavy ceramic switches. My guide did not know if Suarez had a generator or if the electricity was added later. The rooms were bare now, of course, so there was nothing much to see except the view from the windows. For some reason, we could not visit the kitchen or the bathrooms, but what I saw was enough. I was happy to have seen the house that Nicholas Suarez, one of the richest of the Rubber Barons, had built in this isolated place.

Back in the café, I met a Frenchman who worked for a mineral exploration company. He said that the road to Riberalta was impassable, but there was a jeep going back to Guayaramerín that afternoon, so I sat on the veranda overlooking the monument to Esperanza and the rapids named after her and relaxed. I had accomplished almost everything I had set out to do in this journey through Bolivia. I had visited all the five corners of this vast and intriguing land, and now it was time to go home. It was also extremely important that I get back up onto the *altiplano* before the rains arrived and brought all transportation to a halt.

Around noon, I strolled up to the cafe to get a cup of coffee before boarding the jeep and found that it had gone. "It was full, so they left," explained the lady. "But I am sure there will be another one this afternoon," she added cheerfully.

There wasn't. I spent all that afternoon sitting on an antique iron bench, waiting and worrying. A man with a bundle of wild pigskins on his back wandered up and spent an hour selling a few of the hides to the store, one or two women hurried by on their way to the nut factory, a small turtle peeked shyly out of some bushes then retreated, and a sudden wind storm swept through, tearing fruit from the mango tree and then vanishing as quickly as it came. Then an old man came by and explained that as there was a fiesta in Guayaramerín, nobody would be coming to Cachuela today.

At sunset, I retreated to the hotel, where I watched an enormous moon rise over the river and listened to the night chorus. Two of the boys offered to make supper. After considerable noise in the kitchen, they produced some delicious cocoa and chunks of bread and hard cheese. I had returned the flashlight but I did not need it now. I had more important things to worry about than snakes.

Next morning, the hotel manager assured me there would be a truck. I was at the corner long before it was due to arrive. After an hour I heard it and tracked it down to behind the nut factory. I climbed aboard before its cargo was even emptied. I was not going to miss this one. When we stopped at the café, a large crowd clambered aboard, and then we had to wait for an hour for the bandmaster with some drums and saxophones that he was taking back to Guayaramerín. It was a rough but uneventful ride. I started off sitting on my pack, but that was too uncomfortable and I soon stood up. The army was still patching the road, and we saw a very large snake, but the driver was fast and skillful and we soon arrived in Guayaramerín,.

I met the riverboat captain again in the plaza. He was looking very dapper, with dark glasses and shiny shoes and a neatly trimmed mustache, and, as usual, he was eyeing the passing girls. He was horrified at the prices I was paying for hotels when I could be sleeping on his boat. It had been moved half a mile upriver to a boat yard to have its propeller shaft fixed. I wanted to see some boat building, so I took my gear back to the boat. The yard was just a little bay on the river with the remains of a very old paddle steamer lying in the mud. The men were working half in and half out of the water. I was surprised not only at the sizes of some of the boats they were building but also at the complete lack of power tools. Everything was being done by hand. I watched two men using a long saw to cut planks over a saw pit. The man underneath was covered in sawdust, which washed down his body in rivulets of sweat. On the bank, the blacksmith worked his anvil in the blazing sun near a fire in an oil barrel. He used a foot operated leather bellows.

I was getting a haircut that afternoon when a plainclothes Bolivian policeman came in and demanded to know why I had not checked in when I returned from Porto Velho. I explained that I had checked with immigration, but he insisted that I should also have checked in with the police. He took pages of notes and ordered me to get my passport stamped. *Pronto!* So I tried to obey. But the clerk could not find the rubber stamp. He sent me to the mayor's office, where another clerk apologized profusely and told me not to worry about it. I never saw the policeman again.

Just for fun, I took a motorbike taxi out to the small, but very modern radio station, where a charming young secretary in a slinky dress gave me a brief tour. Then I took another motorbike taxi to the offices of the mineral exploration company where the Frenchman worked. I found him in an office with two large fans. He was only too glad to sit and chat about his explorations. He had spent about twenty years in the rain forests of Africa and South America and had a wealth of stories to tell. Hearing that I was on my way home, he advised me not to wait for a plane in Guayaramerín, but to go to Riberalta, where air service was more reliable.

On my way back to the boat in the dark after supper, I stumbled upon the slaughter house where, in the yellow light of oil lamps, men were stripping the hides from the carcasses hanging from wooden hooks. The foreman explained that they could get forty pesos for each hide once it was salted. Hides must be heavily salted to preserve them, and without the salt they stink. But the salt came from the *altiplano*, and it cost them about twenty pesos per hide. Salt from Brazil was even more expensive. At the boatyard, a fire-breathing, sword-swallowing circus huckster with a wooden dummy was selling washing detergent and scented soap to a small crowd. I stood for a while and watched a gaggle of small children squatting on the ground, their eyes and mouths wide open as they stared in awe at the fast-talking salesman. But I couldn't watch for long. I had a bus the catch the next day. I went on my way back to the riverboat.

RIBERALTA

It was a cold, damp night on the Rio Guapore, so I used the mosquito net for a blanket. The morning dawned hot and humid. After I thanked the captain for his generosity and said goodbye to the crew, I contracted with a wheelbarrow porter to take my belongings to the main plaza in Guayaramerín. It was just too humid to carry anything. The bus, which turned up at 9:30, was just a mini bus with no knee room and seats in the aisle. And it was packed. The partially rebuilt road we were traveling on had been ruined by the rain and was in terrible condition, and at the first bridge we came to, all the passengers had to walk across while the bus splashed through the muddy river. The bridge across the next river was also too weak to take the load, so we walked across and carried our luggage while the empty bus crawled slowly behind us to the other side. Then we came to a third river, which had a ferry, only to find the ferry pulled up out of the water. For a third time, we unloaded all of our luggage. We were paddled across this little river by the bus driver and some of the men, in small groups, only to sit in the steaming shade and wait for another bus to come from Riberalta to rescue us. Strangely, there were no mosquitoes just there. Some of the men and boys went for a swim in the dark brown water. The rest of the trip to Riberalta was a slithering, sliding ride through axle-deep mud in a hot and overcrowded bus through thick rain forest. It was no fun at all.

Riberalta, which is in northern Bolivia where the Madre de Dios River joins the Beni River, was a fairly large town of wide avenues and stuccoed houses with red brick sidewalks and white-washed walls along the wide avenues. One side of the plaza was tiled, and the mayor's office was two stories high. Almost every building had columned verandas to offer some shade from the blazing sun. I noticed that although there were jeeps and trucks, there were no passenger cars and the only taxis were motorbike. I also saw wheelbarrow porters and a couple of ox carts with large, solid wood wheels. A fellow passenger suggested a reasonably priced *pension*, and so I followed him there. It was a very open building with a big patio around a brick lined well. I shared an airy room with another male guest. The toilet flushed properly, the shower worked nicely, and on the patio, behind the chrome and plastic bar stood three huge refrigerators.

After a shower, I headed for the airline office, but it was closed for *siesta*, so I had to wait an hour in a corner bar, where I found locally made soft drinks that tasted better than the imported Brazilian beer. Back at the airline office, the lady was very helpful. She warned me against trying to travel to La Paz through Cobija because one flight had already been cancelled due to heavy rain and Cobija was now down to only two flights per week.

I wanted to go back to Oruro before I left Bolivia, if only to thank Ramiro and Barbara for all their kindness, so I booked a seat on the next flight to Cochabamba. That meant I had to wait two more days in one of the hottest and most humid places I had ever been on all my travels on five continents.

Everywhere I went in my travels, I always found the local bookshops and spent time browsing the shelves. Even quite small towns will often have a bookshop whose managers are invariably helpful. In Gayaramerín, for example, I had looked for books about Nicholas Suarez, and the Acre conflict with Brazil at the end of the

19th century, but found very little, so I tried again in Riberalta. The first shop I came to was a Baptist bookshop run by a German who had never heard of Nicholas Suarez. At the next place, where the manager seemed to know everybody in town who owned a book, he made a few phone calls, then directed me to the city hall and the mayor's office.

I have often wondered if the mayor of a small town in the States or Canada or the UK would be as gracious as the mayor of Riberalta was when I wandered in and started talking about old books. The mayor was a knowledgeable woman who spoke English much better than I spoke Spanish. She asked some searching questions about my travels in Bolivia and my interest in Suarez, then made a phone call and her secretary soon came in with an old, worm eaten, copy of the book about the Acre war written by Suarez himself. It was a priceless book and it even had a good map. Then I was ushered upstairs to a large, cool room with a comfortable armchair under a picture of Suarez. I settled in and started reading the book. I was soon so lost in it that I lost all track of time. When it came time to close the offices, the mayor allowed me to borrow the book for as long as I was in town.

To stretch my legs that evening, I walked down to the river and watched the sun set over the junction of the Madre de Dios and Beni rivers. The combined rivers at this point are nearly a mile wide, and the far bank looked like virgin rain forest. It was probably here at the turn of the 20th century that the famous Colonel Percy Harrison Fawcett met with General Pando, the explorer and ex-president of Bolivia. Jose Manuel Pando Solares was one of the better, more liberal presidents of Bolivia. Although he was born on the *altiplano*, he took a great interest in the humid rain forests and acquired a reputation as an explorer in that region. He was president during the Acre War of 1903 and actively encouraged exploration and settlement in the Madre de Dios and Beni regions. He was assassinated by political rivals in 1917, and the northernmost department of Bolivia is named Pando after him. There was a bust of Suarez on a short pillar on the cliff overlooking the river, and along the riverbank below was a busy river port with boatyards and dozens of boats of all sizes. It was soon too dark, however, for me to go down and look around.

Like all tropical towns, the almost empty daytime streets of Riberalta suddenly blossomed with people after sunset. There was an Argentine movie at one theater and a Mexican movie at another, both being announced by a motorbike speaker. I looked through the door where the Mexican movie was playing and glimpsed wooden seats and four large electric fans. I decided not to see a movie, but instead wandered on to a little bandstand where an army band was playing. The soldier-musicians, sweating in their wool uniforms designed for the cold *altiplano*, were playing lively Bolivian tunes in the Andean style that the crowd enjoyed. The conductor stood tapping his baton against his side (possibly keeping time) and from time to time leaned over the iron railing to chat with pretty girls who walked by. He only turned to face the band for the last couple of notes of any song, and he let them start a new song when they pleased. They had obviously played the same tunes countless times, and he was not really needed at all, but it was entertaining to see him pack his baton into his brief case and walk away halfway through the last song.

I was awakened promptly at six by a bugle coming from the army barracks directly across the road. The landlady suggested that I visit an experimental rubber tree plantation, so I had a light breakfast and found a motorbike taxi for an unstable but refreshingly cool ride. The farm got many foreign visitors, so they had printed information sheets in a number of languages and my guide was also eager to answer questions. The most obvious question was, "Why are the trees not in plantations as they are in the Far East?" The trees grown on the Malay Peninsula, my guide said, came from seeds and plants smuggled out of Brazil in the 19th century. In South America, when rubber trees grow close together, they suffer from a number of diseases and fungi that are rampant in the surrounding forest and spread quickly through the rubber trees. The Malay farmers, with their slightly different climate, soil, and native vegetation, can better control the health of their trees, so they plant them in neat rows. The experimental plantation in Riberalta has been for years trying to solve this major disease problem. As we walked through groves ranging from seedlings to mature trees, my guide described the various diseases and how the scientists were trying to combat them. He added that a rainfall of fifty inches per year, plus the heat and extraordinary humidity did not help with disease control. Everybody I spoke to was optimistic, however, and quite sure that one day there would be rubber plantations in Bolivia. "Automobile tires are no longer made of rubber, and plastics have replaced rubber in many industries, but there will always be a demand for pure, natural rubber," I was assured. "In fact, the demand is growing and the *seringueiro* [rubber tapper] can make a good living if he works hard."

Because none of the trees at the experimental farm were being tapped for rubber, it was some years later before I saw a *seringuero* actually tapping a rubber tree. I was in Santarém, on the lower Amazon in Brazil, with a group of English tourists. Our little bus took us miles up a road that paralleled the Tapajós River, then deep into the forest to a cluster of buildings, where we walked even further into the forest to a mature rubber tree, the trunk of which was deeply scarred by dozens of diagonal cuts. The *seringuero* carefully made another small cut and hung a tin cup on a wooden peg in the tree. I was surprised at just how much white sap oozed out of the little cut. Our guide explained that the sap was mostly water and that the constant cutting did not damage the tree. The tree we were looking at was probably thirty years old, and the nearest healthy tree was at least one hundred meters deeper into the forest. Later, we saw how the sap was made into the traditional large ball by heating it on a stick over an open fire.

It was on the Tapajós River, about 100 miles from Santarém, that Henry Ford built Fordlandia in1928. On 2.5 million acres of rain forest, he tried to create a giant rubber plantation complete with a modern town and an electric power plant. Millions of dollars were spent, and Ford, who never actually visited his town, poured a great deal of energy into the project. But it was a complete and utter failure and never produced any rubber. When we asked the guide about Fordlandia, he told us that nothing remained. The forest had reclaimed everything, and even the name had disappeared from the maps.

Along with rubber, the farm was also experimenting with cacao and tea. I saw plots devoted to these plants, and my guide was equally confident that, given enough funding by the government, Bolivia could one day be self-sufficient in rubber, cacao, and tea and even have a surplus for export. He was very enthusiastic, and we spent some time in the laboratories and in sunny rooms filled with trays of seedlings. He also showed me a small factory being built next to the farm. It was going to process rubber and, perhaps in the near future, also cocoa and tea.

Back at the pension, I showered again and then sat in the patio to finish the book about Suarez that I had borrowed. I also drew rough copies of the maps. When I returned the book, the mayor was glad that I had seen the experimental farm and she suggested that I might like to talk to *los linguisticos* at the Summer Institute of Linguistics, where they were recording and preserving the various Indian languages. One of the scholars there showed me books written in a variety of languages. The Institute seemed to be a very efficient organization that used the latest linguistic techniques. The scholar said they also used light planes for transport and mentioned that they often sent a plane to Santa Cruz or La Paz. There was, he added, one due tomorrow morning. And there was the faint possibility that there might be room for an extra passenger.

Back at the river, I saw boats being loaded and unloaded. Ship builders were busy, too, so I spent the afternoon watching. One of the boats was quite different from the others. Most riverboats are flat bottomed and quite shallow, but for this boat, the builders were using a thirty-foot dug-out canoe as the keel. Of course they had no blueprints or plans and could not show me what it would look like when finished. The most interesting boat I saw that afternoon was an old wood-burner with a tall funnel and a huge black boiler that had the date 1909 on it. There was a Swiss flag painted on the funnel, which reminded me that the House of Seiler was a Swiss trading company that had founded the town of Riberalta in the early days of the rubber boom. The company's headquarters were still in Riberalta. The old riverboat, which was loaded with balls of rubber and sacks of nuts, looked like she still had plenty of good years ahead of her.

That evening, I found a plastic table outside a cafe decorated entirely with old calendars and sampled a wide selection of interesting soft drinks made from locally grown fruit. A Maryknoll priest I had met in Gayaramerín joined me, and we discussed the history of the area. When I commented on the generous width of the main avenue, he said, "That was going to be a railway. When they built the Mamoré railway and the Brazilians promised to build a bridge across to Gayaramerín, the Bolivian government said that they would build a railroad from La Paz to link up with it. It was a marvelous idea. Riberalta planned for the line to run right through the middle of the town. But, as you know, the whole thing collapsed. The bridge was never built. La Paz never had the money to build the railway, and Riberalta now has a nice wide avenue." He sat back and smiled. "Frankly," he added, "I doubt if anybody could build a railroad through that country. They'll be lucky if they ever finish the road." Then he shook my hand and said, "Drop around for dinner tomorrow night. Anybody will tell you where we are."

I was packed and ready to go at 8:30 the next morning, but the airline office said that there would be no plane that day. I met one of the priests, however, and he told me that he had been on the mission radio and there would be a plane next day. He was going to Cochabamba himself. I had seen all that was worth seeing in Riberalta, so I went back to the river and the boats. The river was noticeably higher and moving faster, and there were gray clouds far to the east. Strolling along the river bank, I ran across a metal shop downriver and watched men riveting metal plates the old way, with iron rivets heated red-hot in a furnace. They inserted the red-hot rivets into the holes with tongs, then beat them into shape with huge hammers before they cooled and shrank. That is one of the hottest jobs in industry, and these men were doing it out under the blazing sun. As I stared across the wide Rio Beni, I found it hard to remember that this was the same small mountain river that I had seen in Coroico in the Yungas and the road that the priest had talked about was the same road that ran down to Caranavi. They all seemed so far away.

Then an extraordinary sight drifted into view. It looked like a floating village, but it was actually a huge log raft, about sixty feet long and covered with palm thatch shelters, plus pigs, chickens, people, and baskets of fruit and stems of bananas. There was a very large steering oar at each end, and soon the raft slowly swung toward the shore and beached itself. A man in the crowd that had gathered to watch told me it was a *calappa* from far up the Rio Beni. "It is probably from Reyes," he added. "About fourteen days away. Very damp!" I further learned that the logs the raft was made of, an insect-proof, tropical hardwood, would be sold in Riberalta and the various families who had joined in the enterprise would take more ordinary riverboats back home. "Sometimes a big *calappa* takes a year of hard work," my informant told me, "and sometimes they break up or get stuck on a sandbar. It is a gamble. But is that not how you get rich?" he asked. Compared to the gambling I have seen in Las Vegas, riding a *calappa* would be vastly more exciting.

Further along, I came across the House of Seiler. It had real concrete steps down to the water and a small capstan on the cliff top with a little set of lines so that heavy cargo could be hauled up to the warehouses. There was also a small railroad track running down the bluff. Their riverboats looked ship-shape and quite smart, but by now it was getting too hot to do any more touring, so I headed back to the *pension* where I spent the *siesta* chatting with a big man in a white tropical suit who showed me some ore samples and claimed they were tin. He insisted that the Brazilians were dredging tin in Porto Velho, but I had been there and seen no sign of it, nor heard anything.

As we were talking, a baby started to cry. The man said, "This is not a good climate for children. The death rate is too high for the little ones. But, if they get to be six years old, then they will live." As he started listing all the various diseases that a child could get, I found this too depressing, so I made an excuse and walked up to the market, where I found why there were so few cafes in town, There were food stalls everywhere, and the selection was excellent.

Among the various offerings were some foods I did not recognize. One lady was frying things about as big as my thumb that could have been anything. As I was in an adventurous mood, I tried a small plateful. They were crisp on the outside, but quite soft and tender on the inside, and they had a faintly sweetish flavor. When I asked what they were, she could only give me the local name, though she did make clear that they came from old trees in the forest. My guess is that they were some type of insect larvae, or perhaps a grub or caterpillar. Another lady was frying what looked like shrimp. When I bought a small plateful, she showed me how to remove the tough outer shell. What I was eating was apparently a type of locust or grasshopper. These tasty appetizers heightened my appetite, so next I had a large bowl of meat stew that the lady assured me was genuine capybara. It was heavily spiced and tasted a little like rabbit.

While I was nibbling on a coconut pastry for desert, I was greeted by the elderly gentleman who had donated the old Suarez book to the mayor's office. He told me he had known Suarez. We sat down together and drank coffee Brazilian style, black and loaded with sugar in tiny cups, while he told me stories of the old days in Cachuela Esperanza.

At sunset, I was picked up at the *pension* by a priest wearing khaki shorts and driving a motorbike and taken out to their mission. This was a fairly large complex that included a convent, a hospital, and a school. I saw two jeeps parked outside. There were half a dozen missionaries in casual clothing, and one of them described the very up-to-date radio system he operated and told me who he talked to in the United States. These missionaries were mostly Americans, some of whom had been in Bolivia for years and liked it so much that they were not interested in a transfer back to North America.

At supper, the conversation was almost entirely about the rapidly disappearing wild life. They said that while the alligators were getting smaller and scarcer each year, the snakes were getting bigger. A twenty-foot anaconda was no longer unusual. I also heard some slightly exaggerated stories of domestic animals being swallowed by anacondas. Then they told me about all the children they had known who had been bitten by poisonous snakes, and a couple of the older missionaries traded stories of the days when jaguars were big and roamed the streets of Riberalta after dark. One had been shot right outside the hospital. Back in Corumba, I had seen photos posted in the windows of shops that sold guns and hunting equipment and had noticed that the old and faded photos showed very large jaguars, but as the photos got more recent, the jaguars got smaller. One of the younger priests, who had been in Bolivia only about two years, said that he had never actually seen a live jaguar.

When I brought up the subject of missionaries, they rattled off a long list of sects from both North America and Europe that had missions in the Beni, a list that even included a group of Norwegians from across the river. "There are barely 10,000 people in the whole territory," somebody said, "so I guess that averages out to half a person per missionary. Most of them are just wasting their time and money. But some of them, like the medical ones, are very useful. The *linguisticos* really do a fine job with the languages thing, but I wonder if what they do has any real value. Think about it," he added. "Very soon these little tribes will either have died out or been assimilated into Bolivian or Brazilian society. So what do the *linquisticos* have? A lot of information about a lot of dead languages."

One of the priests who had not said very much until now turned to me and asked, "Are you writing a book?" I nodded and said, "Yes, but it's a history of Bolivia, not a travel book." He sighed. "Thank the Good Lord for that. I've read quite a few books about traveling in Bolivia, and almost all of them have been sheer garbage. It's unbelievable what some people will say." The others agreed. I assured everybody that I kept careful notes and that I had no intention of writing a travel book, anyway.

It had been a very nice meal with fascinating company, but everybody was busy, and so I was given a motorbike ride back to the hotel, where I found that my roommate was holding a business meeting in our room. I walked over to a nearby church to watch a wedding, after which the happy couple left in a well polished jeep and the wedding party and guests followed on motorbikes. Later, the band began to play in the plaza again, and the girls walked in little groups in their best clothes past stores selling Christmas decorations, including garish plastic Christmas trees.

THE PLANE BACK TO COCHABAMBA

I woke next morning in a panic. I heard no sounds coming from the army barracks. Had I overslept? But then I remembered it was a Sunday. When I phoned the airport at 8:00, they said the plane would arrive at nine, so I got myself and my baggage to the airport on a motorbike. I was the first passenger there. The clerk said that the plane would arrive at 10:00. There was a small stack of rubber waiting to be loaded onto the plane and the sky was clear, so I was optimistic. Then a red and white Cessna landed and disgorged a group of Americans I guessed to be *linguisticos*. Two of the priests arrived, and one went immediately to the pilot of the light plane to try to bum a newspaper or any magazines in English. A crowd of other passengers began arriving now, and it began to look as if there would not be enough room on the plane. I was becoming quite anxious, but then at noon, the DC-6 landed in a cloud of red dust.

The passengers were barely off the plane before the priest grabbed my arm and said, "Every man for himself!" We shoved and elbowed our way to the front of the crowd and were among the first ones on the plane. I grabbed a window seat next to a grandmother with a little girl who had to stand. The plane was soon packed. When the baggage was loaded, the ground crew filled what little space remained with balls of rubber and blocks of valuable hardwood. The plane looked to me to be heavily overloaded, but she took off quite smoothly. I breathed a huge sigh of relief.

There were neither steward nor any radio announcement from the pilot, but somebody said that they would not stop at Trinidad because the airstrip there was soaked. We would go straight to Cochabamba.

The window was clean and the plane did not fly high, so I had a clear view of the land below and was quite surprised at the number and the size of the lakes. South of Riberalta is a large region of dense vegetation, but then we reached patchy savanna and forest with wildly meandering rivers yellow with mud and lakes of all sizes, ranging from the giant freshwater Lake Rogaguado to tiny puddles. The lakes were a strange mixture of colors, some red from minerals, some yellow from mud, others green from algae, and many dark brown from rotting vegetation. Close to some of the lakes I could distinctly see the ancient prehistoric earthworks of a forest civilization that until quite recently nobody knew had ever existed. The neat house circles were raised above the floods, and the ridged fields stood out quite clearly.

The forest thickened as we approached the mountains then, quite abruptly, bare ground appeared below us. The land rose steeply, and I held my breath as the old DC-6 skimmed the mountain tops and dropped into the valley of Cochabamba.

TIME TO GO HOME

The air felt dry and cool in Cochabamba, and it was a pleasure to carry my own luggage without immediately breaking into a sweat. One of the teenagers from the riverboat shared a cab with me to the hotel, where I dumped my stuff and went immediately to the post office, which, strangely enough, was open on a Sunday. There was no letter from Lily. I was feeling a trifle unhappy when I went to the plaza. There I ran into the doctor and her husband, who had driven up from the Chapare. I had been wondering how I was going to return the hammock and mosquito net to their rightful owners, and they had been wondering what I had been up to in the Beni. We went to a café and I told them all about my travels since I had last seen them in their little jungle clinic at least six weeks ago.

Heading back to the hotel, I detoured past the post office and went in and asked to see their pile of dead letters. Sure enough, I found a letter from Lily. I celebrated by getting a shoe shine and munching on a firm, sweet Argentine apple. As I was sitting there, it gradually dawned on me that my travels in Bolivia were at an end. I had been everywhere I had planned to go, I had seen everything I could see and had talked to countless people in every walk of life. I had had many great experiences. All that remained was to say good-bye to Ramiro and his charming family.

The train ride back up to Oruro was uneventful. It took a couple of days to get my plane reservation from La Paz to Lima to Los Angeles. I used this time to describe my travels to Ramiro and his father. Ramiro's father still had the instincts of the old fashioned prospector who sees the possibility of valuable minerals in the wildest places. He and his son agreed that the rock sample from Puerto Siles contained some low-grade iron ore, but they disagreed on the possibility of alluvial tin deposits in Porto Velho.

Eventually my ticket was confirmed. It was with strangely mixed feelings that I left Oruro for La Paz, whence I went on to Lima and then home to Los Angeles. As much as I wanted to get home to my lovely wife, I also hated leaving Bolivia. I wanted to continue my studies at the university, but I also felt that there was a lot more to see in Bolivia, that extraordinary land of contrasts and great beauty.

I was home in Long Beach, California, in time for Christmas, and Lily, who had been worried about yellow fever, piranhas, and poisonous snakes, was glad to see me in one piece. Within days, I was caught up in the whirl of modern life—freeway travel, apartment hunting, graduate studies, and car repairs. But my memories of Bolivia—the high Andes, the deserts, the mighty rivers, and the charming people—have never faded. I worked on researching my history of Bolivia and kept in touch with Ramiro Miranda in Oruro. We also traveled whenever we could, usually together, occasionally separately. Eventually, I had visited very

Latin American country south of the Rio Grande and as far south as Tierra del Fuego and Cape Horn. But for some reason I never went back to Bolivia.